HERDER ON NATIONALITY, HUMANITY, AND HISTORY

McGill-Queen's Studies in the History of Ideas
Series Editor: Philip J. Cercone

HERDER ON NATIONALITY, HUMANITY, AND HISTORY

F.M. Barnard

McGill-Queen's University Press
Montreal & Kingston · London · Ithaca

© McGill-Queen's University Press 2003
ISBN 0-7735-2519-x
ISBN 0-7735-2569-6
Legal deposit second quarter 2003
Bibliothèque nationale du Québec

Printed in Canada on acid-free paper

This book has been published with the help of a grant from the Humanities and Social Sciences Federation of Canada, using funds provided by the Social Sciences and Humanities Research Council of Canada. Funding has also been received from the J.B. Smallman Publication Fund, Faculty of Social Science, The University of Western Ontario.

McGill-Queen's University Press acknowledges the support of the Canada Council for the Arts for our publishing program. We also acknowledge the financial support of the Government of Canada through the Book Publishing Industry Development Program (BPIDP) for our publishing activities.

National Library of Canada Cataloguing in Publication

Barnard, Frederick M., 1921–
    Herder on nationality, humanity, and history/F.M. Barnard.

(McGill-Queen's studies in the history of ideas 35)
Includes bibliographical references and index.
ISBN 0-7735-2519-x (bound)
ISBN 0-7735-2569-6 (pbk.)

    1. Herder, Johann Gottfried, 1744–1803 – Contributions in political science. 2. Herder, Johann Gottfried, 1744–1803 – Contributions in philosophy of history. 3. Political science – History – 18th century. 4. History – Philosophy. I. Title. II. Series.

B3051.Z7B37 2003   320'.01'1   C2002-905580-6

This book was typeset by Dynagram inc. in 10/12 Baskerville.

Contents

Preface

IN RECENT YEARS I have witnessed a growing and widening interest in Herder's thought. This interest now extends beyond Germany, where it seems to have focused chiefly on his literary criticism and his theory of aesthetics.[1] Judging by the increasing number of requests I have received from editors of anthologies for permission to include excerpts of my work on his social, cultural, and political philosophy, Herder's seminal contribution in these fields also can no longer be in doubt. Since my original study on Herder's social and political thinking has been out of print for years, and since 2003 marks the two-hundredth anniversary of Herder's death, it occurred to me that I might combine under one cover the works I have published in articles and symposia with some previously unpublished material on the themes selected for this volume. I was pleased that this suggestion was warmly welcomed by Philip Cercone, the editor of McGill-Queen's University Press's series on the history of ideas, and generously supported by the press's reviewer.

In selecting the central themes of this book I had students of the history of ideas principally in mind, although my emphasis on Herder's philosophy of language and culture, as well as on his highly effective use of metaphors, may possibly also attract a broader readership. I have tried to indicate in my introduction what appear to be the core elements linking the themes under discussion, but, clearly, this judgment is ultimately a matter of individual interpretation. I therefore made use of

---

1. A notable exception is *Vom Selbstdenken*, a recently published symposium that focuses on Herder's *Ideas on History*, ed. by Regina Otto and John H. Zammito (Heidelberg: Synchron, 2001).

secondary sources only when they significantly assisted in, or diverged from, my own interpretation.

Although references to earlier relevant publications of mine will be found in the notes, I would like especially to thank Professors Hanna Spencer and Stanley Winters for their permission to include parts of my contribution to their respective symposia on Heine and Masaryk. I also want to acknowledge my appreciation to the editors of the following scholarly journals for allowing me to use earlier versions of themes discussed in the following pages: The *Modern Language Review*, the *Journal of the History of Ideas*, the *Canadian Journal of Political Science*, the *American Political Science Review*, *History and Theory*, *Jewish Social Studies*, *Political Theory*, and the *Deutsche Vierteljahrsschrift für Literaturwissenschaft und Geistesgeschichte*.

My greatest debt, however, is once again to Margot, without whose encouragement I might not have persisted, although I must confess that Herder's own extraordinary way of expressing his thoughts and feelings has been the most abidingly potent stimulus. Few writers before or since could rouse readers more vibrantly by their language than he did.

F.M.B.
Dyers Bay, Ontario
Spring, 2002

HERDER ON NATIONALITY, HUMANITY, AND HISTORY

Introduction

"If only the books produced in Germany were of a more republican tone, how much more openly could I have said what I wanted to say instead of having to speak darkly or in parables and hazardous allusions."

I

SO WROTE HERDER in his (unpublished) postscript to *Fragmente*, his first major work. The chapter on government in *Ideas for a Philosophy of the History of Mankind* – the work for which Herder is best known to students of nationalism and history – had to be rewritten four times before it passed the censor. Germany, which Herder described as a *terra obedientiae*, was virtually a political desert. None of the princely states that composed the only nominally existing empire offered any scope for shared political activity. There was no parliamentary life to speak of, no political parties, few, if any, political clubs, and the mere semblance of a popular press. "Politics" was tantamount to personal rule by the princes, assisted by councillors so privy that no one ever heard them utter a word, in public at any rate. Herder indeed doubted if there was at all such a thing as a "public," let alone a *demos* with which it could be identified.[1] Under these circumstances, it is scarcely surprising that persons of humble birth like Herder could cherish little hope of making any impact on the political realm by word or deed. Intensely aware of these impediments, Herder felt he had no choice but to confine his political thinking to private letters or disguise it within non-political contexts.

1. J.G. Herder, *Sämtliche Werke*, ed. B. Suphan, 33 vols. (Berlin: Weidmann, 1877–1913), I, 14–16; the quoted postscript is in I, 528. All subsequent Herder references are to this edition.

This is not to suggest that Herder had the makings of a political thinker *par excellence*. It may well be that the sporadic nature of his forays into recognizably political issues was largely attributable to the constraints under which he lived – and his official church position at the court of Weimar did not help matters – but it probably also had a good deal to do with the heterogeneity of his intellectual interests, which ranged from literary criticism, aesthetics, philology, folklore, and psychology to history, anthropology, and the philosophy of culture and education. Yet, despite the fragmentary nature of his political writings and the array of his intellectual pursuits – which must seem exceedingly odd in our age of specialization – Herder's multi-dimensional approach to human creativity does have the merit of yielding a synoptic view of things. In his case this view revealed an unusual amalgam of empirical realism, imaginative insight, and a lively sensitivity for the unique and incommensurable. Seen in the context of his passionate commitment to "entering into" connections and interrelations previously unexplored, Herder's breadth of vision on the nature and dynamics of human cultures makes up for what his writings at times lack in systematic elaboration. Indeed, more often than not, his insights disclose a perspicacity in capturing the patterns of thinking and the values of peoples and periods to an extent that we only now can appreciate to the full.

At the same time, Herder for the most part looked upon the past less as the professional historian than as the reflective spectator for whom historical research was important not simply in order to study the past for its own sake. Although he was genuinely intrigued by the origin of things, it was the pastness in the presentness that aroused his foremost interest. In point of fact, much of this interest projected into the future. Here Herder possibly saw himself following the "golden rule of politics," as he called it, according to which gauging the course or direction of things demanded a realistic assessment of the present through an imaginative tracing of the past.[2]

By and large, Herder does indeed seem to have followed this rule in determining the "stream" of historical continuity and, in its light, the portents for the future. And in viewing the past and present as pregnant with the future, Herder was undoubtedly among the first to acclaim the French Revolution not as a cataclysmic lapse of continuity but as the most continuously significant occurrence since the Reformation. Similarly, despite pioneering the idea of nationhood in its modern

2. Herder, *Werke*, I, 8.

sense, he was fully awake to the dangers of racist variants and ethnic imperialism. Although Herder (unlike Rousseau) welcomed the advances in science, technology, education, and commerce, he also warned against the hazards of social disintegration in the wake of industrialization and urbanization, if such developments were not tempered by measures of "humanization" – a term he used almost synonymously with *Humanität*.

Historians may justly wonder to what extent Herder, in following the "golden rule of politics," managed to enlist the degree of detachment that he demanded of the authentic historian and which he claimed for his own historical judgment. Few, however, could justly deny – historians or non-historians – his uncommon gift for grasping the interpenetration of past, present, and future. As with the incisiveness of a scalpel, Herder laid bare the sores of his age, in which people were forced into treadmills, and cities into slagheaps of human vitality. So much, he observed, had become mechanized that the "*human* machine" had lost its zest to function, having become alienated from itself. European culture itself had become a mere "paper culture," and its ideals mere rhetorical abstractions in the service of mass deception.[3] These substantive issues apart, Herder also strikingly anticipated such future methodological trends as, for instance, the dialectic interplay of opposites, the non-replicative dynamics in the transmission of cultures and traditions, and the problematic fusion of persistence and change. Even his speculations on a nationhood free from norms of political centrality appear less utopian in the light of contemporary anthropological findings regarding stateless national communities and variants of political pluralism that opt for "polyarchy" and decentralized autonomies in place of a single focus of power.

I I

So many words and concepts that Herder pioneered have entered the thought and speech patterns of intellectual discourse that their users are no longer aware of their Herderian origins. Some, such as *Nationalcharakter, Volkslied*, or *Zeitgeist* have more or less easily found their equivalents in English. But this cannot be said of *Einfühlungsvermögen*, the essential requirement Herder posited for understanding cultures and peoples of the past and the present. Its closest rendering as "the capacity to feel

3. Herder, *Werke*, V, 532–41.

oneself into" the minds, motives, moods, purposes, aspirations, habits, and customs of those different from ourselves is an awkward circumlocution, while "empathy," its less awkward rendering, seems somewhat wooden, or too coldly clinical – if not altogether sterile – to convey the imaginative sweep of the German word; its vivid flavour is lost in translation. This loss tellingly illustrates the essence of the uniqueness and incommensurability of national cultures that Herder (and Vico before him) so emphatically insisted upon. We cannot, accordingly, assimilate one nation to another any more than we can fully render the meaning of a word in one language through the vocabulary of another. Each language, each culture, in this view, expresses a particular way of seeing and feeling, a distinct perception of the world, together with a certain manner of responding to its challenges. The word *Weltanschauung*, in its most literal sense, captures perhaps best the compass of divergent ways of encountering the outside from the inside.

Take, for instance, the word *Einfühlungsvermögen* itself, and contrast its reception by English-speaking peoples with that of German-speaking ones: what seems embarrassingly elusive to the former appears luxuriously rich to the latter. To the English speaker, that one could grasp things from the inside by an act of imaginative projection implies a degree of sensitivity that smacks too much, and too suspiciously, of romantic fancy, irrational enthusiasm, or wilful subjectivism to be at all taken seriously. To the more idealistically inclined German, on the other hand, such an attitude wholly typifies an excessively hard-nosed empiricism. These may of course be rather crude stereotypes, but, whether they are or not, they point to a cultural gulf that cannot easily be bridged by argument, however rational.

Herder, himself, for example, apart from having been viewed as a racist, a relativist, a parochial nationalist, and a vapid universalist, has not infrequently been dismissed as a whimsical romantic for whom intuition was the only valid path to knowledge. In most, if not all, these respects, he was the undoubted victim of apparently irreconcilable clashes of cultural seeing and perceiving. In actual fact, as we shall find, the complexity of his thought defies any of these labels. All the same, as critical though he was of "enthusiasm" and romantic *Schwärmerei* as any hard-nosed empiricist, he did favour imaginative "in-dwelling" when confronted with periods, peculiarities, and problems of the human world. There *was*, he argued, a process of understanding that could at times prove superior to established methods of enquiry, to the deductive form of *a priori* reasoning and the *a posteriori* form of empirical induction. It consists in grasping connections *creatively* by bringing a combination of different modalities of the mind into play. And while Herder felt that deduction and induction may be adequate for the observation, description, and classification of external nature, they may fail to tell us what we want to know about human action. Herder does not suggest, however, that attempting to "enter into" what people aspire to, enjoy, or resent is a matter of mystical divination or superhuman powers of intuition. It is therefore sadly misguided to read into his conception of empathy metaphysical propensities that in truth were entirely foreign to him. While he granted that, in the final analysis, imaginative understanding entailed an irreducible element of subjective judgment, he denied that this foreclosed objectively valid findings or the possibility of attaining what Kant has called an "enlarged mentality."

Verstehen, thus conceived, has since been celebrated as Herder's most lasting achievement by such outstanding scholars as Wilhelm Dilthey and Max Weber, but the most vivid account of its depth of meaning that I have come across is a story that Yehudi Menuhin recalls in his autobiography, *Unfinished Journey*. Menuhin remembers playing a violin sonata to the Hungarian composer Béla Bartók which Bartók had written specially for Menuhin. Bartók, although known to be pitilessly severe with his comments, was delighted. He did not think, he remarked, that music could be played like that except long after the composer was dead. In relating this episode, Menuhin is not boasting; however, the knowledge that he succeeded in penetrating to the heart and innermost meaning intended by the composer in and through his music, and that the living composer himself felt *understood*, was an experience of infinite worth to him.

By the same token, plumbing the depths of the past and feeling its pulse was for Herder like breathing life into the "dead bones in the burial grounds of the past."[4] The knowledge thus gained, moreover, is *sui generis* and cannot be assimilated to Gilbert Ryle's classification in terms of "knowing that" and "knowing how," since it is exclusively confined to the world of human thought, human feeling and, above all, human creativity, the only world in which, in Herder's words, "man can be his own god."[5] And, to know this world is to know it from the *inside*, by

---

4. Isaiah Berlin's description of Herder's gift of imaginative reconstruction, in *Vico and Herder* (London: Hogarth, 1976), xxvi.

5. Herder, *Werke*, VI, 64.

knowing *what it is like* to partake in what Herder meant by distinct *Lebensformen*, by distinct configurations of human existence.

III

It is better for individuals to actively participate in forging their own collective forms of life by their own concerted efforts – whatever they achieve – than to be efficiently (or stupidly, or criminally) governed by others who claim superiority over them. For propensities deteriorate if they are not used. To be truly human, therefore, humans must reach a stage of acting together (*Zusammenwirken*) when they no longer need a master to rule them. Everybody should be a "somebody," a master in some sphere, but no one should be a master in all spheres. Surely, Herder proclaims, it is the most blatant example of unreason to think that those yet unborn should be destined to rule over others yet to be born, just because of wealth or dynastic pedigree. Also, there is no such thing as a "father of the nation": a wife requires a husband, a child parents, a herd a leader; these are natural relations. The notion of a father who keeps his children permanently under age, however, is anything but natural. Similarly, what is natural about a *Herrenvolk* or master race subjugating other people or continents, defrauding and plundering them? There is no *Favorit-Volk*; humans lose their humanity if they live on others, their labour, ideas, and creations. They rob themselves of something essential to themselves as selves by exploiting and dominating others, just as they do if the whole purpose of their existence lies in obeying others as their overlords.

These are but salient themes of Herder's political creed and of his doctrine of reciprocal *Zusammenwirken* within and between cultural groupings that he identified with distinct nationalities. Enquiring into the genesis of such culture groupings, Herder asks what characterizes humans as creatures of culture as opposed to beings in nature whose existence rests wholly on their biological make-up. In his first major philosophical work, *On the Origin of Language*, he emphatically parts ways with the "naturally derived" thesis that humans are essentially rational animals, with reason as a special "faculty" merely superimposed on their animal nature. Herder insists instead on viewing humans as *fundamentally* different since, unlike animals, they have the capacity for speech, by virtue of which they no longer are "infallible mechanisms" in the hands of Nature, or not totally so. And, although not endowed at birth with conscious self-awareness, humans are conditioned to acquire it by dint of their "entire economy" of cognition and volition and of the direction of their energizing powers. As a result, and in complete contrast to the animal, they can "mirror themselves within themselves" by *reflection*.[6]

Not being wholly determined by biological forces, however, humans face problems that no animal is faced with in the same way. Both as individual persons and as members of cultural groupings, they encounter obstacles that are not susceptible to "natural" resolution, as impediments are in the animal world. Herder attributes the chief source of this difference to the existence of an acute consciousness of imperfection that produces in humans a permanent form of self-questioning which, in turn, leads to constant restlessness and desire for change. This sense of imperfection keeps humans always in motion and prevents them from ever being wholly satisfied. Unlike the bee, "which is perfect when building her first cell," human life is characterized by "continuous becoming" and the urge for creative self-enactment through self-improvement.[7] On the other hand, having language and possessing the capacity for reflection, humans are able to develop a mental horizon far surpassing that of animals. While animals are confined to the sphere of action for which they are equipped by natural instincts, humans, not thus provided, are not thus limited either: they are creatures of *freedom* as well as of nature. Their perfectibility, as well as their corruptibility, is bound up with this distinguishing feature. "Man alone has made a goddess out of *choice*," writes Herder in the *Ideas*, "and can accordingly explore possibilities and decide between alternatives." And though he can "most despicably abuse his freedom," Herder adds, "he is still king, for he is still able to choose, even if he chooses the worst."[8]

Herder posits a sense of imperfection and a sense of freedom, then, as the foundation for the emergence of human culture and the formation of distinctive national entities. It follows that neither "culture" nor "nationhood" is simply a product of nature in the manner in which the growth of a plant is. Likewise, states based on national cultures are no more natural than other states. Nationalists and others misread Herder if they think that he said, or implied, that nation-states, unlike

6. Herder, *Werke*, V, 28, 95. (I discuss these themes in the subsequent essay on nationality.)

7. Herder, *Werke*, V, 98.

8. Herder, *Werke*, XIII, 110, 146–7.

multi-national states, are natural. For, in point of fact, Herder was hostile to *all* states, and merely conceded that, though they were also artifacts, nation-states could be considered the least unnatural. Nor did he
say or imply that national cultures were simply the work of nature and,
as such, blessed by unswerving solidarity, entirely free from inner tensions. All he did maintain was that, despite the possibility of conflictual
relations, the mode of overall thinking (*Denkart*) was more similar
within nations than *between* nations.[9] Indeed, it was essentially a certain
consciousness of having ways of seeing and feeling in common that made
people think of themselves as *belonging*.

This idea of a collective consciousness was taken over by Hegel, who
associated it with the sense of a shared history, while the idea of social
tension reappeared in Kant's essay on universal history as "mutual antag-
onism in society." Unlike Herder, however, Kant identified this antago-
nism with the motor of "all the culture and art that adorn humanity"
(Fourth and Fifth Propositions). But, then, Kant defined culture in a narrower sense than Herder, and opposed it to "civilization." Herder (we
shall note) rejected this dualism: "culture" for him included *all* creative
activities, whatever their content or place in the hierarchy of values. Nor
did it exclude myths, legends, or even prejudices; for, to dismiss any of
these, together with religion, as irrational vagaries, would be to deprive
national cultures of significant moulding agents. And, while Herder by
no means disputed or ruled out that religious beliefs may serve to prop
up authoritarian structures, he could not agree that this stance ruled out
their autonomous origin or their self-validating significance.[10]

I shall return to this point in a later chapter, but, clearly, here too
Herder impressively anticipated not only anthropological findings but
also what subsequent generations could learn from their own experience. For anthropological findings, no less than the experience of people living under autocratic and totalitarian regimes, have disclosed that,
contrary to the optimistic expectations of prevailing currents of thought
in the Age of Reason, authoritarian structures have defied disappearance with the suppression or decline of religious institutions and religious practices. Conversely, as Herder also boldly declared, the demise
of authoritarian structures need not imply the demise of myths, legends,
prejudices, or religious festivals, in that these have a life of their own
and will outlive those who use them for self-serving ends. Not rarely,

9. To be discussed in the subsequent essay on culture.
10. Herder, *Werke*, XIII, 307.

however, Herder points out, those using them have themselves not ceased to believe in them. For the myths, legends, or religious beliefs have become deeply ingrained in the tissue of collective cultures and common habits of thinking and feeling.

I V

While Herder inveighed against the "facile rationalism" of the Enlightenment, he did not mistake the part for the whole. Even in his most spirited attacks on *a priorism*, he never denied the power of reflective reasoning, just as, in his dislike of the "cosmopolitanism" of his day, he neither questioned the equality of humans as an anthropological or ethical assumption, nor abandoned the idea of universality. If he repudiated cosmopolitanism, therefore, or expressed misgivings about creating a supra-national "world-government," this did not at all stop him from advocating ways of combining universal with national thinking, provided that such conceptual fusion did not militate against the recognition of plural diversity and the right of all nations to their distinctive cultural existence. In essence, Herder's idea here was not very different from Rousseau's central theme in the *Social Contract*: the question of how to associate with others without sacrificing one's own individuality – a theme which, as Herder records in his earliest notebook, "is most closely akin to my own."[11] To put it slightly differently, even though Herder's own conception of nationhood as the essential foundation for the complex fabric of social and political entities *was* the alpha and omega of his nationalism, this nationalism by no means ruled out international fellowship, for it was not tantamount to an exclusionary chauvinism in the light of which nations had to view themselves as superior to others or face each other as mortal enemies.

Herder's conception of nationhood in this non-exclusionary sense was an attempt to go beyond thinking in terms of opposed camps, so that, while the envisaged oneness of nationality and humanity *was* a complex oneness, not bereft of potential tensions, it no longer was a question of having one foot in two "camps." At any rate, in his more optimistic moods, Herder did wish to believe that, given renewed efforts of "joint endeavour" (*Zusammenwirken*), a *modus vivendi* among nations was an attainable aspiration. The route to this end was not, however, primarily a matter of "scientific method" or superior organization, or of discovering

11. Herder, *Werke*, XXXII, 41.

an all-encompassing formula; it was through a concerted effort of nurturing a reciprocal sensitivity that would enable people to extend their capacity for experiencing the pain and humiliation of the deprived and marginalized in this world as if it were their own.[12]

However, except for "Herderians" such as Guiseppe Mazzini, Alexander Herzen, or Thomas Masaryk, to whom Herder's philosophy of humanity meant at least as much as his philosophy of nationality, it was not Herder's "humanity" that made the deepest inroads into nineteenth-century thinking. To nationalists and romanticists, at any rate, it was rather his vibrant defence of native languages as incommensurable treasures or his emotionally charged critique of the European Enlightenment that mattered first and foremost, and created the greatest flurry and excitement. But the fact that this was so had to do not only with *what* Herder had to say; it had at least as much to do with *how* he said it.

Clearly, the importance that Herder attached to language was not confined to his theorizing about the genesis of human culture but extended powerfully to his own eloquent use of it. It was his eloquence and the imagery which he so effectively employed that undoubtedly aroused the enthusiastic response of his followers within and beyond the borders of Germany. And although the essays included in this volume focus on Herder's ideas themselves rather than on their influence, I feel that before ending these introductory remarks I ought to turn briefly to Herder's own language as something that crucially enhanced that influence.

V

Being a poet first and a philosopher second, Herder learned early in life the use of words. Already in his first writings on literary criticism he tells people in the most persuasive, if not beseeching, terms that, without a language of their own, they are but a monstrous absurdity. "No greater harm can befall a nation than to be robbed of its character by being deprived of its language, for without its language it loses its own mode of thinking" (*Denkart*). Every effort must therefore be made to cultivate a community's language in order to create "that level ground upon which it can erect its national edifice."[13]

12. For a contemporary expression of this position, see Richard Rorty, *Contingency, Irony, and Solidarity* (Cambridge: Cambridge University Press, 1989), xvi.

13. Herder, *Werke*, I, 147–8, 162, 366; see also II, 103, where Herder speaks of the realm and growth of a people's language as "a democracy which tolerates no tyrants."

In particular, Herder came to recognize the force that the language of metaphor conferred upon the intelligibility of conceptual discourse. Indeed, he goes so far as to state that without the use of metaphor such discourse would be virtually impossible because of the inherent limits of the human mind. In the absence of what he calls the *spirit* of metaphor (*Metapherngeist*), understanding and explaining would be exceedingly difficult, because no human mind could cope with the "ocean of impressions." What is more, Herder interestingly adds, it is precisely by means of metaphor that things, ideas, and concepts are *humanized,* are given a form with which humans can come to grips. To ban metaphor from language, therefore, would mean to "dehumanize" it. By the same token, since metaphors embody "the labyrinth" of a people's "imagination and passion," thereby making it what it distinctively *is,* any attempt to ban them from language would empty it of its most precious content and thereby "denationalize" it. Metaphors, in short, are not a matter of choice; they are the essential ingredients which, embedded "in the very soul of a nation," are comparable to the heartbeat that gives life to every sentient creature. Only, unlike the heart, the language of metaphor is the creation of humans, and not a direct gift from God, for "no angel or heavenly spirit would have need of any metaphor."[14]

So profoundly steeped in metaphor is Herder's own language that it at times gets somewhat carried away by its own imagery. An example is his use of the "growth" metaphor, in which he loses sight of the distinct causality of "purpose" in nature and "purpose" in culture and human action.[15] Metaphorical blurrings did little, however, to diminish the rhetorical force of his appeal to suppressed nations. Even though Herder's words were not infrequently quoted out of context, the case he made overstated, and elements combined with it that were altogether foreign to his line of thinking, there was, distortions apart, enough punch in his actual language to carry his message. Especially in Central and Eastern Europe his apotheosis of national belonging, its necessity – if not sanctity – created an extraordinary stir, for such rousing talk was clearly celestial music to nationalist ears. No wonder, therefore, that Herder was acclaimed as the father of Slav national revival. Czechs, Poles, Latvians, Slovenes, and Ukrainians, as well as the

14. Herder, *Werke,* V, 51–90. See also the section on "Reflections on Myth, Prejudice and the Imagination" in his *Travel Diary,* translated in my *Herder on Social and Political Culture* (Cambridge: Cambridge University Press, 1969) 71–86. (Herder, *Werke,* IV, 356–65, 448–60.)

15. For an elaboration of this point, see my "Natural Growth and Purposive Development: Vico and Herder," *History and Theory,* XVIII (1979), 16–36.

slavophiles in Russia, enthusiastically followed Herder's call to resuscitate their hallowed traditions, their ancient literatures, their folksongs and, above all, their indigenous languages.

The most directly influential source of Herder's inspirational power was undoubtedly the chapter on the Slavs in his *Ideas*. In it he expressed in ringing tones the hope that "ye deeply bowed, but once so industrious and happy peoples, you will at last awake refreshed from your long listless slumber and, having shaken off the chains of slavery, will enjoy again the possession of your fair lands from the Adriatic to the Carpathian Mountains, from the Don to the Moldau, and celebrate on them your ancient festivals in peace together with the prosperity of your industry and trade." These times, Herder confidently adds, will surely come and produce in their wake a true "garden of humanity."[16]

Soon after its publication this chapter appeared in several translations and was most likely the first piece of Herder's work that people in that part of the world encountered.[17] To anti-nationalists, on the other hand, it seemed an insidious threat to the continued existence of supranational states such as Austria. Indeed, the Austrian censors did everything in their power to prevent Herder's message from spreading. Nevertheless, I doubt that Herder's influence was such as to constitute a major cause of the break-up of Austria-Hungary, as has been suggested.[18] For, however inflammable his words, it required an explosive situation – such as Austria's defeat in World War I – to give them an incendiary effect.

Strangely enough, it was Thomas Masaryk, the least aggressive of national leaders, who was one of the foremost to ignite Herder's inflammatory words, in that he was without a doubt the chief architect of Austria's dissolution. And yet it was Masaryk who came closest to putting into practice what Herder had only dimly envisaged, in founding one of the most democratic successor-states to the Empire. Masaryk's writings, too, bear witness to an unusual grasp of Herder's attempted fusion of nationality and humanity and disclose a remarkable affinity with his republican sentiments. Indeed, no other of Herder's nationalist followers, with the possible exception of Mazzini, went so far *beyond* Herder's philosophy of nationalism as Masaryk. The magnitude of con-

16. Herder, *Werke*, XIV, 280.

17. As H. Barry Nisbet observes in "Herder's Conception of Nationhood and its Influence in Eastern Europe," in Roger Bartlett and Karen Schönwälder, eds., *The German Lands and Eastern Europe* (Houndmills: Macmillan, 1998), 115–35, here 130.

18. For example, R. Schierenberg, *Der Politische Herder* (Graz: Schmidt-Dengler, 1932), 77.

ceptual parallelism is in truth so astonishing that I could not resist juxtaposing their thoughts on the bounds of humanism and the hazards of titanism.

The themes included in this volume yield, I believe, a fair portrayal of Herder's ideas on nationhood, humanity, culture, and history, many of which have by now permanently entered the texture of intellectual history. What, however, is rather elusive to capture is the evocative mood of Herder's language itself, the *feelings* it has kindled, notably in directions in which the political is not easily separable from the apolitical, or the visceral from the cerebral.

As for the identifiably "ideological" content of Herder's thought, its liberal and democratic leanings were to an extent known by the end of the nineteenth century, although possibly more widely outside than within his own homeland – with one notable exception, that of the liberal writer and statesman Wilhelm von Humboldt (1767–1835).[19] His most radical views, however, have only subsequently surfaced with the discovery of Herder's uncensored drafts and a closer reading of works that, by and large, had been considered wholly apolitical.[20]

Finally, if I were pressed to summarize what lies at the core of the ideas that form the substance of the subsequent pages, I would single out five points: (1) the conviction that optimal human creativity requires a national matrix of embeddedness: (2) the need for caution, lest one mistake embeddedness for sameness, or relationship for identity; (3) the recognition that historical progress involves the cost of excluded alternatives; (4) the counsel that relating the particular and the universal – such as nationality and humanity – must resist absorption of one by the other if their interaction is to preserve what is distinct and

19. For further details on Herder's political influence, see my *Herder's Social and Political Thought: From Enlightenment to Nationalism* (Oxford: Clarendon Press, 1965, 1967), 153–77. Although Kant's impact on Humboldt, together with that of Friedrich Schiller, may have been more direct than Herder's writings, there are nonetheless remarkably Herderian parallels in his thought, not only in his emphasis on the limits of the state, but also as regards his understanding of the origin of language, the distinctiveness of national cultures, and the problematic question of progress in human history.

20. As, for example, Herder's *Spirit of Hebrew Poetry*, referred to in the following chapter on nationality, and commented upon at greater length in my *Self-Direction and Political Legitimacy: Rousseau and Herder* (Oxford: Clarendon Press, 1988), 261–7. For a lucid recent assessment of Herder's significant contribution to social and political philosophy as well as to the philosophy of language, see Charles Taylor, "The Importance of Herder" in *Philosophical Arguments* (Cambridge: Harvard University Press, 1995), and his *Sources of the Self* (Cambridge: Harvard University Press, 1989).

incommensurable in each; and (5) the realization that coming to grips with history's tangled sequences of events may call for different methods of enquiry than the application (or sole application) of theoretical formulas, methods that demand a cognitive sensitivity toward the uniquely individual in order to yield the possibility of imaginative seeing and empathetic understanding.

Within these core issues there is, despite a number of perplexities – notably in Herder's philosophy of history – a remarkable degree of consistency and inner unity amidst their broad-ranging diversity. Each of these issues discloses penetrating insights and opens up trails that previously were but poorly charted or not charted at all. And while Herder voraciously drew on a vast array of sources, he nevertheless brought an approach to bear on the themes under discussion that was at once boldly exciting and challengingly provocative.

Besides the impressive approach and the pioneering surge of Herder's ideas, there is, as I indicated, an incalculably distinctive aura that hovers over it all and, like a magnet, helps to hold it together, making it of a piece as what is quintessentially Herderian.

1

The Hebraic Roots of Herder's Nationalism

THE IDEA THAT A SHARED CONSCIOUSNESS of cultural identity based on a common language constitutes a valid, if not compelling, reason for claiming the right to political self-government has become a familiar theme in demands for separate statehood. Johann Gottfried Herder (1744–1803) is widely credited (or charged) with having pioneered this idea. Without challenging this view, I nonetheless want to suggest three explanatory or qualifying points. The first is that Herder's vision of nationhood has little to do with an emergent national consciousness in his native Germany, but is to a far greater extent the upshot of his interpretation of ancient Isra4el. The second point is that Herder's conception of *Volk*, with the Hebrew people in mind, is at variance with his conception of *Volk* within the context of his own times. And, thirdly, that in both conceptions Herder emphatically sets apart "relationship" from "identity" – a distinction that tends to be overlooked in characterizations of Herder's nationalism that pay exclusive attention to his "ethnic" message.

I

As early as 1769 Herder had planned an account of the Jewish people's role in the development of learning in its diverse forms,[1] and in his later reflections on history, the *Ideas on the Philosophy of History* (1784–91), he expressed the wish that someone would "collect data for

---

1. Herder, *Werke*, XII, 405. All citations of Herder's work are from: J.G. Herder, *Sämtliche Werke*, ed. B. Suphan, 33 vols. (Berlin: Weidmann, 1877–1913).

a history of the Jews in all the countries into which they were dispersed, since such a history would yield a revealing example (*Schaustück*) of humanity, equally remarkable as a natural as well as a political event."[2] Its principal impulse was to discover how the Jews managed to preserve a sense of identity for nearly two thousand years within an alien and largely hostile environment.

Viewing it as *the* age-old problem of world history as a whole, Herder kept returning to the past and future of Jewish existence, and when, at the turn of the century, he came to write what he called his "poetical testament," he reopened the subject at some length.[3] That people no longer sharing a common homeland should regard themselves as *a* people has puzzled many students of history and politics before and after Herder, but I believe that few non-Jews have disclosed as deep an insight into this phenomenon, or derived as much inspiration from it, as this eighteenth-century German writer and philosopher of history.[4] While his original impetus was undoubtedly religious, prompted by his home background and his contact with Johann Georg Hamann, an eminent Old Testament scholar, during his student years in Königsberg, Herder's later interest in the Hebrews of antiquity, and in the contemporary situation of the Jews, increasingly assumed a distinctly political complexion. The Bible, Herder came to urge, was not intended solely for spiritual edification but should be read also as a political-historical document of prime importance, portraying a people's aspirations and failings within the context of its national development.[5]

Similarly, when in 1783 he published one of his most mature works, *The Spirit of Hebrew Poetry,* he told his readers to study it not simply from

2. XIV, 66.

3. As Herder wrote not long before his death to the poet Johann Gleim (January 1802) when engaged in writing his *Adrastea* (H. Düntzer, *Von und an Herder* [Leipzig, 1861–62], i, 297). Herder's "classical" biographer Rudolf Haym, commenting on this part of the *Adrastea*, writes that nothing Herder wrote on the principles of *Humanität* is more instructive than his treatment of the "Conversion of the Jews" (the title of the seventh *Adrastea*). (In his *Herder nach seinem Leben und seinen Werken*, Berlin: Gaertner, 1880–85, ii, 793).

4. Apart from Haym's standard biography, two biographies in English have appeared: Alexander Gillies, *Herder* (Oxford, Blackwell 1945) and Robert T. Clark Jr, *Herder, his Life and Thought* (Berkeley and Los Angeles: University of California Press, 1955).

5. VIII, 543–4; see also VI, 64, VIII, 235, XI, 178, XIV, 322–4, XVII, 120–1, XX, 178, 232, 239, 265, and Herder's letter to the Swiss theologian and writer Johann Caspar Lavater, dated 30 October 1772 (H. Düntzer and F.G. Herder, eds., *Aus Herders Nachlass*, 3 vols., Frankfurt: Meidinger, 1856–57, ii, 15–16.)

a literary and theological point of view but as something of profound political import.[6] Oddly enough, this recommendation has remained virtually unheeded, thus depriving Herder scholars of an invaluable source of his expressly political views and of his speculations on nationality. This is unfortunate, for it was there rather than in the censored chapter on government in the *Ideas* that Herder dared to give expression, under literary and theological disguises, to his most radical social and political convictions.[7]

When Herder wrote about the Jews, he thought of them chiefly as a collectivity, indeed as a nation *par excellence*, which he called a "genetic individual," portraying its collective self-creation in the world of culture as comparable to organic growth in the world of nature.[8] This "national" approach did not stop him, however, from sharing the sentiments of men such as Voltaire and Montesquieu in France, or Mendelssohn and Lessing in Germany, in support of Jewish emancipation. But Herder sharply distinguished emancipation from assimilation and categorically rejected proposals for the conversion of the Jews to Christianity – advocated by well-meaning contemporaries, mainly theologians, as both futile and presumptuous.[9] To blur or obliterate the existence of the Jews as a people with its own "national character" was to remove the most "excellent model" of a people "inextricably tied by its own confession to that ancient law given to it under a distant sky."[10] Assimilation would amount also to the admission that nationality was a purely surface phenomenon easily replaceable by simply superimposing one faith upon another, one tradition upon the other, one mode of thinking upon another.

In his firm denial that a people was no more than a collection of individuals, Herder strikingly foreshadowed central communitarian themes in subsequent nationalist aspirations, including those of Jewish nationalists. Furthermore, in stressing the connection between conditions of a people's freedom and the character of collective traits, he revived the value of collective liberties, using as an illustration the unattractive traits

6. XII, 119.

7. When in his first draft of the *Ideas* Herder attempted to voice his political views more openly, he was instructed by Goethe, then chief minister of the court of Weimar, to revise that section. (*Aus Herders Nachlass*, ii, 268.)

8. X, 139, XVII, 285.

9. XXIV, 62–3; see also Haym, *Herder*, ii, 793.

10. XXIV, 63–4.

into which Jews as individuals were forced within the moulding conditions of unfreedom.[11]

In *The Spirit of Hebrew Poetry* Herder seems directly and indirectly bent on demonstrating this contrast by focusing on the shared traits that distinguished the Hebrews when they lived in freedom in their ancient land, as the oldest illustration of nationhood itself. How could Moses, Herder asks, create a free people out of twelve independent republics? Significantly, he speaks of the twelve tribes of Israel as "republics," and, no less significantly, of their union as a "nation," without implying that its creation coincided with the founding of a Hebrew *state*. The two evidently did not necessarily go together for him. Just as Germany in his days was a nation of many states and Austria a state of many nations, so ancient Israel portrayed "a most excellent example" of a nation long before its emergence as a *state*. In trying to account for the creation and survival of Hebrew nationhood, Herder lists five principal components as causal determinants:

(1) the land, as the people's common heritage;
(2) the law, as a covenant freely entered into;
(3) the existence of a shared language and folklore memory;
(4) the emphasis on family ties, fostered and perpetuated by;
(5) the love and reverence for their forefathers.

However, in his view, it is the interacting fusion of these determinants that sustained Jewish nationhood and enabled it to survive even when some of the components as such were no longer operative. Thus it is particularly by so closely interweaving the land and the law that Moses bound the hearts of his people to their native soil and made them look throughout their dispersal upon Palestine as their true homeland.

---

11. Here, too, Herder revealed his exceptional historical and psychological insight and empathy. Moses Mendelssohn, a philosopher and leading voice in support of the emancipation of the Jews, greatly admired Herder's ability to identify himself with the outlook and experience of people in different lands or periods of history. He wrote to Herder: "You have the gift to feel yourself, whenever you wish, into the situation and mentality of your fellow-beings." (The letter is dated June 1780; *Aus Herders Nachlass*, ii, 216.) It was mainly through Mendelssohn that Herder became familiar with the lot of the Jews in Germany as well as with the philosophy of the Jews in the Middle Ages and more recently.

"The Land belonged to the Law, and the Law belonged to the Land of Jehovah." Hence, however dispersed and distant from its shores, the eyes and hopes of the Jewish people did not cease being focused on their ancient land, a nostalgic focus that helped them retain their identity.[12]

Indeed, so intimate was the merging of the principal components that, buttressed as it was by Israel's holy literature, it in effect resulted in the closest possible identification between religious, moral, and political sentiments. Coupled with these sentiments is a highly "genetic" reverence that the Hebrews held for their forefathers, a reverence reflected and reinforced by the emotive significance of the word "father" itself, merging feelings of love and esteem. Combined, these elements helped to create a sense of relatedness that was at once familial *and* political. In Herder's view, it was above all this quasi-organic symbiosis that constituted the source of the intense historical continuity within Jewish national survival.[13] And because for Herder the existence of a national holy literature is indicative of the still earlier possession of a common language, cultural and associative forces incessantly interact.

It was arguably this tight linkage of religious, moral, cultural familial, and institutional components in Hebrew nationhood that induced Herder to envisage a form of political entity that was free from the power of a central source of coercion. This, however, is not all there is to it. For Herder points to additional characteristics that illustrate further indigenous traits essential for his portrayal of ancient Hebrew society as a communitarian-republican order rooted in the legal provisions of the Mosaic "Constitution." First and foremost among these added characteristics he postulates a spirit of reciprocity capable of engendering a social fabric permeated by widely shared overarching interests and supported by a fairly undifferentiated political structure. Thus while not a monolithic entity – by virtue of being a tribally-conditioned pattern of many-centred allegiances – ancient Israel is nonetheless presented as a polity in which there are no real divisions between rulers and ruled, and in which laws rather than men assume supremacy. "Nomocracy" is the term Herder applies to Israel's confederation and to the Mosaic "groundrules" that are to have inspired it.[14]

12. XII, 115. In the *Ideas* Herder compares the association of the tribes of Israel with the Confederation of Switzerland (XIV, 61). See also VIII, 355 and XVII, 312.

13. Herder observes in a footnote: "The reasons of his (Moses') legislation were not only moral and philosophical but also national." (XI, 462); see also XII, 107 and VI, 60.

14. XII, 82.

But although Herder attached such great importance to the sovereignty of law, he did not view Moses' work as a legislator to have been the final word on the way things ought to be. In other words, he did not look upon the Mosaic Covenant as a rigid contract in the manner in which Althusius and Pufendorf spoke of the agreed basis of the *corpus symbioticum*.[15] He held it to have been intended as a flexible document, amendable to suit changing circumstances. Moses himself, Herder observes, never hesitated to alter the constitution when the situation required it. For example, whereas the original framework provided for a form of law-making in which the elders of all tribes should participate equally, both in decisions affecting the administration of law and public affairs generally, Moses found it necessary to confine administrative functions to one tribe only, namely the Levites.[16] Their paramount concern, Herder contends, was to make sure that the institutions created by the Mosaic Constitution never became obsolete. One of the principal objectives of Israel's prophets, therefore, was to do everything in their power to maintain the Law of Moses as a living heritage and prevent it from becoming a "dead letter."[17]

For Herder the Law of Moses was first and foremost a political document, and he regarded Moses himself as one of the oldest and wisest legislators not only of the Jewish people but of all peoples, surpassing in stature even Lycurgus.[18] And this was so, Herder explains, because Moses could combine effective political leadership with utmost personal humility. Evidently, nothing was further from his mind than self-glorification. "Not his name, but the genius of his *Volk* was to go down in history; throughout it was *Israel* that he wanted to see flourish and prosper – Moses never thought of himself as supreme, as the overarch-

---

15. XI, 452. Johannes Althusius (1557–1638), political theorist and constitutional jurist, whose main work, *Politica methodice digesta atqua exemplis sacris et profanis* (1603), has been judged by Otto Gierke to constitute the first systematic treatise on politics since the ancients. (In *Johannes Althusius und die Entwicklung der naturrechtlichen Staats-theorien*, 3rd ed. (1913). Samuel Pufendorf (1632–94) was a German jurist and historian. His chief works, *De jure naturae et gentium* (1672) and *Elementa jurisprudentiae universalis* (1660), had a profound influence on legal and political theorizing in Germany.

16. XI, 453. But Moses made sure, Herder adds, that the Levites had no executive or legislative powers, for he was careful not to curtail his people's political freedom. "The tribe of Levi was the most learned but not the ruling tribe; every *political* decision rested on the deliberations of the tribal elders of the *whole* people" (XII, 120).

17. XII, 114.

18. VIII, 349, XI, 450. There is a marked contrast between Herder and Goethe (who urged Herder to come to Weimar) in their treatment of biblical history and their appraisal of Moses; see especially Goethe's *Israel in der Wüste*.

ing person (*Hauptperson*)."[19] Hegel's "historical individual," therefore was not the man Moses, but the nation Israel. And the fact that Moses claimed divine origin for his laws was simply an act of exceptional political wisdom, but never a case of self-aggrandizement. For how could he have succeeded, Herder asks, in controlling and persuading some 600,000 rebels by appealing to the dim light of political reason? To be truly efficacious, Moses felt, laws had to enjoy almost divine reverence, at any rate at any given time, for only thus could they be the supreme arbiter of men and the most sublime authority of nations.[20]

No less intriguingly, Herder sought to contrast his understanding of the Mosaic Constitution with that of the Natural Law tradition, which put chief emphasis on basic individual rights. There was not a shred of evidence, he declared, that Moses thought in terms of innate inalienable rights that the individual could be said to have possessed before the constitution came into being. Indeed, he added, it is more than doubtful whether the individual as such was Moses' chief concern at all; for the main purpose of his constitution was the creation of a free *people*, subject to none other than its laws; it was *its* right to liberty and the pursuit of happiness that, says Herder, Moses had primarily at heart. All the same, the very fact that the constitution provided for a *republican* system in which laws rather than men were to rule precluded, in Herder's view, the danger of arbitrariness and injustice in the conduct of public affairs. Hence, as long as the law was the supreme arbiter, the individual citizen had no grounds for fear: "That law should rule and not the legislator, that a free nation should freely accept and honour it, that invisible, reasonable, and benevolent powers should guide us and no chains enslave us: this was the idea of Moses."[21] To ensure that no man should ever assume political dominion over another, God himself was to be King and Keeper of the Law. Thus, with the institution of kings, Herder concludes, the paramount object of the Mosaic Constitution had become vitiated.[22]

III

The essence, then, of the Mosaic Constitution, in Herder's interpretation, is the rule of law. Good government is associated with impersonal government. Only as long as a society can dispense with personal rulers,

19. XII, 123, XXXII, 207.
20. XII, 122.
21. XII, 117.
22. XII, 82, 121.

only as long as it succeeds in functioning without having recourse to physical power as a sanction of authority, can it remain compatible with the dignity of the human spirit. Arguing that in a true republican system it is laws and institutions that matter, and not superior individuals, Herder, like Rousseau, does not identify governing *authority* with any particular administrative *body*. And even though the elders of each tribe do constitute a governing authority, their actual legislative power is not meant to be very substantial, for they are to meet only if and when circumstances demand. Moreover, when they do meet, customs and reverence for existing laws will act as a brake on their effective authority, not least because "reverence" is likely to be backed by the various sectional *foci* of influence, such as the Levites, the priests, the prophets, and other associations and semi-corporate bodies.

It would appear, therefore, that Herder envisaged the organization of Hebrew society on quasi-pluralistic lines, as a socio-political framework within which diverse sectional entities operate and cooperate. Indeed, government is virtually reduced (or elevated) to "cooperation." Strictly, there are no rulers at all; their existence is viewed as a denial of the rule of law, if not as a symptom of political bankruptcy.

The next section will disclose how essential this portrayal of Hebrew society was as a backdrop to Herder's pluralist conception of republican politics. For the present, however, I wish to underscore his evident bias toward a communitarian rather than individualist ethic in his approach to ancient Hebrew society, since, with a remarkable degree of consistency, he applies the same bias in his approach to the Jewish question in his own times and his own society. For he viewed the situation of European Jewry as first and foremost a *collective* problem requiring a *political* solution.[23] Only by resuming the threads that had been broken over two thousand years previously could the Jews attain full maturity as a nation in their own land. Only then could they recover their self-respect and find national fulfilment as *a people* among other nations.[24] But in this collective and political solution, Herder explicitly adds, they need the assistance and understanding of the rest of the world which, Herder feels sure, they are more likely to get if they present their problem as a *national* problem. In other words, only by collectively thinking of them-

---

23. XXIV, 63. Jacob L. Talmon, in *Political Messianism: the Romantic Phase* (London: Secker and Warburg 1960, 256–92) sees in Mazzini's political thought the first major illustration of this switch.

24. XXIV, 67.

selves nationally could the Jews expect recognition as a distinct people internationally.[25]

The similarity of Theodor Herzl's lines on this theme, laying the foundations of political Zionism, is truly striking, especially if it is borne in mind that Herzl probably had never set eyes upon Herder's writings. In his "blueprint" for the proposed Jewish State, *Der Judenstaat*, Herzl wrote in 1895: "I consider the Jewish question to be neither a social nor a religious question, even if it assumes this or that colouring. It is a national question, and in order to solve it, we must make it above all a world-political issue, which will require settlement in the councils of the civilized nations."[26]

In one important respect Herder actually more than anticipated Herzl's conception of the *Judenstaat*. For Herzl did not there as yet commit himself to Palestine as the sole territory qualifying as the Jewish homeland. He only spoke of *a* territory. Herder, though he doubted that all Jews would wish to go to a national homeland of their own, had no doubt whatsoever about its location; in this he was correctly assessing the power and fascination that historical continuity and tradition exert over people's minds: "What bliss when a Messiah-Bonaparte will victoriously lead them to Palestine!"[27] Even if only part of Jewry returned to Palestine to re-establish the State of Israel, this would greatly affect the fortunes of those who stayed behind, for it would engender in them as well a national self-respect they were in real danger of losing. Moreover, Herder maintained, they would thereby also evoke respect among non-Jews.[28] Here, too, Herzl shared Herder's view when he told his fellow-Jews: "If you become untrue to yourself, you must not complain if others become untrue to you; a man could only be true to himself if he continued to stand by the particular world in which he had grown up and into which nature and history had placed him."[29]

In effect, Herder called for a *national* solution as the condition for any *individual* solution. Individual Jews, wherever they were, stood a far better chance of achieving emancipation and full civil rights, he argued, by helping to bring about their national rebirth in a country of their own.

25. XXIV, 63–75.
26. Theodor Herzl, *Zionistische Schriften*, ed. L. Kellner (Berlin: Jüdischer Verlag, nd), i, 47–8.
27. XXIV, 67.
28. XXIV, 74.
29. Alex Bein, quoting Herzl, in his *Theodore Herzl* (London: East and West Library, 1957), 106.

At the same time he urged his fellow Gentiles to do all that was in their power to assist the Jewish people in this undertaking. As for those who would not or could not uproot themselves to create a new existence in their own homeland, "toleration," Herder made clear, was not good enough. Beyond recommending in Christian countries legislation that would accord to those Jews who remained behind the civic privileges that hitherto had been denied them, he pleaded for a fundamental change of attitude, amounting to a metamorphosis of people's minds, a change of heart he hoped would create what he called a "common culture of the soul." As with Rousseau's notion of a *civil* religion, this common culture would promote the *overall* reciprocity of citizenship through a massive effort of educational *Bildung*.[30]

If it is remembered that in Herder's Germany Jews were still confined to the ghetto, that public schools and most of the universities as well as many professions were closed to them, and that citizenship was denied to them in many European states until the second half of the nineteenth century,[31] Herder's plea for full emancipation of the individual Jew in the diaspora was as bold as his demand for a collective and territorial solution for the Jews as a nation.

IV

The main thrust of Herder's thinking was nevertheless in the direction of helping to bring about a *national* solution for the Jews as well as for all the other peoples viewing themselves as suppressed and unrecognized.

30. XIV, 284. It is of interest that Herder stressed the correlation between the legal treatment of the Jews and the political enlightenment of a state: "All those laws that treat the Jew worse than a beast indicate the barbaric constitution of a state" (XXIV, 71).

31. Goethe's reminiscences in his *Dichtung und Wahrheit* (*Fiction and Truth*) give a vivid insight into eighteenth-century conditions of the Frankfurt ghetto and the precarious situation of the Jews. For this see William Rose's study "Goethe and the Jews" in his *Men, Myths, and Movements in German Literature* (London: G. Allen and Unwin, 1931), 157–80. See also Mark Waldman, *Goethe and the Jews* (New York, London: Putnam, 1934). Where Jews were admitted to a university, as in Göttingen, the university authorities were required by law to warn Jewish undergraduates that the attainment of academic qualifications would not necessarily entitle them to enter the professions. An excellent account of the Jews in eighteenth-century Germany can be found in Karl Biedermann, *Deutschland im achtzehnten Jahrhundert* (Leipzig, 1880), iii, 1113–27. It is not without interest that a decree by the elector of Mainz, aiming at the emancipation of the Jews in this tiny city-state, was met by the majority of citizens with considerable hostility, as the eighteenth-century historian and publicist A.L. Schlözer noted in his *Staats Anzeigen* (Göttingen 1784), VI, 502.

In so doing, Herder signalled a marked ideological shift from doctrines of individual rights to doctrines of collective rights which, despite his organismic metaphors, foreshadows not so much racist Nazism – as has at times been claimed – as the emergent gulf between "liberal" and "communitarian" positions. For Herder's national-political thinking rested on his belief in an individual's *embeddedness* within a larger whole that forms the matrix (in its most literal sense) of a person's existence and development. But this matrix, it should be noted, Herder identified with shared *institutions* rather than with a shared *race*. Hence, while in his preferred scheme of things the individual is viewed as an integral part of the nation to which he or she belongs, this "whole" is itself thought of not in terms of a homogeneous *substance* but rather in terms of an *ensemble* made up of a great variety of smaller wholes that are self-regulating units in their own right. What Herder envisions, therefore, is not centralized collectivism, in which constituent parts are forged into unity by a dominant centre of power, but a kind of partnership between distinct institutions and associations within a political structure free from any major pressure point.

This pluralist conception of political nationhood does not stop Herder, however, from speaking of the Hebrews as a single *Volk*, synonymous with the *whole* of the Jewish people; *Volk* and nation are one. And, in contrast to his thinking about *Volk* within the context of his own times, he identifies the ancient *Volk* of Israel with a vertically undifferentiated society, politically structured to form an "organic" entity, in sharp opposition to his contemporary states, which he dismisses as purely "mechanical contrivances" glued together by administrative fiat or military conquest, "machine-states, without any inner source of life."[32] While Herder does not suggest that it is "race" that makes a *Volk* an organic community, he does in this connection make use of a well-tried device in political argument: he invokes "nature." Contemporary states, like

---

32. XIII, 385. What is lacking, Herder makes clear, is not "race" but "national character"; it alone can give life to a state and prevent it from "playing around with peoples and humans as though they were lifeless bodies." See also XIII, 252, 257, where Herder flatly declares that he sees no grounds for employing the concept of race. Yet it was not only Nazi sympathizers in Germany such as Benno v. Wiese, for example, who acclaimed Herder as a precursor of racism (in *Volk und Dichtung von Herder bis zur Romantik*, Erlangen, 1938, 18), but also R.G. Collingwood, in *The Idea of History* (Oxford, Clarendon Press 1946), 86–92, or K.R. Popper, in *The Open Society and its Enemies* (London: Routledge, 1952), ii, 52, and H.S. Reiss, in *The Political Thought of the German Romantics* (Oxford, Clarendon Press, 1955), 2, 8. Perhaps Hitler's use of *Volk* had this effect.

their governments, have arisen out of emergencies, of conditions of crisis (*Not*), and, like bad doctors, keep their peoples in permanent dependency. By contrast, nations *are* natural if they grow spontaneously and unfold from *within*, not unlike plants, sustained as they are by life-forces of their own and adapted to exist among others.[33] In principle, therefore, nations emerge, exist, and survive, not because of rulers, states, or governments but because they can draw on sources of *internal* strength.

External factors are not, to be sure, ignored in Herder's vision; but, in contrast to Montesquieu's more balanced interaction between human (internal) elements and physical (external) elements, Herder's scheme centres primarily on internal elements, which he refers to as "genetic" forces. This internalization accounts in part for its originality, but it also contributes to its problematic repute, despite the fact that Herder expressly links "genetic" not with biological but rather with cultural characteristics and with processes that he describes as constituting a *spiritual* genesis.

Furthermore, whatever ethnicity is involved in the internal elements is closely linked with a political impulse *sui generis* that is an integral part of Herder's teleological assumptions about the destiny of humankind as a species. Accordingly, human beings, by their intrinsic nature, are not intended to see the point of their existence or the fulcrum of their happiness in ruling or being ruled. Anyone who cannot exist without being ruled is not fully human yet, and the same is true of a people as a whole. For, once humans *are* fully human, "they no longer need a master to permanently lord over them."[34]

V

With this lofty, yet negative, stance on the need for states and governments, Herder transparently discloses how essential his "organic" conception of nationhood is, if social life is not to disintegrate in the *homo-homini-lupus* manner outlined by Hobbes. Only the strongest inner cohesion can provide a chance of survival for a nation in which political rule is replaced by what amounts to a pluralistic coexistence of economic and social activities. And, since he is not advocating anarchic lawlessness, Herder apparently presumes that in a spontaneously grown nation the most diverse pursuits do not demand a central body

33. XIII, 384.
34. XIII, 383.

to coordinate them. Hence "government" is turned in effect into a degree of self-rule that yields little if any scope for central control, let alone for the assertion of hereditary rulers.

However, apart from recommending self-government in this pluralis-tically diffused understanding, Herder sees little point in speculating on the ideal form of political government. "A best form of government never has existed and hardly ever will exist."[35] All the same, Herder does mount a more specific argument, rooted for the most part in his pro-found dissatisfaction with things as they are. Thus he emphatically rejects every kind of absolutism, including that of the "enlightened des-pot." Indeed, *any* sort of personal dominion is odious to him, not only because it breeds servility on the one hand and arrogance on the other, but because it altogether corrodes the soul of a nation and erodes its true nobility.[36] Reform has to come "from below," and whatever "nobil-ity" is required to promote it must come "from the people themselves, and their natural leaders," for "why should anyone, by right of birth, reign over thousands of his brethren? Nature does not dispense her most noble talents among particular families." In an added, but sup-pressed, statement Herder is even more outspoken. "In our age," he writes, "there is hardly anyone who anymore believes that birth makes people wise, gentle, or deserving."[37]

As for size, while the city-state of Riga remained for Herder what Geneva was for Rousseau, this personal preference nevertheless did not induce him to follow Rousseau in declaring that the republican form of government was less suitable for large states, since he could not agree that large republics were *in principle* less viable than small ones. Size as such, Herder felt, discloses little about the public spirit or the intensity of mutual ties among a republic's citizenry.[38] And it is these attributes that make all the difference. Almost axiomatically, therefore, Herder concludes that it is the nature of a nation's inner bonds that matters first

---

35. XVIII, 283.
36. XIII, 381, XVIII, 310.
37. XVIII, 312. See also J.G. Müller, *Aus dem Herder'schen Hause* (Berlin, 1881), 109: "Er (Herder) ist dem Adel schrecklich feind," (He is terribly hostile to the nobility) "because it goes against human equality and all principles of Christianity, apart from being a monu-ment of human stupidity." It has been variously stated by Herder biographers that Herder's ideal form of government was that of constitutional monarchy. I can find no evidence for this. Although he possibly preferred constitutional monarchy to absolutist monarchy as the lesser evil, he left no doubt about his firm belief in republicanism.
38. XVIII, 317.

and foremost. The stronger and, at the same time, gentler these are, the more permanent a state's political institutions will be, and the less likely it is that they will fall victim to the rule of one or the few.[39]

Admittedly, Herder was rather vague about how to bridge the gap between what is and what ought to be, between visibly imposed ties and ties that are invisible because they are genuinely spontaneous. This vagueness had partially to do with the political censorship in virtually all German states at the time, but in some measure it must be attributed to Herder's use of the concept of "*Volk.*" When talking about the ancient Hebrews as a *Volk*, he always meant the people as a whole, and thought of them as both a nationally homogeneous entity and an almost undifferentiated social entity. In his critique of contemporary society, however, its meaning is no longer the same. *Volk* is only part of the nation; its most numerous, to be sure, and, as Herder insisted, by far the most valuable as well. But the main thrust of Herder's efforts now is to help the part to become the whole by shedding both its aristocratic rulers and their servile hangers-on. And, by claiming that the *Volk*, composed of the ordinary *Bürger,* make up not only the majority of the population but also the most creative source of a nation's culture, Herder most effectively strengthened the fortunes of those anxious to present their case for nationalism and democracy as one and the same argument.[40]

VI

Broadly, Herder identified the *Volk* with people who by virtue of their own industry have a certain sense of independence, in the knowledge of standing squarely in a world of their own, in and through which they earn their livelihood. These Herder distingushed not merely from the aristocracy but also from a stratum of society that he called the *Pöbel*, a drifting mob or rabble, with no self-location within society. As opposed to those who, despite diverse occupations, share a sense of collective identity and social mutuality, the rabble is a mere aggregate of individuals, with no abiding loyalty whatsoever, who are thus easily manipulable by the powers that be. These "dregs of society, ever roaming the streets," cannot be depended upon to assume the kind of duties

39. XII, 117; see also XIII, 381.

40. I, 392. This is particularly true of the tenor of argument in the case of Giuseppe Mazzini and Thomas Masaryk.

expected of members of a given trade or calling.[41] Although Herder does not apply the criterion of property ownership in order to distinguish the *Volk* from the rabble – a common practice by many political thinkers of the time – he does associate the rabble with a fundamentally different mentality, a mentality separating it from the *Bürger*, the mainstream citizenry. And it is this middle-class sort of segment that is to replace the aristocracy as the "pillar of the state."[42] Following Montesquieu, Herder attributes England's attainment of political freedom, together with her rise as a commercial power, to the early participation of this class in public life.[43]

Indeed, it is only through this kind of transformation that Herder sees the possibility for the emergence of a *public* realm properly so called. The rabble, therefore, is perhaps best defined by what it is not, since, unlike the mainstream citizenry, it neither embodies, nor expresses, an identifiable social or national consciousness. Having no sense of abiding existence, no sense of stable location, its loyalties are exceedingly fluid and dangerously prone to rapid and unpredictable shifts – it simply cannot be trusted.

In singling out the lack of any shared consciousness and the absence of any self-location as the defining hallmark of the rabble, Herder remarkably prefigures Marx's thinking, since for Marx, as for Herder, some people clearly form no part of *the* people. Just as members of the rabble for Herder lack civic consciousness, and hence cannot be trusted as citizens, no more can they be trusted, in Marx's scheme, to be militant fighters for a new social order. Marx identifies the rabble with the *Lumpenproletariat*, with that unpredictable "scum on the streets," always susceptible to the basest treachery, banditry, and corruption. In the *Communist Manifesto* he describes it therefore as that "dangerous class" which, thrown off "by the lowest layers of old society" constitutes in its "passively rotting mass" the bribed tool of "reactionary intrigue."[44] Similarly, in *The Class Struggle in France*, the rabble is as sharply marked off from the people proper as it is from the *Volk* in Herder's account. The

41. XXV, 323; see also I, 157 and III, 413.

42. XXIII, 429. Herder indeed comes close to suggesting a two-nation version of the *Volk*, the majority of the nation, the *Volk* of the *Bürger*, and its learned minority, the *Volk* of *Gelehrsamkeit* (XXXII, 60.)

43. XVIII, 108.

44. Karl Marx and Friedrich Engels, *The Communist Manifesto* (New York: International Publishers, 1932), 20.

recruiting ground for *any* undertaking in which quick gains are to be made, it yields all sorts of opportunists, thieves, and criminals, "vagabonds *sans feu et sans aveu,* varying according to the degree of civilization of the nation to which they belong, but never renouncing their *lazzaroni* character."[45]

Finally, and again recalling Herder's refusal to put the rabble into any particular *economic* category, Marx (in *The Eighteenth Brumaire*) places the *Lumpenproletariat,* because of its parasitic nature, within the full spectrum of society – "the whole indefinite, disintegrating mass thrown hither and thither," from pickpockets to brothel-keepers, from discharged soldiers and jailbirds to ruined offshoots of the bourgeoisie. Bonaparte himself Marx considers the "chief of the *Lumpenproletariat,*" of this "scum, offal, refuse of *all* classes ... upon which he can base himself unconditionally."[46]

Yet, while Herder judges no less harshly the *product* of the process resulting in the emergence of the rabble, he is more charitable in tracing its origins. He blames the existence of this drifting mob on the decadence of the political *status quo* and on its failure "to make use of man's divine and noble gifts, [allowing] these to rust, thereby giving rise to bitterness and frustration." For what is involved, Herder explains, is not merely that human assets are sentenced to be destroyed and buried but that no such sentence can be executed because, being "life forces," human assets "invariably *defy* burial." And since unwanted humans cannot rest while they are still alive, they create a great deal of confusion and disturbance and, in their frustration, "are likely to use their creative gifts for destructive ends."[47]

On this view, the existence of the rabble is not so much the work of individual deficiencies as it is a symptom of sociopolitical bankruptcy and the tragic result of blindness to the fact that discarded human assets cannot help being alive. That frustrated individuals can lose every sense of belonging and, in turn, threaten to wreck the texture of social mutuality has almost become a truism in our own day. This was not, however, quite so when Herder wrote and, evidently, not altogether realized even by Marx himself.

45. Marx, *The Class Struggles in France* (Moscow: Selected Works, Progress Publishers, 1952), I, 155.
46. Marx, *The Eighteenth Brumaire of Louis Bonaparte* (Moscow: Progress Publishers, 1952), I, 295.
47. XXX, 234.

The reason I am drawing attention to this intriguing parallelism goes, however, beyond the similarity of Herder's and Marx's concern over the drifting outsider. For I believe that it casts additional light on the symbiosis of source and structure – and each in its own right – in Herder's speculations on nationhood and popular self-government. Clearly, within this symbiosis, while ethnicity provides bonds of *identity*, it does not by itself define the *relationship* of these bonds. This is significantly evident in his treatment of *Volk* in both the ancient Hebrew context and in the contemporary social context. In both, Herder leaves no doubt whatsoever that the sovereign rule of law, as the safeguard of reciprocal fairness and overall equity (*Billigkeit*) is every bit as important to ensure civic rights (*Bürgerrechte*) and a sense of common belonging as linguistic or broadly cultural requirements.[48] Similarly, by virtue of his extraordinary sensitivity for, and reflective perspicacity about, social ills, Herder powerfully anticipated subsequent concerns with structural problems in society, with defects causing alienation, and with the bifurcation of its members into haves and have-nots. In short, by stressing bases of cultural identity, Herder was not blind to bases of civic relations that bear upon a shared consicousness of nationhood and societal inclusiveness without having much to do with "ethnic" characteristics.

VII

That the major part of humanity should have so little to say on public concerns was as unpalatable to Herder as to several of his forerunners and contemporaries. Unlike them, however, he had – except for a short period in his youth – little, if any, confidence in reform from the top in and through enlightened monarchs, for he doubted their ability (or frequently their real desire) to change things. He therefore pinned his hopes on the emergence of popular leaders, of "men of the people" who, imbued with missionary zeal, would spread the gospel of *Bildung*, of active self-creation, with a view to helping others reach a stage when they no longer were in need of intrusive guidance and could, as a result, eventually dispense with political masters altogether. The popular leaders Herder had in mind were to "come from that part of the middle segments of society that has hitherto initiated most of the advances

48. XIV, 246, 487.

of mankind; by exerting their influence up and down the social scale, they would give life and meaning to the whole."[49]

The term Herder applied to these popular leaders was "aristo-democrats." Although far less charismatic, if not less mysterious, than Rousseau's Lawgiver, they were to assume functions not altogether different, at any rate during the transition from "government" to "self-government," to enable the *Volk* to attain political maturity. And while he had no doubt that persons as individuals would profit from this transitional process, Herder went beyond Diderot and the encyclopaedists in stressing the need for mutuality through active reciprocity by making people realize that as individuals *per se* they could exist only most imperfectly. Aristo-democrats were therefore to strive toward creating a society, not of isolated individuals exclusively bent on promoting their own interests, but of citizens engaged in maximal cooperative sharing, jointly employing their creative energies, their *zusammenwirkende Kräfte*.[50]

Active social cooperation is therefore the central idea in the communitarian republic that Herder visualized. Only through inter-dependent reciprocity could he see any scope for fostering a livelier *social* consciousness as the condition of an enhanced *national* consciousness that implied a high degree of *civic* inclusiveness. In essence it was this vision that sustained his ultimate goal: the compatibility of nationality with humanity (*Humanität*), the combination of distinctive particularity with international universality. He sums up this goal in a simple maxim, rightly celebrated for its succinctness, but no less problematic for all that: "If you must, serve the state, and if you can, serve humanity,"[51] It expresses poignantly, however, what Herder missed in the reality he knew, as against what he strove for in a reality that might be.

---

49. XXIV, 174. Although maintaining that most people could apply judgment and reason to whether or not their interests were taken into account, thinkers of the Enlightenment were more concerned with the *how* than with the *who* of political rule. Locke, Leibniz, Wolff, Thomasius, Kant, Voltaire or Diderot, for example, had no serious problem with the existence of the monarchy or the aristocracy, provided their demands for tolerance, the abolition of torture, the emancipation of the serfs, and the dissemination of education were heeded or at least not entirely ignored. The young Herder largely shared this outlook, even contributing an enthusiastic poem on the occasion of the coronation of Catherine II (of Russia) in 1765 (XXIX, 24–7). He also expected great things from Joseph II (of Austria). In both instances, however, he was to be deeply disappointed; and this disappointment marked a turning point; absolutism and enlightenment, he now concluded, were totally incompatible (XVII, 61).

50. XIV, 227, XVIII, 331.

51. XIII, 456.

Yet Herder was no starry-eyed utopian. We noted that he was by no means unaware of roadblocks, for he knew that *Fortgang*, the passing of time, was not tantamount to *Fortschritt*, the advancement of moral or material progress. Again and again he therefore points to what lies ahead, and how arduously long and frequently interrupted the process of *Bildung*, in its literal meaning of conscious shaping, will be before people can hope to approximate to the political and moral ideal that he believed to have found in the Mosaic legacy, associating it, as he did, with his own most cherished aspirations toward nationality *and* humanity, *Volk* and *Humanität*.

It is conceivable that Herder's "organic" conception of nationhood, with its emphasis on "genetic" characteristics, lends itself to racist interpretation, if not antisemitic perversion, when taken out of context. However, no one with the slightest familiarity with Herder's overall thought could doubt for one moment that he would have recoiled at the mere suggestion. For nothing was more abhorrent to his very being than persecution of any kind. "From early childhood," he writes, "I have found nothing more abominable or detestable than oppression or personal insults of anyone for his religion or outlook (*Gesinnung*) ... Retribution for such persecutions has never been wanting and never shall be."[52] Herder, we noted, had no use for the concept of race and denied that national differences could be explained in terms of racial differences. Humanity, to him, was biologically alike, and nothing was gained by bringing "race" between *Volk* and *Humanität*.[53] Nor was he insensitive to the danger of nationalist chauvinism, "the most fatal malaise throughout history ... a fearful mania, to which in all epochs the feeble-minded are particularly prone ... especially if politically induced." Against this "national fanaticism" Herder repeatedly sounded his most earnest warnings.[54]

There is no need to labour the point. Herder was singularly unfit for the role of a precursor of Nazi ideology. If anything, in eliciting the core

52. XVII, 273–4.
53. XIII, 252, 257.
54. XXIII, 214, XVII, 230, 319; see also XVIII, 137, 271, and XXXII, 519. It was not that Herder sought to drive a wedge between the cultural and the political in his vision of national self-government – a central point of the next chapter. Rather, he was anxious to keep apart the political from the pathological – *Nationalbewusstsein* from *Nationalwahn* – (Herder *coined* both terms), by insisting upon the transitional process of aristo-democracy. In this process he saw indeed the defining characteristic of "reform from below" by viewing it as *itself* a democratic process.

problem of the Jewish question as a *national* problem, Herder was anticipating political Zionism, not racist Nazism, while his portrayal of communitarian nationalism discloses a republicanism that is as democratic
as it is pluralist – and a far cry from Hitler's *Volks-gemeinschaft*, his community through Aryan purity.

Always sceptical, however, regarding the extent to which perfectibility
could be carried, Herder went out of his way to make clear that the idea
of progress could be accepted only as an ideal, as a hypothesis of faith. It
was precisely such an affirmation of faith that Herder associated with
"the idea of Moses"; it was an idea, he declared, that "could not be sur-
passed by a higher or truer one." Unfortunately, he adds, it and all the
institutions Moses based on it "came three or four thousand years too
early, just as another Moses might still be in another six thousand
years."[55] Doubt mingles with hope, resignation with faith, despondency
with expectancy: all typically Herderian moods which, on different occasions, and in different proportions, underlie his nationalism as much as
his humanism.

And yet, while Herder emphatically strove to distinguish the passing
of time from a smooth advance toward beatitude, he nonetheless was
man of the Enlightenment enough to believe, as we shall note, that
ultimately time *qua* "history" was itself an agent of human progress, a
harbinger of better things to come. But there was no necessary contradiction involved. For even in his optimism Herder remained a relativist
in that he kept insisting that few gains are made without loses, and that
advances in some directions are therefore wholly compatible with decline in others.[56] Indeed, he went so far in the *Ideas* – his most mature
reflections on history – as to express the fear that the rapid diffusion of
inventions and techniques on a global scale might be followed by the

55. XII, 117. Likewise, he argued, the reconciliation of *Volk* and *Humanität* must be
accepted as an article of faith, although Herder wished to believe that persistent human
striving toward it might attain it – the recurrent theme of his *Letters for the Advancement of
Humanity*. Thus, whether or not another Moses would come to help the fusion along was
an issue separate from what was in essence a clarion call to *self*-directed action in which
men and women, in seeking their shared identity as members of a distinct nation, would
at the same time recognize their belonging to universal humanity. But muted as this call
was by Herder's acute consciousness of the uncertainty of progress, it had little in common
with sanguine political romanticism or ecstatic political messianism. (Regarding this consciousness of uncertainty and the mingling of hope and doubt, see, for example, XVIII,
314, 328.)

56. See, for example, XIV, 233–7.

"gradual extinction of national character."[57] Herder clearly was by no means unaware that moves to augment "globality" might come at the cost of national distinctiveness and vitality. His optimism, therefore, such as it was, was anything but unqualified.

Much the same applies to his vision of oneness amidst manifold plurality, in the absence of any government over and above self-government. He guardedly cherished this hope because, in addition to a sense of national belonging in ethnic terms, he assumed the eventual possibility of a comparable degree of social and civic mutuality. Ultimately, therefore, Herder appears to have made the attainment of rightful association far less restrictedly contingent on ethnic identity than is widely believed; there was for him evidently more to nationhood than speaking the same tongue, if it was to sustain relations among people without rulers and nobles at the upper end or "prowling riffraff" at the lower. In a real sense, if I am right in stressing the distinction between sources of identity and sources of relationship, it might not be wrong to conclude that Herder's conception of nationality not so much pioneered nationalism – as it came to be most widely understood – as it gave a highly novel expression to the idea of culturally rooted civic association, to a sense of collective belonging within a republic that was maximally inclusionary in social and cultural terms and minimally exclusionary in political-legal terms.

57. XIV, 288. This is surely in sharp contrast to the cosmopolitanism of such contemporaries as Kant, Schiller, or Lessing. And a similarly qualified enthusiasm for a universal humanity also colours Herder's ideal of *Humanität* in the sense of international brotherhood, despite Herder's sincerely felt moral fervour. It evidently, too, cannot be viewed as an *absolute* gain. (See, for example, XIV, 213, 230–5). This note, like the previous one, illustrates Herder's pioneering principle of displaced alternatives, which recognizes that every gain invariably entails the cost of some loss; it likewise bears out what Herder has had to say about the burdens of human freedom, in that the essence of freedom consists in the possibility of choosing between alternatives. Evidently, Herder himself preferred to interblend things rather than categorically set them apart. For example, he sought to combine an essentially communitarian ethic with the liberal idea of individual rights and freedoms. This foreshadows contemporary attempts in a similar direction, such as those of Will Kymlicka; e.g., his most recent *Politics in the Vernacular: Nationalism, Multiculturalism, and Citizenship* (Oxford: Oxford University Press, 2001).

2

Cultural Nationalism and
Political Romanticism

IT MAY WELL MAKE HISTORICAL SENSE to distinguish the nation-state from the state-nation, as Friedrich Meinecke has done.[1] I am less certain, however, that it makes conceptual sense to make a distinction between cultural nationalism and political nationalism, especially if the juxtaposition rests on the assumed divergence between Herder and Rousseau in those terms. Instead, I wish to suggest in this chapter that, if a contrasting variant to Herder's cultural nationalism is to be singled out, it is not political *nationalism* but political *romanticism*. For, while the latter shares its evocative mood and metaphorical terminology with Herder's cultural nationalism, the two are poles apart.

I

I should first like to resume the point made in the previous chapter, which questions the belief that in his philosophy of nationhood Herder put exclusive emphasis on ethnic characteristics. And I propose to do this by taking issue with a widely held thesis that, while Herder identified the source of national belonging with sharing a common language, Rousseau equated it entirely with the articulation of a common will. There clearly is more to it; and the "more" I would locate not simply in Herder's celebration of folksong in addition to language but in his provocative contention that national belonging is not the same as membership of a state. For it was above all this contention that prompted nationalists, as members of multinational states, to embrace

1. Friedrich Meinecke, *Weltbürgertum und Nationalstaat* (Munich: Oldenbourg, 1963), 10–26.

the "cultural" properties that Herder put forward to establish the congruence between a particular people and its particular habitat. To them these were important chiefly, if not only, because, within the context of their aspirations, they could serve as the justification or legitimation of political claims in support of linking a distinctive national identity with a distinctive national home-land. And once this is granted, the opposition between cultural nationalism and political nationalism loses force.

By the same token, the opposition between Herder and Rousseau can no longer be *essentially* viewed in terms of "cultural" *versus* "political" categories, since, if Herder *linked* these categories to establish the indentifying congruence between *a* people and *a* territory, so did Rousseau. Should, therefore, significant divergences exist between their respective visions of the legitimate polity, they would need to be looked for elsewhere.

In an attempt to trace these divergences, I shall make use of three principal distinctions: the distinction between "creation" and "emergence," the distinction between substantive and accidental wholes, and the distinction between "unitary will" and "dialogical consensus." In so doing, I intend to affirm a twofold thesis: (i) that Herder's contribution to nationalist doctrine involves not a depoliticizing of the idea of nationhood but rather, not unlike Rousseau's, its redefinition; and (ii) that Herder's undertaking toward this end, though different in important details, nonetheless embodies in essence a common quest for uncovering sources of a society's rightful existence. Accordingly, I propose first to sketch what Herder and Rousseau have in common.

To start with, both are prone to blurring the difference between "nature" as an empirical description and "nature" as a promotional prescription. Possibly, the blurring is neither accidental nor entirely unintended, since nature is almost invariably invoked in order to oppose the contrived and artificial to the authentic and original. The truly natural, therefore, consists of the stream of human development that underlies the "surface culture" that has become disconnected from it. Rousseau and Herder likewise seek, accordingly, to retake possession of a people's true heritage, so that the national and the natural coincide. And to make this fusion, it was evidently of minor concern to both if Nature as she is and Nature as she should be were strictly kept apart.

Second, both Herder and Rousseau repudiated Hobbes's image of the state of nature. Even though Rousseau viewed humans as naturally non-sociable, he, no less than Herder, portrayed their basic dispositions as peaceable. Once people realized that other selves had affinities with them, their similarities patently mattered more to them than their dissimilarities, in that they suggested the basis of a common bond. While Herder and Rousseau saw the transition from national becoming to political becoming in divergent terms, there was full agreement between them that some matrix of national becoming must precede political becoming for the latter to be able to build upon the former. Therefore, although they had to interrelate in order to constitute nationhood proper, national culture and political culture were nevertheless not identical.

Third, both Herder and Rousseau had a deep distrust of cosmopolitanism. The source of this distrust was for the most part a shared sense of the importance of law. In the absence of an established legal order in the international realm, cosmopolitanism was for Herder as much as for Rousseau nothing but an empty formula, a mere abstraction, if not a mirage.

Fourth, though not subscribing to radical egalitarianism, Herder, like Rousseau, detested inherited social privileges and the inequality they helped to exacerbate. So-called high culture was suspect to both because it had grown out of an unequal society.

The fifth resemblance in their thinking is rather intriguing; both held that religion and nationality were not easily separable. Impressed as they equally were by the extent to which religion deepened the sense of collective identity in ancient Israel, Rousseau made a point in urging the Poles to follow the example set by Moses and the Hebrews, while Herder, we saw, viewed the Hebrews as "a model nation of all times."[2] On Christianity, too, their ideas converged closely. Herder accused Christian missionaries of having cruelly deprived peoples of their national "character, heart, and history,"[3] and Rousseau went even further, seeing organized Christianity as a constant threat to distinct nations everywhere, which frequently caused their destruction by separating political institutions from religious institutions. In this separation Rousseau saw the seed of the "internal divisions that have never ceased to stir up Christian peoples."[4]

Finally, although both thinkers upheld the principle of national uniqueness, they did not associate the principle, as a number of political romanticists did, with a divine mission analogous to the Messianic tradi-

2. J.G. Herder, *Sämtliche Werke*, ed. B. Suphan, 33 vols. (Berlin: Weidmann, 1877–1913), XII, 128, 168.
3. Ibid., XXIV, 42–9.
4. J.J. Rousseau, *The Social Contract*, Bk. IV, ch. 8.

tion of the chosen people. For in agreeing that each nation, by fully realizing its inherent nature, enriched the quality of humanity at large, they by no means said or implied that universal redemption rested on the self-realization of any *one* nation.

II

Regarding the questions of what transforms people into *a* people and, secondly, what enables a people, once founded, to survive, Herder (as much as Rousseau) was greatly indebted to Montesquieu, as he fully acknowledged. Like Montesquieu, Herder grappled with the interrelations between institutional-cultural and environmental-natural forces. In addition, however, Herder, following Rousseau, was deeply concerned with the specifically normative issue of what might be the most desirable unit or configuration or form of life for a particular people to live in, and which kind of political association accorded most suitably and least unnaturally, with such a people.

In order to establish such a congruence between a people and its national institutions, both Rousseau and Herder search for characteristics that might disclose the most basic features in the customs of a collectivity that distinguish it from other groups. In these basic features both see causal forces at work in the formation of the "spirit" of a nation's institutions, its distinctive ethos or "personality." They differ, however, about the *process* in and through which the causal forces are to take shape; how, that is, a custom-guided mode of life is to turn into a politically regulated mode of life. The divergence, therefore, has to do with the road from one to the other. Herder favours the idea of *emergence* in the course of which standards of civic relations unfold, without calling for the intervention of an external lawgiver. Rousseau, on the other hand, does favour such intervention in order to facilitate the *creation* at a given point in time of a constitutional framework. This point is reached, Rousseau specifies, during the "final stage in the state of nature," a stage he describes as halfway between unsociable animality and unconscious sociability, a stage characterized by the use of language as communication beyond the family circle.[5]

For, although Rousseau, as subsequently Herder, refers to "shared customs" as the source of national cultures, he does not include *legal* traditions as part of historical evolvement. In short, Rousseau's early

5. Rousseau, *Discourse on the Origin of Inequality*, ed. and trans. Lowell Bair (New York: Mentor, 1974), Pt. I, 162.

collectivities are merely the rudiments of nationality, the *foundations* upon which the nation proper is to be built. In Hegelian terminology, these unreflective collectivities are merely nationalities *in* themselves, not nationalities *for* themselves.[6] Interestingly, in the transition from nationality to nationhood, language itself, Rousseau suggests, can serve as evidence of political development. Thus, if words and sentences are short and precise, as in commands, and no time is wasted on eloquence – since persuasion is unnecessary to ensure compliance – this shows that a nation as a *legitimate* association has not as yet come into being. It is only when language is resonant and prosodic that persuasion will assume centrality and political freedom will be manifest.[7]

Confined to bringing about the transformation from a non-reflective and non-political stage to a reflective and political stage, the lawgiver *has* to be a charismatic personality, an almost god-like man, for he has no recognized place within the institutions of the nation he has helped to create, and hence no power other than the force of his superior personality.[8] As for the dynamics of the transformation, Rousseau is at the same time explicit *and* paradoxical. Although the transformation involves a radical change, it must not eradicate the basic character of a people; in other words, the change is not to be *dis*continuous. On the other hand, Rousseau just as explicitly insists that the transformation never leaves a people what it was before. Herder, too, we shall note, seeks to reconcile discontinuity with continuity; change must never be total. However, since to him the *context* of national becoming is one of *emergence* rather than *creation*, Herder's postulate of continuity *within* discountinuity seems less starkly paradoxical, apart from also being a good deal less mysterious than Rousseau's account.[9]

All the same, the mysterious intervention of Rousseau's law-giver or the seemingly paradoxical requirements characterizing Rousseau's dynamics of the transformation must not be allowed to cloak the profound realism in Rousseau's account. Precisely because he recognizes that what is done cannot easily be undone and change is for the most part irrevocable, Rousseau takes great pains to make sure that creating a political nation is not taken lightly. Three requirements are of the essence: timing, suitabil-

---

6. Rousseau, *Social Contract*, Bk. II, ch. 10.

7. Rousseau, *Sur l'origine des langues* (1781) (Paris, 1974), 173–4. Language alone is not a cohesive force for Rousseau, but it is instrumental in making agreement possible. Thus it is only indirectly that language contributes to the formation of nationhood.

8. Rousseau, *Social Contract*, Bk. II, ch. 7.

9. Ibid., Bk. II, ch. 8.

ity, and manageability. Peter the Great is taken to task for thoroughly bad timing; as a result, instead of transforming a nation *in* itself into a nation *for* itself, he turned Russians into Germans and Englishmen or, at any rate, did his level best to do so. "By convincing them that they were what they were not," he prevented them from becoming what they were meant to be.[10] Similarly, the most excellent constitution is of no avail if it has no applicability to the people for which it is written – if it is simply not suitable. "The wise lawgiver ... does not start by drafting laws that are merely good in themselves, but he examines first whether the poeple for whom he intends them are suited to bear them."[11] Third, Rousseau knew well – and Herder learned from him equally well – that a political nation cannot be created independently of its nature and its history. The political culture must therefore be in harmony with a people's non-political culture, and should serve only to "secure, accompany, and rectify" it.[12] Otherwise the outcome could be dismal in the extreme and would leave people worse off than they were before – and most certainly less manageable.[13] Manageability, accordingly, is not simply a matter of size. Rousseau is anxious not to sound dogmatic on this point. As in his account of the state of nature, in these observations he merely offers as a "reasonable conjecture" that, generally speaking, "a small state is proportionally stronger than a large one" because "the more the social bond stretches the looser it becomes."[14] It follows that it is not in the interests of the wise nation to extend its territorial borders if it wants to intensify its national consciousness – an empirical insight Rousseau may have gained from the history of his native Switzerland. What matters most, in this view, is that a nation experience itself as a tangibly distinctive self, and Rousseau, not unreasonably, believes that this is more likely to happen if a nation remains small. Not surprisingly, therefore, Rousseau advises the Poles that their principal trouble is that their country is oversized – something he knew they would realize themselves were they more mature as a nation.[15]

Clearly, the overarching goal for both Herder and Rousseau, whether the emphasis is on *creation* or *emergence*, is to help a nation gain maturity. Admire as they both did ancient Israel as the earliest nation

---

10. Ibid., Bk. II, chs. 8 and 10.
11. Ibid., Bk. II, ch. 8.
12. Ibid., Bk. II, ch. 11.
13. Ibid., Bk. I, ch. 8.
14. Ibid., Bk. II, chs. 10 and 9.
15. Rousseau, *Considérations sur le gouvernement de Pologne*, in C.E. Vaughan, ed., *Political Writings* (Cambridge: Cambridge University Press, 1915), II, 442.

with a self-reflective image of itself as a distinctive people, Herder, as Rousseau before him, deplored the fact that it was unable to attain full political maturity. Although it had passed the threshold from apolitical nationhood to political nationhood in and through the foundation of constitutive laws and the formation of public standards, it did not have enough time and tranquility to entrench its distinctive political culture of nomocracy within its ancient land. Thus, despite putting maximal emphasis on emergence rather than creation in respect of political institutions, Herder wholly shared Rousseau's emphasis on the rule of law and on standards of mutuality as essential conditions for the maturation of nationhood as a rightful association *sui generis*.

III

On the second critical issue, the question of the viability of a political nation once founded, Rousseau almost sounds Herderian when he proclaims that the laws and institutions that make a people a *political* association are alive only if they are lived (*vécues*), if they are "engraved not on marble or bronze but in the hearts of the citizens."[16] Unlike Herder, however, Rousseau measures the intensity of national belonging by the dedication to the state. Individuals should keep asking themselves whether what they think, say, or do is of advantage to their state.[17] Herder, we noted, was reluctant to draw so close an affinity between experiencing a sense of nationhood and a sense of service to the state. Nor would he go so far as to demand the total abandonment of individual rights.[18] But, then, Herder was a liberal of sorts, whereas Rousseau, whatever else he was, certainly was no liberal in its political understanding. He saw state and society as wholly integrated, and the monistic consensus he advanced was unconditional.[19]

This may have at least been one reason why Herder chose spontaneous emergence rather than deliberate (or instant) creation. And although

16. Rousseau, *Social Contract*, Bk. II, ch. 12. Rousseau's insistence on "daily renewal" of a citizen's consciousness of national belonging was not, however, ultimately related to the work of law or other formal institutions, but to habits, customs, and, above all, to a shared *public* opinion. The "daily renewal" idea rather strikingly foreshadows the historian Ernest Renan's notion (over a century later) of a "daily plebiscite."

17. Ibid., Bk. IV, ch. 1.

18. Ibid., Bk. I, ch. 8, Bk. II, ch. 7.

19. Ibid., Bk. I, ch. 7.

he was no less aware than Rousseau that a people's *patrie* was quite unlike a natural family, Herder nonetheless likened the nation to an "extended family."[20] He did so in order to affirm two related but inherently distinct ideas. One was that the nation did not displace families, clans, tribes, and other historical groupings but was continuous with them and thus, in its way, as natural a growth as the family.[21] The other was that the cultural bonds that linked members of a nation into a relational whole were not *things* or artifacts imposed from above but living energies (*Kräfte*) emanating from within, shared meanings and sentiments which form a people's collective soul. They were what lent a sense of identity and a sense of continuity to a people, and aroused feelings of solidarity not dissimilar to those experienced by members of a family who remained united not out of physical necessity but out of choice, out of the desire to remain a family.[22] Interestingly, Rousseau, anxious to make a similar point, speaks of *agreement*, where Herder speaks of *choice* – a nation is like a family by agreement.[23] This difference in terminology revealingly illustrates the divergence of their approach and accounts for the shift of emphasis in their respective visions of political nationhood and the mode of its coming into being. For, while Rousseau insists on the drawing up of strictly formal contracts, Herder prefers informal bonds that have grown out of historical evolvement.

The main clue to the gap between "agreement" and "choice" is in their having strikingly different philosophical-anthropological starting points. And this difference also casts added light on why "creation" looms prominently in Rousseau's approach and gradual "emergence" in Herder's. Each typifies a fundamentally contrasting perception of what underlies the transformation from apolitical culture to political culture, each perception in essence, amounting to a vastly divergent portrayal of the state of nature. Unlike Rousseau's solitary savage "wandering in the forests, without industry, speech, a fixed dwelling, war, or ties of any kind,"[24] Herder's primitive human is no "isolated rock" or "egotistic monad," since from the very origins human beings are creatures of society and

20. Herder, *Werke*, XIII, 384.
21. Nations are compared to plants, to so many diverse flowers in the garden of humanity. The "garden" symbolizes human creativity in conjunction with nature.
22. Herder's philosophy of *Kraft* recalls Leibniz's *vis viva*, as it anticipates, in Herder's use, Bergson's concept of "life force."
23. Rousseau, *Social Contract*, Bk. I, ch. 2.
24. Rousseau, *Inequality*, Pt. I, 169.

possessors of language.[25] Language itself is for Herder something quite distinct from what it is for Rousseau, because in Herder's theory its primary function is internal: it serves internal speech first and foremost, not external communication. In embodying thoughts and feelings, it simultaneously expresses them. To be human, therefore, is to articulate one's inner world for oneself *and*, by living with others, to articulate it for them as well; the internality of language is accordingly *at once* individual and social, so that "communication" is not something externally added at a later stage. In contrast to Rousseau, there is for Herder consequently no reason to speculate about what came first, language or society. Moreover, in Herder's theory of language, humans are from the beginning creatures of a *particular* language and members of a *particular* society, in that they are what they are by dint of their embeddedness in a distinctive cultural matrix, a matrix that is coterminous with *every* stage of human existence.[26]

In view of this difference about both the origin of language as such and about the origin of a particular language group, there is for Herder from the start a simultaneous existence of nature and culture, of language and social ties, and of the grasp and expression of meanings. In effect, Herder's rejection of Rousseau's tracing human language to animal language, and his making the emergence of a particular language contingent on the prior emergence of a particular society, is *the* key to their divergent conception of the state of nature. Clearly, since for Herder the difference between humans and animals is not a matter of degree, of more or less, but a qualitative difference – human language being inherently unlike animal language, there can be no question of culture invading nature at a given point in time. Language to a human being simply is not native in the same sense in which the hoarding of honey is native to the bee. Rather, it is *sui generis* a mix of nature *and* culture from the very beginning.

The have situated the origin of human language in the animal world seemed, therefore, to Herder totally incomprehensible.[27] Society is by definition cultural as well as natural, unlike the world of plants and animals; therefore, human action – being mediated by language and linguistic meanings – is ontologically different from processes in nature.

25. Herder, *Werke* (*Abhandlung über den Ursprung der Sprache*, 1772) V, 5.

26. For a more detailed discussion of language and nationality, see my *Herder on Social and Political Culture* (Cambridge: Cambridge University Press, 1969), 17–32.

27. Herder, *Werke*, V, 135; see also 23, 25, 98–9, and XIII, 116–17.

And, not being the product of the "blind determination" of nature, it implies possibilities denied to the rest of nature.[28] Among these possibilities, there is above all the exercise of choice and the exercise of reflective judgment. Both of them distinguish membership in a nation from membership in a herd; the capacity to create, to act by choice rather than from necessity, and the capacity to reflect upon oneself – "mirror oneself within oneself" – enables humans to consciously unite with or differentiate themselves from others.[29] Becoming conscious of being a Russian or a German is a wholly integral process that is inherent in the dynamics of human and social existence, an internal culture, so to speak, that requires no external assistance by a lawgiver and no formal drawing up of a social contract.

At the same time Herder does acknowledge that the emergence of a particular *political* culture is not implicit in a particular *linguistic* culture. The switch from a hereditary monarchy to a self-governing democracy, for example, does not happen just because a particular people speaks a particular tongue: it does not enable ordinary folks to pull themselves up by their own bootstraps. With all his metaphorical rhetoric, Herder is forced to face up to the fact that decay from above, the collapse of aristocratic rule – which he persistently foreshadows – does not in itself ensure growth from below.[30] Nonetheless, if any leadership is required, it is not to come from above or from some semi-divine source. Instead, as we noted earlier, Herder's aristo-democrats come from the people and, unlike Rousseau's lawgiver, are therefore not outsiders, but are "one of them." Nonetheless, Herder's popular leaders are similarly intended to be the architects of a social order in which laws, rather than men, govern.[31] In that sense, they are guardians of a sort. At the same time, they are not meant to assume a permanent role comparable to Plato's guardians; on the contrary, they are supposed to do everything in their power to make themselves dispensable. Their function is thus a limited function: their guidance is to cease as soon as the majority of citizens can walk by themselves.[32] How the "democratic" leaders are to emerge

28. Ibid., V, 28.

29. Ibid., V, 29.

30. Ibid., V, 124–34. For a more detailed discussion of this point, see my *Herder's Social and Political Thought* (Oxford: Clarendon Press, 1967), 72–87, and my "Culture and Political Development: Herder's Suggestive Insights," *American Political Science Review*, 63 (1969), 379–97.

31. Herder, *Werke*, XVIII, 331.

32. Ibid., IV, 454, XIII, 149, XVIII, 339.

Herder does not disclose; he throws out hints that scholars, teachers, or writers like himself would be eminently suitable, not least because he believes them only too eager to step aside from political leadership to resume their research, teaching, or writing. There is undeniably an air of unreality hovering over Herder's projected transformation, only slightly less far-fetched than Rousseau's, and it might justifiably be argued that the contrast between Herder's aristo-democrats and Rousseau's lawgiver should not be overdrawn. All the same, even if this point is granted, the difference between "creation" and "emergence" does signal an important parting of their ways, as well as a fundamentally different starting point.

I V

What the previous section principally demonstrates is that, Herder was evidently not so preoccupied with ethnic pecularities that he overlooked distinctly political concerns. Commentators anxious to present Herder's "cultural" nationalism as essentially unpolitical, or at best apolitical, could therefore be wrong. Perhaps they took the negation of the importance of states as such or Herder's profound hostility to the status quo as the rejection of politics *tout court.* But, whatever the reasons, they strangely failed to recognize that Herder's basic objective was the same as Rousseau's: to redefine politics and, in redefining it, make it legitimate, even though he went his own way about it.

I pointed out earlier that, unlike Rousseau, Herder could not accept that national belonging required the abdication or total subordination of partial concerns to an overriding reason of state. The reader may recall that in his interpretation of the Mosaic Constitution (as Herder called it), the pluralist structure of Hebrew society, its division into diverse institutional and tribal entities, did not detract from Israel's understanding of itself as *one* people.[33] The emergence of political nationhood, therefore, was not intended to displace a plurality of segmental components; rather, the nation was envisioned as a composite structure, as a configuration of self-sustaining groups and associations, and not as a substantive body comprising individually atomized citizens. Guided by this pluralist model, Herder, we found, denied the need for a permanent central authority. He wished to replace existing centralized state-nations, to which he contemptuously referred as "patched-up

33. For more on this point, see the previous chapter.

contraptions" forced into submission under one sceptre, with the nation-state – "one people with its own national character" – which, in a sense, was a non-state, insofar as it was thought able to dispense with a central focus of power.[34] Ethnic ingredients, in conjunction with customs, legal traditions, and established standards of reciprocity, were apparently sufficient agents of coordination and integration once a nation had attained political maturity.

Evidently, Herder did not draw a sharp distinction between political society and a community of unmediated fellowship and spontaneous mutuality, or see a potential threat to overall unity in the existence of plural autonomies. Consequently, he must have cherished the belief in a large measure of complementary diversity, in the light of which he preferred the principle of informal *Zusammenwirken* by multiple agents to Rousseau's idea of formal contractuality.[35] To be sure, both spontaneous cooperation and contractually based agreement rest on shared standards and common understandings of what is or is not done, but the former, suggesting dialogical consensus, unlike the unity of Rousseau's general will, does not demand the elimination of divergent positions, but merely a *modus operandi* under which they do not cause societal disruption by unbridled fragmentation. Putting it slightly differently, the assumption made here is that dialogical consensus is inherently more compatible with plural diversity than formal agreement based on a unitary will.

What Herder in effect envisions is an association comparable to a composite *ensemble*, in contrast to an association comparable to a corporate *body*. Once again, the difference reflects a divergent sense of what is politically attainable. To Rousseau nationhood as a composite ensemble – what St Thomas called an accidental whole – manifestly seemed too risky an analogue, too contingent on imponderables of one kind or another, to guide a nation once founded; the threat to its survival was simply too alarming to contemplate. Far less hopeful about the cooperative propensities of diversity, he preferred to build the nation-state on a more solidly integrated basis. It is possible that Rousseau, viewing himself primarily as a spectator and giving advice as a detached outsider, opted for maximum circumspection and the tempering of loftiness of vision with the institutionally realizable. Herder, on the other hand,

34. Herder, *Werke*, XIII, 384–5.
35. Ibid., XVIII, 137, 271, 300–2, 408, see also XIII, 346; XIV, 227; XVI, 119, 551; XVII, 116; XXIV, 375; and XXIX, 129, 133.

liked to view himself as another self-enacting Solon or Lycurgus and, as such, as a man of daring vision.[36]

More fundamentally, however, the source of their divergence about the viability of the political nation, once it was founded, was the difference in their thinking about its ongoing operative *how*, a difference that was closely bound up with their contrasting emphasis on the relation between "nature" and "culture." Whereas Rousseau viewed culture as a marked departure *from* nature, Herder viewed it as a simultaneous development *with* nature. The involved transformation, therefore, was in a real sense profoundly more radical for Rousseau – for whom external statehood and internal nationhood were essentially of a piece – than it was for Herder. Clearly, the national consciousness of being a German, for example, was not synonymous for Herder with being a citizen of Prussia or, for that matter, Wilhelm's or Hitler's *Reich*, or the *Bundesrepublik*, just as being a nationally conscious Québécois would not have implied for him the existence of a separate sovereign state. This statement does not, however, alter the proposition I have advanced throughout that the concept of nationhood is at once cultural *and* political, and is so for Herder as much as for Rousseau. All it does allow for is a greater latitude in the interpretation of the "political."

V

My concern in this comparative discussion has been primarily with nationalism as a doctrine rather than with nationalism as a movement. There can be little doubt that both variants I tried to juxtapose lend themselves to ideological distortion. What is principally at issue, however, is whether or not there is such a thing as an apolitical or nonpolitical form of nationalism. The thrust of the foregoing argument points to a negative answer, as it implies that to suggest otherwise would in practice amount to making a distinction without a difference. For what the argument considers of crucial importance about both variants is their redescription of politics in the direction of making "culture" not merely relevant to politics but indispensably necessary. In its light, a nation is no longer simply a group of people governed by a common sovereign; it

---

36. In projecting himself as the detached spectator rather than the persuasive ideologue, Rousseau writes: "My function is to tell the truth, not to make people believe it." (*Confessions*, 1782), trans. J.M. Cohen (Harmondsworth: Penguin, 1954), 192.

is a collectivity bound by spiritual ties and cultural traditions. Seen this way, nationalism is unthinkable without the appeal to cultural values. Indeed, there is a twofold process at work: the infusion of the political with cultural content *and* the infusion of culture with political content.

The reception of, or the objections to, this double infusion in the modern understanding of nationalism is beyond the scope of this essay.[37] It may well be arguable whether nationality is part and parcel of human nature; whether a person *needs* to live with others who share a given ethnic culture; and whether states not grounded in such a culture fail to be rightful states.[38] Perhaps these questions, thus put, are intrinsically unanswerable. The marriage between culture and politics may indeed prove a source of lasting bliss but, by the same token, culturally based states may turn out to be no more just or harmonious than non-culturally based states. Much the same might be said about the international sphere. Potentially, given the extension of the standards of reciprocity upheld within a nation – the operative idea of Herder's conception of *Humanität* – it could be more peaceful. But just as potentially, relations could be greatly more acrimonious and conflicts more intense, since gains and losses in cultural terms may prove far less negotiable than those involved in purely pragmatic bargaining. When the sanctity of language and hallowed traditions or the sacredness of religious ikons are at issue – and with them the soul or spirit of an entire nation – compromises do not easily suggest themselves; the stakes simply are too high.

Interestingly, Herder is by no means unaware of this. Thus he attributes enmity between nations not primarily to disputes over wells and pasture grounds but rather to the "far more dangerous spark" arising from conceptions of national pride and collective honour. Cultural nationalism, therefore, only contingently favours international harmony. Similarly, even *within* nations, cultural components only contingently

37. The most incisive (if not always balanced) critique is probably still Elie Kedourie's *Nationalism* (London: Hutchinson, 1960); see also Anthony D. Smith, *Theories of Nationalism* (London: Duckworth, 1971), and his *Ethnic Revival* (Cambridge: Cambridge University Press, 1981), esp. 45, where he rightly questions the identification of nationality with language; on this see also his *The Ethnic Origins of Nations* (Oxford: Clarendon Press, 1986), 138–40. The collection *Nationalism*, ed. John Hutchinson and Anthony D. Smith (Oxford: Oxford University Press, 1994) is also of interest.

38. For a sophisticated elaboration of this point, see James S. Fishkin, *Tyranny and Legitimacy* (Baltimore: Johns Hopkins University Press, 1979).

ensure national solidarity, although it may no doubt be true that, whenever they do so, they effectively reinforce strictly political components.[39]
However, it may be no less true that in post-Herderian nationalism it
has increasingly been rather problematical to speak of culture and politics as *distinct* components. For it is precisely the ingenious fusion of
culture and politics that has conferred upon the doctrine of national
self-determination its impressive ideological comprehensiveness, its persuasive power, and its quasi-ethical vigour.

At the same time there can be little doubt that the ideological force of
this doctrine – which resists the driving of a wedge between cultural nationalism and political nationalism – is apt to conceal the fact that political legitimacy is not purely a matter of getting the ethnic composition of
a collectivity and its territorial boundaries right.[40] Nor is the political extension of "self-determination" any the less contestably problematic than
its application to individual autonomy. All the same, it is not without
irony that this unquestionably problematic doctrine has become one of
the most effective legitimizing and rallying devices in modern politics.

What makes it all the more ironic, is that the man who has launched
this originally Kantian ethical principle as a national doctrine by marry-
ing it with the powerful, if not explosive, mixture of culture and politics
is still widely thought of as an apolitical thinker.

V I

Herder's ideas on nationhood, in and through this symbiosis, have
gained additional force by their use of the language of metaphor. So
much so, in fact, that I felt prompted to suggest (in the Introduction)
that Herder's thought is practically structured by metaphor. There is a
sort of interaction between thought, image, and further thought. As
mutually reinforcing clusters of images, metaphors form a conceptual
stimulus as much as a conceptual framework, and, cumulatively, they

39. Herder, *Werke*, V, 132–4. On the political nature of Herder's cultural nationalism,
see John Hutchinson, *The Dynamics of Cultural Nationalism* (London: Allen and Unwin,
1987), 35, 42.

40. Legitimacy in politics generally involves at least three levels of applicability: the who,
how, and where of government. By concentrating on the third level (ethnicity), national
self-determination either disregards the first two levels – who should properly rule and in
what manner – or views them as necessary entailments of the third, thus collapsing the
three levels of legitimacy into one.

provide a powerful discursive momentum to his argument.[41] Clearly, metaphors had greater meaning for Herder than purely rhetorical tools, although he certainly knew how to use them to enhance the impact of his writings, not only regarding cultural nationalism, but equally regarding political romanticism.

Admittedly, Herder got himself occasionally carried away by his metaphorical reasoning, as I observed earlier; yet it is remarkable to what extent he succeeded in avoiding its obvious pitfalls and dodging the traps of hyperbolic excess.

Herder's romantic "successors" were not quite as successful in this. If Herder, for example, merely likened the nation to an organism, a significant fringe of political romantics maintained that the state was not merely *like* an organism but was *in fact* an organism, and therefore suggested that the laws which control a biological organism should apply equally to the political and social organism.[42] And they lamented that this was far from being the case.

Laments, like metaphors, have a long and honourable tradition in Western political thought. From the Hebrew prophets on, people have lamented defeat in battle, subjugation, exploitation, and the exactions of unjust governments, not to mention their more private and personal griefs. Not infrequently, however, laments have been the harvest of disenchantment, of shattered hopes, of misplaced confidences. Modernity, especially since the European Enlightenment, has grown to cherish an unprecedented faith in continuous progress. Defects of human institutions could supposedly be solved as easily as problems were being solved in physics and mechanics, so that the existence of any social problem virtually entailed the possibility of its eventual, if not immediate, solution. This confident approach to the human world of the future undoubtedly yielded marked benefits, but it also reaped its measure of disillusionment.

---

41. See Hans Dietrich Irmscher, "Beobachtungen zur Funktion der Analogie im Denken Herders," *Deutsche Vierteljahrsschrift für Literatur und Geistesgeschichte*, 55 (1981), 64–97; see also Heinz Meyer, "Überlegungen zu Herders Metaphern für die Geschichte," *Archiv für Begriffsgeschichte*, 25 (1982), 88–114; and Walter Moser, "Herder's System of Metaphors in the *Ideas*," in W. Köpke and S.B. Knoll, eds., *Johann Gottfried Herder: Innovator through the Ages* (Bonn: Bouvier, 1982), 102–24.

42. Morley Roberts, for example, stressed the *literal* identity of the body politic with an organic body. "States are," he writes, "really and not metaphorically true organisms." *The Behaviour of Nations* (London, 1941), 1. See also his *Biopolitics* (London, 1938), xii. Clearly, organismic political theorizing was not confined to Germany.

Disillusionment over unfulfilled expectations as a cause for lament may assume at least two contrasting complexions. One, mainly of the specific kind, may be thought of as merely temporary, a setback occasioned by this or that miscalculation, and hence a matter that can be remedied by improving theory, correcting practice, more effectively disseminating knowledge, and so on. The other complexion may, however, take on the form of more lasting and more profound gloom, having its origin in the growing realization that some expectations *cannot* be fulfilled.[43] Two events in particular, one economic, the other political, which originally had held out every promise that the success achieved in science and technology could be transferred to industry and society, gave rise to doubts and misgivings, and eventually to a formidable chorus of laments over unfulfilled expectations. Something, it became increasingly evident, had gone wrong somewhere.

To be sure, some voices had questioned the efficacy of social and political engineering some time before the disenchantment with the industrial and French revolutions, and the questioning had a good deal to do with the loss of the prestige that mechanistic metaphors had recently gained in social and political theorizing. Ever since Leibniz introduced the concept of *vis viva*, organic metaphors, prominent in classical and medieval writings, made a gradual re-entry into intellectual discourse. Thus, some time before Edmund Burke was to lament in eloquent organismic imagery the havoc caused by the French Revolution, or Friedrich Schiller – the father of the concept of alienation – was to express his grief over the effects of the industrial revolution, writers such as Rousseau, Justus Möser, and Herder, were striking chords that found a resounding echo in the organismic philosophy of the political romantics.

The predominant drift of romantic thinking after what was perceived as the failure of the French Revolution was to turn the clock back. But in this leap into the political bygone, Herder was no real guide. Paradoxically, perhaps, it was the liberal Kant on the one hand, and the arch-conservative Möser on the other who figured more prominently. Most romantics now readily accepted Kant's proposition that in the realm of politics humans were like animals in need of a master to tame

---

43. See, for example, W.G. Sumner, who had doubts about the extent (or wisdom) of trying to make the world over, in *Folkways* (Boston: Ginn Co., 1907), esp. ch. 2, secs. 83–91. I have enlarged on this point in an article on Sumner, in the *Encyclopedia of Philosophy*, ed. Paul Edwards (New York: Collin Macmillan, 1967), 8, 47–8.

and control them, or Möser's defence of the status quo.[44] If political romantics, therefore, adopted Herder's organismic imagery, they could see no point in applying it in Herderian terms, not least because it would have conflicted with what they borrowed from Kant. For, as we noted, Herder flatly challenged Kant, contending that *humans* required no political master to lord over them, and that, if he had to choose between the efficient government of an enlightened despot and the less orderly regime in which the people had a share, he would always opt for the latter.[45] Likewise, in his biological metaphors, Herder nowhere stipulated a subordinate relationship such as that of a leaf to the tree or of a given limb to the human body. There is, on the contrary, a remarkable degree of consistency between his imagery and his idea of horizontal *Zusammenwirken* within a non-hierarchical pluralism.

Clearly, the political romantics, whether they lamented the French Revolution itself, or merely its outcome, were selective in picking the doctrinal components of their creed. Just as they ignored Kant's liberal philosophy but built on his anti-democratism, so they ignored Herder's democratism but built on his organismic imagery. In one way or another, they were also inclined to interpret Herder's cultural nationalism as wholly unpolitical and, therefore, as posing no danger to multinational empires. Some, indeed, went so far as to recommend it to the ultra-conservative regime of Austria as a viable way of preserving it.

VII

Most conservative political thinkers, particularly since Burke, have invoked organism in their defence of the status quo and in their warnings against the dangers of change based on rational principles. Burke himself, to be fair, seems to have shown greater insight than his self-professed followers in recognizing the limits of the organic concept of growth as a rationale for conservatism. It is no accident that Bruke,

---

44. Immanuel Kant, *Ideen zu einer allgemeinen Geschichte in weltbürgerlicher Absicht* (1784), in *Gesammelte Schriften* (Berlin: Preussische Akademie der Wissenschaften, 1902–13), VIII, 23. "It is manifest violence," Justus Möser maintained, "if members of the lower class unite and attempt to claim the same rights to property as members of the higher class by simply basing such claims on a common human origin." *Werke* (Berlin: Abeken, 1842–3), V. 182.

45. Herder, *Werke*, V, 516; see also XIII, 383. Even Rousseau, the great advocate of a new social order, urged the Poles to venerate their ancient nobility as the surest safeguard of preserving their political freedom as a nation. *Considérations sur le gouvernement de Pologne*, ch. XI.

after making ample rhetorical use of the metaphor of organic growth when dealing with the British constitution up to the beginning of his own century, makes much less use of it when dealing with contemporary institutions. Growth was good imagery for the formative period of the constitution; it had little relevance to the finished or virtually finished product, or, to apply biological terminology, to something that had attained the stage of maturity. For Burke the British constitution had grown up; it had reached maturity. To have pursued the organismic imagery beyond this point would necessarily have implied either that maturity had not really been achieved or that decay had already set in. Organisms simply do not grow *ad infinitum*; hence neither the implication of delayed maturity nor that of early decay were palatable to Burke. Only very slight change, or no change, seemed now desirable. What such a perfect instrument as the British constitution now demanded was no longer growth or change, but preservation and permanence. As far as the present and future were concerned, therefore, Burke felt no compunction in abandoning biological imagery in favour of the imagery of mechanical construction. Buildings suggested far greater durability than organisms; there was infinitely more scope for keeping buildings in a state of good repair. Maintenance, not change, accordingly, became the operative rhetoric of Burke's political stance.

Admittedly, Herder, too, preferred "gradual, natural, reasonable evolution" to revolution.[46] Yet he saw this gradual evolution, which he also liked to identify with "growth," in terms of continuing change. And, whether or not this makes biological sense, it made good political sense within the context of Herder's Germany. Unlike Burke, Herder found little in his country's political institutions worth preserving. His traditionalism, therefore, could not dispense with the idea of change. If social and political life had thus far failed to emerge in a form that befitted the nature of humans, it was so, Herder argued, because the process of development had been artificially arrested. Traditions had become warped because growth had been denied them. In other words, tradition itself must be made subject to change, to a process of continuously revitalizing forces. Instead of opposing tradition to progress, Herder consequently preferred to view each as mutually bound up with to other within the historical "stream" of development; one without the other had only a shadowy existence, for if progress without tradition

46. Herder, *Werke*, XVIII, 332.

was like a plant without roots, tradition without progress was like a plant without water. Stagnant traditionalism was therefore to be shunned; acting like opium on the spirit of a people, it could eventually sound its death-knell.[47]

In this conjunction of progress and tradition Herder's ability to reconcile apparent opposites again comes into play. We have observed how he sought to resolve dichotomies generally believed to be irreconcilably opposed, by suggesting *interpenetration*, treating the liberal stress on the self-governing individual and the conservative stress on communitarian embeddedness, for example, as though they were complementary requirements. But, apart from thus venting his distaste for the prevalent anti-traditionalism of the Age of Reason as well as intriguingly foreshadowing Hegel's use of the dialectic, Herder's brand of progressive traditionalism indirectly suggests that the link between organismic metaphors and doctrinal conservatism may be more tenuous than is often supposed.

Unlike Burke's static, and Herder's progressivist, conception of tradition, the orientation of the political romantics was distinctly reactionary, in the most literal sense of this much-abused word.[48] Disenchanted with the results of the French Revolution, they saw the best hope for mankind in a return to the type of society that they associated with the Middle Ages. In their craving for order and stability they projected into the past what they most fervently desired in the here-and-now. The French Revolution, they held, was but a climax of a process of social atomization that could be traced to the destruction of medieval values and institutions, and hence to disconnectedness from an epoch in which every person, every belief and custom, were inseparable parts of a tightly knit social whole. In short, for the romantics the Middle Ages provided the model of organic embeddedness, by virtue of which, in contrast to the Enlightenment, the community and not the individual constituted the irreducible unit of society. Scoial stability rather than individual autonomy, therefore, embodied the supreme ideal of a just order. Not surprisingly, Herder's highly sympathetic treatment of the Middle Ages – dismissed by most of his contemporaries as a dark and barbaric era – had a profound appeal to the political romantics, in that it most strongly affirmed community values as the bedrock of national

47. Ibid., XIII, 347; XIV, 89.
48. Although political romanticism did not amout to a unified ideology, the features singled out here were common to the views of most leading representatives.

cultures. In addition to Herder's organismic imagery, therefore, his positive sentiments about a prerationalist age were undoubtedly fertile impulses on which the political romantics abundantly feasted.

Because of their almost compulsive obsession with the Middle Ages, the romantics preferred to think of the ideal community structure in strictly hierarchical terms. Herder's notion of *Zusammenwirken* was not abandoned, but it was thoroughly transmuted. In place of Herder's novel conception of integrative pluralism within an essentially undifferentiated or horizontal sense, the romantics put the much older notion of vertical subordination. And, in contrast to Herder's advocacy of multiple affiliations, where individuals can move between, or belong to, a diversity of groups, the romantics revived the medieval idea of social immobility and the total and exclusive submission of an individual to a single group.

Metaphorically, this divergence is reflected in the romantics' return to a wholly anthropomorphic image of organism. The state, said Novalis, was *in fact* a *macro-anthropos*, the anatomy of which was composed of the different social orders that formed a political whole. The guilds were its limbs and the source of its physical strength, the nobility represented the moral element, the priests the religious, and the teachers the intellectual, while the king embodied its will.[49] Definitionally, therefore, the body politic is characterized by a social structure whose viability *depends* on the inequality of graduated "orders," of which obedience and subordination form natural corollaries. Some people, accordingly, are *born* to rule and others are *destined* to serve; each order of persons has to perform the role that Providence has assigned to it. Obedience to authority does not degrade; on the contrary, there is joy in obedience.[50] The soul craves elevation in voluntary surrender; it finds freedom in complete submission; without a state and fatherland, the individual person has no anchorage and no purpose beyond physical existence.[51]

Usually, the land-owning nobility were identified with the natural ruling class and favourably contrasted with commerce and trade as the most reliable custodians of order and stability. Their superiority was as generally and readily accepted as the force of natural elements; their

---

49. Novalis, *Werke*, ed. Carl Seelig (Zürich, 1945, 5 vols.), IV, 158; see also II, 193: "The State is a person like any individual"; similarly, III, 298.

50. Ibid., V, 32–3.

51. Adam Müller, *Elemente der Staatskunst* (Berlin, 1809, 3 vols.), III, 327.

authority was beyond question.[52] Obedience to this natural authority could never be debasing; hence, disobedience, not obedience, disgraces, as it also forms the most common source of alienation. Once you move away from your assigned place, anguish presses around you; you become king of your own misery, a degraded sovereign in revolt against himself, without bounds, without duties, without society.[53]

Allied with the glorification of the medieval social structure, especially among German romantics, was a somewhat incongruous notion, the idea of the supremacy and all-pervasiveness of the state – incongruous because it clearly is totally foreign to the medieval mind as also to its political realities. Obviously, historical accuracy had no high priority among nineteenth-century romantics. Adam Müller spoke of the state as an all-embracing organic whole, the interest of all interests, the supreme end of all human pursuits outside of which human life was virtually inconceivable. An individual belonged entirely to the state, in mind and in body and with all his earthly possessions. It was not, therefore, for subjects to question the purpose of the state, for to do so implied that there was a purpose beyond the state – a utilitarian notion too despicable even to contemplate.[54] More than simply an institution serving particular material needs, the state was viewed as something wholly beyond the sphere of ordinary, everyday experience. Anticipating Hegel somewhat, Müller spoke of the state as the epitome of an "extremely moving realm of ideas."[55] In speaking of the state as an *idea*, Müller wished to distinguish it from a *concept*. Being purely static, and related to phenomena at any given point in time, a concept, he said, is susceptible to rational analysis, the formulation of definitions, and the construction of hypotheses. Ideas, on the other hand, refer to dynamic phenomena, and the analytical method of the sciences was therefore wholly out of place; what was required instead was direct intuitive insight.[56] For Müller the utter indefinability of the state was indeed its outstandingly distinctive hallmark, and for Schleiermacher the idea of the state was accordingly a truly *divine* idea.[57] In both cases, the

52. See, for example, S.T. Coleridge, *The Constitution of Church and State* (London, 1829), 20–32, and his *Lay Sermon* (London, 1817), 414.

53. F.R. Lamennais, *Oeuvres* (Brussels, 1839), II, 150–1.

54. Müller, *Elemente*, I, 62–8; II, 85; see also Novalis, *Werke*, IV, 225 and 274.

55. Müller, *Elemente*, I, 63.

56. Ibid., I, 20.

57. Ibid., I, 27. Friedrich Schleiermacher, *Vorlesung über den Staat* (1829), trans. in H.S. Reiss, *Political Thought of the German Romantics* (Oxford: Clarendon Press, 1955), 198.

intention was to endow the state with a mystique and transcendence that was as ontologically unique as it was spiritually sublime.

VIII

On purely logical grounds it could undeniably be argued that the romantic conception of functional subordination was every bit as valid as Herder's conception of functional coordination; for both conceptions are compatible with the image of an organism. One may, of course, legitimately question the adequacy of the organic analogy in either conception as a description or an explanation of social and political structures. But the real point at issue here is whether the diverse claims made by the political romantics for the political community do not involve an almost absurd overextension of the metaphor originally chosen. Clearly, when we think of an organism we do not at the same time think of the whole as being on an ontologically higher level than its parts. The political romantics, on the other hand, maintained both: (a) that the political community is an organism; and (b) that it exists on a level that is in every respect intrinsically superior to its individual members. And they seemed to believe that the first statement entailed the second or, more precisely, that the two claims were substantially identical.

Similarly, it does not follow from the analogy of organism that the state cannot be conceived in an instrumental sense. One may properly hold the state to be an organism – or like an organism – without holding also that it is an end in itself. Conversely, one may properly uphold the thesis that the state is something final, in the nature of an absolute in some metaphysical sense, without committing oneself to the view that the state is an organism. There simply is no necessary connection between these two assertions.

A further confusion arises from the romantics' attempt to identify the image of an organism with that of a person. For not only is the unity of a person an altogether different notion from that of the unity of an organism; it is also difficult to see how one can speak of the *parts* of a person. One may arguably contend that the state is an organism made up of other coordinate organisms – as Herder tried to do – or of subordinate organisms – as the romantics did – but it is surely intelligibly problematic how one can maintain that the state as a person is made up of other or lesser persons. Although neither the organic model nor the model of a person may be regarded as fruitful devices of political analysis, nothing but total confusion must result from mixing the two models, let alone considering them identical.

Finally, even if it were conceded that in the organic model the parts can be explained only with reference to the whole, this would not imply that their value is derivative from the value of the whole. For, surely, ethically speaking, members of a social or political whole may be more or less valuable than the whole, or of equal value. Herder seems to have had an inkling of this because he increasingly switched (in the *Ideas*) from the organic to the mechanic image. Instead of illustrating the "flow" of things by having recourse to events in nature, he there chooses the metaphor of a chain, since its links are individually separable entities.[58]

In light of these observations one may wonder whether the political organism of the romantics was not in truth a pseudo-organism. By making the sort of claims for the state which they did, they both distorted and obscured the image of an organism as a political model. Herder, by refraining from associating such claims with the organic model of national culture, was for this reason a more consistent organicist than his romantic "followers." What is more, by insisting on functional co-ordination rather than subordination, and on multiple rather than single-group membership, he disclosed also the feasibility of an organic community theory that was both pluralist and democratic. And, whereas the political romantics looked upon the state as a unified organism from the outset, the organic unity of Herder's image of nationhood was that of a relational texture, a sort of tapestry woven by diverse attachments into a scheme of concerted action, in and through free and equal participation.

Once again, what reappears in Herder's vision of nationhood is the distinctness of "identity" and "relation" as well as the prospect of their coming together, once identity as a *fact* combines with the working out of a relational whole as a *process*. Unity, on this argument, demands both if it is to be neither physically enforced nor doctrinally presupposed. In other words, in order to be in keeping with Herder's affirmation of spontaneous emergence or growth and his negation of the associative legitimacy of mere centralizing power, national unity must be seen as potentiality seeking realization, and not as implicit actuality.[59] It is meant to render all forms of arbitrary coercion obsolete and superfluous.[60] Government is to be impersonal and non-physical, if it is not to be a burden

58. See, for example, Herder, *Werke*, XIV, 229.

59. Herder, *Werke*, XIII, 149, XIV, 227; XVIII, 339. Herder's preference for the diffusion of power between diverse sectional groupings is in marked contrast to Rousseau's open hostility to any form of pluralism, although here, too, he could be inconsistent.

60. Ibid., XIV, 217.

upon the citizenry. The *nation*-state, we noted, is envisioned as a territorial system in which citizens, sharing a common cultural heritage, order their lives within a legal framework of their own making. It is *at the same time* the area of a people's political self-determination *and* the space in which they are able to pursue diverse social goals and interests. The emergence of plural communitarian autonomies was to signal the disappearance of the state as an administrative and coercive organ and its replacement by a pluralist diffusion of self-governing entities – a vision not very different from that of the guild pluralists in early twentieth-century England.

It may perhaps be objected that in his repudiation of central government Herder seriously underestimated the degree of coordination that multiple autonomies require. Similarly, and in sharp contrast to the political romantics, Herder may be said to have misjudged the importance of hereditary monarchy as a symbol of unity and continuity. Yet, in both respects, in his hostility toward bureaucracy as an administrative medium of governmental control as much as in his staunch republicanism, Herder's thinking has a striking affinity with prevalent opinion during the American Revolution (1775–83). What is more, his hostility to bureaucratic organization extended to his ideas about world government. Herder rejected such visions as "utopian phantoms" designed to deceive humanity into believing that international fellowship was essentially a matter of administration, when in fact bureaucrats were parasitic on peoples, and, instead of uniting them, were the source of further divisions.[61]

But, above all, it should be borne in mind that Herder's pluralist communitarian organicism was an essentially normative theory. As such, it undoubtedly has its use as a heuristic device for judging the extent of social and political cohesion in actual states. But it has its dangers as well. The concept of power may be irrelevant to a theory that views society as a pluralist network in which shared cultural traditions combine with latent tendencies to fuse multiple loyalties with a sense of overall oneness and reciprocal obligatoriness. Yet, when actual conditions widely diverge from those envisioned by Herder's community theory, the application of his political terminology may disguise the realities of unequal power and misleadingly imply, as several political romantics did, that political matters are indistinguishable from human concerns in which power is not involved.

61. Ibid., XVII, 125; XVIII, 283, 346.

The extent of this danger has been amply illustrated by the diverse expressions of twentieth-century totalitarianism. But to suggest a link between political romanticism and totalitarianism is also open to challenge, at any rate if it is too closely forged. For, by opposing the atomization of society into what is at times referred to as mass society, both Herder and the political romantics revived the belief in the importance of intermediary groups as buffers between the omnipotent Leviathan and the individual citizen. What, however, can less plausibly be maintained is that a theory which lays as much stress on hierarchy of status as the romantics did leaves much scope for intermediary groups to serve as effective brakes upon central autocracy, especially if it is overlaid – as it frequently was – with transcendental images of the state that confer upon it an absolute pre-eminence over every other form of social organization.

Political romanticism, then, conflicts as much with the notion of an open society as with that of reciprocal pluralism, let alone democracy, in any recognizable sense. Even if it were conceded that the political romantics were imbued with a Christian ethos and that they cherished the hope that those who govern would do so with paternal concern for the governed, it nonetheless remains true that they allied this faith and hope with a complete trust that rulers would be infallible arbiters of what was best for the ruled. In effect, therefore, if not always in intent, their political theories came to provide a basic ideological sanction for authoritarian, if not absolutist, regimes, even though, in historical fact, the most reactionary romantics were originally enthusiastic supporters of the French Revolution, welcoming it, as Herder did, like a new dawn.[62] But, then, Herder did not live long enough to witness the events that followed in its wake, whereas the romantics whose views I sketched did. They became reactionaries not because they favoured absolutism – many in fact opposed it – but because they felt betrayed by the principles in which they had placed their trust. Their lament over the gods that failed kindled their post-Revolutionary faith in the idols of the past.

---

62. Ibid., XIII, 317. Johann Gottlieb Fichte, for example, would have preferred a liberal path; certainly in his earlier writings he championed the rights of the individual. Similarly, Wilhelm and Friedrich Schlegel espoused republicanism, and Friedrich Gentz and Johann Görres demanded democracy during the Wars of Liberation. But, as Frederick Beiser puts it, the more the romantics "lost faith in the power of the people to develop a community through their own spontaneous efforts, the more they trusted the powers of the state," or looked back "with longing on the corporate order of the Middle Ages." (in *Enlightenment, Revolution, and Romanticism*, [Cambridge, Mass., Harvard University Press, 1992, 223.])

Disillusioned over the eagerly hoped-for reform from below, they reverted to the belief that political initiative could be expected only from above, and that, moreover, it could be effective only if it was glorified and invested with an aura of overwhelming wonder.

I X

It is not the purpose of this essay to assess the validity of the laments that gave rise to political romanticism. Words such as "mass society," "alienation," "atomization," or "embeddedness" have by now acquired an ambiguity of overtones that is liable to impair the cognitive status they may originally have possessed. Should it, however, be objected that, in spite of having become somewhat overused clichés, these words still contain kernels of meaning, it could nevertheless be maintained that the "forces" alleged to have brought in their train the separation of selves from their community roots have also helped to liberate humans from servitude to time-hallowed conventions and group pressures. Many of the thinkers of the Enlightenment assuredly believed this to be the case. Post-Enlightenment reflections, on the other hand, have cast uncertainty over the unmixed blessings of this liberation. It was the merit of Herder's trenchant critique of Enlightenment boasts in this direction, together with the laments of the romantics – who generously drew on this critique – to have yielded early glimpses of this doubt.

As with all might-have-beens, it is perhaps futile to speculate what the course of ideas and events would have been – and in particular the fortunes of nationalism – had the political romantics adopted and propagated Herder's organic imagery in the service of social regeneration and built on his vision of progressive traditionalism as the true bedrock of the modern nation state. One thing, however, is beyond doubt: Neither the excesses of ethnic nationalism, nor the quaint aberrations of political romanticism can be viewed as part of Herder's legacy. Herder, as we noted, despised the idea of structuring society into rulers and underlings, just as he had no use for racist interpretations of nationhood, let alone for the suggestion of any master race. "There could be no order of rank; the Negro was as much entitled to think the white man degenerate as the white man was to think of the Negro as a black beast ... for there simply is no such thing as a Favorit-Volk."[63] In point of fact, Herder's extreme distaste for the concept of race provoked

63. Herder, *Werke*, XVIII, 248; see also XIII, 252, 257, and XVII, 115.

rather severe strictures from Kant. Indeed, Kant considered it as one of the major defects of Herder's *Ideas*, and in his review of the work castigated Herder for his highly "inadequate and unsympathetic treatment of race."[64] Kant was referring especially to Book VII in the *Ideas*, where Herder concludes that there are neither four nor five races, nor exclusive varieties thereof, on this globe. Complexions run into each other, and, in the final analysis, there are only different shades of the same great picture.

There is another thing that seems to me beyond any doubt. If Herder had no ambition to be a precursor of an arrogantly overbearing racism, nationalism, and ethnicity, or of an absurdly reactionary romanticism, on the other hand, he never veered far from his political aspiration to make Rousseau's "great theme" – as he called it in his notebook – very much his own. Certainly, he shared with Rousseau a crucially important thesis in his own philosophy of nationhood: the idea that a nation, properly so called, must build on the foundations of prior collective customs and cultural traditions.[65] I do not know if Herder's political vision will ever be regarded as an intriguing complement to Rousseau's doctrine of participatory politics, but I have a hunch that, were this to happen, it would give Herder immense posthumous gratification.

---

64. Kant's review of the *Ideas* appeared in the *Allgemeine Literatur-zeitung* of 15 November 1785.

65. For a contemporary account of the prepolitical foundations of a nation, see Bernard Yack, "Popular Sovereignty and Nationalism," *Political Theory* 29 (2001), 519–21.

3

Nationality and Humanity: Heine and Herder

OF THOSE WHO WOULD HOVER *BETWEEN* FRONTS without ceasing to be valiant fighters for humanity, Heinrich Heine was perhaps, from his earliest youth, the most self-consciously torn by conflicts of allegiance. To ask, therefore, if Heine viewed himself principally as a German or a Jew is not only to pose a true or false antithesis but to raise the more fundamental question of commensurability and meaning. For, troubled as he undoubtedly was over his self-identification as a German and a Jew, he also strove to be a broker between Germany and France – as a German living in Paris. What was he, and what was he to do? Heine sensed the inadequacy of simple answers. True, he saw his situation as an exciting challenge, yet he also perceived it as an agonizing predicament. Most frequently he professed to stand above nationalities, sects, parties, and factions of every conceivable kind, as a man, an artist, a citizen of the world. Could one, however, shun allegiances to party and nationality, defy political authority, and still join battle "as a soldier in mankind's war of liberation"?[1] Karl Marx, whom Heine befriended in Paris, expressed similar sentiments, but he had no desire to associate them, as Heine did, with the universalist dream of the Hebrew prophets or the messianic tradition of Israel, in both of which Heine saw the "great civilization of the heart," and the profoundest expression of universal humanity.[2]

---

1. Hans Kaufmann, ed., *Heinrich Heine, Werke und Briefe*, 10 vols. (Berlin: Aufbau, 1961), III, 265. All further references are to this edition, hereafter cited as Heine, *Werke*. Surprisingly little has been written about the problem of conflicting loyalties. For a brief but illuminating discussion of this problem, see Milton R. Konvitz, "Loyalty" in *Dictionary of the History of Ideas* (New York: Scribner's, 1973), III, 108–16.

2. Friedrich Hirth, ed., *Heinrich Heine: Briefe* (Mainz: F. Kupferberg, 1950–57), III, 562–3 (hereafter cited as Hirth, *Heine: Briefe*).

In his struggle for humanity Heine, therefore, saw himself closer to Spinoza, Moses Mendelssohn, Ephraim Lessing, and Herder than to Marx, his younger contemporary in Paris. Above all, the "great Herder," as he admiringly called him, was nearest to his own thinking.[3] There is indeed, quite astonishingly, a remarkable kindredness of vision between the two men; astonishingly, because of their undeniable differences in background, personality, and the spatial and historical context of their lives. Most strikingly, perhaps, Heine shared with Herder an unusually perceptive – though at times decidedly unorthodox – understanding of the Bible as a national document and a profoundly imaginative drama of universal strivings and human failings.

The mingling of the dual strains within the Hebrew tradition, of uniqueness *and* universality – which so intensely captivated both Heine and Herder – forms the focus of this chapter, which with the following chapter, grapples with the problematic application of *Humanität*. Its principal thrust is to suggest that the tensions between uniqueness and universality characterize the more general question that I have mentioned in the Introduction and the preceding chapters; namely, the interaction of forms of relationship and forms of identity. The comparative discussion in both this chapter and the next attempts to indicate that this question contains at its root a truth that is paradigmatic of human existence *per se*: the opaqueness of one's self-location in a world in which each of us is constantly reminded of a simultaneous otherness that is particular and a sameness that is universal.

Although there are remarkable parallels of thought between Heine and Herder, and although Herder is invariably mentioned with praise, the parallels are not at all times the work of direct influence. No doubt, by the time Heine was writing, Herderian ideas had become so deeply ingrained in the texture of contemporary thinking that Heine, in some of his themes, was no longer aware of their Herderian origins.

I

Heine, not unlike Herder, could not speak of the Bible without being overcome by its poetic majesty and political wisdom. "What a book! As great and vast as the world, rooted in the depth of creation and soaring up into the blue mysteries of heaven ... Sunrise and sunset, promise and

3. Heine, *Werke*, V, 60.

fulfilment, birth and death, the whole human drama, it is all in this book ... the Book of Books."[4]

We observed earlier that for Herder the Bible was a book intended not merely for religious edification but also for the guidance of a particular nation. Heine expressed much the same thought when he wrote that it was the Bible which enabled the Jews "to console themselves for the loss of Jerusalem and the Temple and the Ark of the covenant and the golden vessels and the jewels of Solomon," for it somehow replaced their fatherland, their national birthright, and their political sovereignty.[5] From the Bible they drew the strength to defy men and wordly powers, and through it they acquired a culture of mind and a civilization of the heart which prepared them for two thousand years of dispersal among the most diverse cultures and civilizations.[6] How did they manage this? "I believe," Heine responds, "that the reason why they were able so quickly to participate in European culture is that they had nothing to learn in regard to feeling and only needed to acquire knowledge."[7]

Heine's admiration for Moses is also strikingly similar to Herder's. Herder had praised Moses not only as the great lawgiver of the Hebrews but as a great creator and artist, and a most sagacious statesman and legislator not only of the Jewish people but also of the entire human race, far surpassing the renowned lawgiver, Lycurgus;[8] and so did Heine. How, he asks, could Moses have done it? How could he take poor shepherd tribes and create out of them a nation that was to brave the centuries? How could he form "a great, eternal, holy people, a people of God who could serve all the other nations as an example"?[9] Moses, Heine remarks, worked on a grandiose scale, and his edifice, though not of brick and granite, was nonetheless a monument for the whole of mankind, a prototype to be followed by the rest of humanity.[10] The creation of Israel evidently was "that great human pyramid" which, for Heine, dwarfed all the giant constructions of the Egyptians.[11]

4. Ibid., VI, 118.
5. Ibid., 118–19.
6. Hirth, *Heine: Briefe*, III, 180.
7. Ibid., 562–3.
8. J.G. Herder, *Sämtliche Werke*, ed. B. Suphan, 33 vols. (Berlin: Weidmann, 1877–1913), VIII, 349, XI, 450 (hereafter cited as Herder, *Werke*).
9. Heine, *Werke*, VII, 135.
10. Ibid.
11. Ibid.

Herder, we noted, shared this awe. In almost identical words he wondered how Moses could have succeeded in controlling and convincing an unruly mob of rebels to form a nation.[12] Was it by appealing to cold reason? By no means, Herder replies. Moses, possessing an incredible degree of political wisdom, displayed utmost personal humility, sensing correctly that self-glorification would never work.[13] No Jew, Heine shrewdly observed, could ever bring himself to believe in the divinity of another Jew; hence, only a law of wholly divine origin stood any chance of becoming for Israel "the supreme arbiter of men and the most sublime authority of the nation."[14]

Practically echoing Herder in affirming that the main purpose of the Mosaic Constitution was the creation of a free people subject to none other than its laws, Heine describes the Hebrews as through-and-through republicans who revered not the person of the prince, but the majesty of the law. The law *was* the prince, the true ruler and supreme sovereign.[15] Heine, like Herder, considered the enthronement of kings to be out of keeping with the republican character of the Mosaic Law. And, since in no other people did the law capture so completely the essence of holiness and infinity as in the Hebrews, this change could not but mean a drastic change, if not the end of an epoch. Indeed, for both Herder and Heine, it was the beginning of the end of Israel's being a nation whose crucial significance for Heine was neither the monotheistic creed, nor its ethical content, but the reverence an entire nation professed for an impersonal authority, the supremacy of the idea of right acting. For it was the supremacy of this idea that transcended the conception of nationhood in its purely secular and finite meaning of power. By virtue of it, the Hebrews saw themselves as a nation *in* this world, but not exclusively *of* this world. And it is principally this transcendent character of their nationhood which, Heine argued, conferred upon its uniqueness a quality that combined distinct particularity with intrinsic universality.[16]

12. Herder, *Werke*, XII, 122.

13. Ibid., 123.

14. Hans Houben, ed., *Gespräche mit Heine* (Frankfurt/Main: Rutten and Loerning 1926), 812–15, cited in William Rose, *Heinrich Heine: Two Studies of his Thought and Feeling* (Oxford: Clarendon, 1956), 124. See also Herder, *Werke*, XII, 122.

15. Heine, *Werke*, V, 551.

16. Herder, *Werke*, XII, 82, 121. Heine, *Werke*, V, 551. If universality is indeed integral to Jewish particularity, the contrast frequently drawn between Christianity and Judaism seems overdrawn.

Although neither Heine nor Herder before him *identified* the arrival of the perfectly just society with this unique expression of nationhood, both applauded its emphasis on freedom, in both its national *and* individual understanding. "Freedom," Heine declared, "was at all times the great emancipator's ultimate thought; this thought breathes through all his laws concerning poverty and, like a flame, it burns with the same intensity as his contempt for human bondage."[17] While he was in sympathy with Marx and the latter's critique of the status quo, Heine nevertheless refused to reduce the source of all social ills to the existence of private property. Indeed, he says, Moses was wise in demanding not the abolition of private property but rather its wider diffusion as a safeguard against slavery, so that no one should lose his freedom out of dire poverty. Moses, according to Heine, feared nothing as much as the spread of a servile mentality, for in it he perceived the greatest threat to a people's continued existence as a people. So great was his hatred of slavery that he found few things more detestable than the refusal of a slave to be freed. Such a slave "he ordered to be nailed by his ears to the doorpost of his master's house." If only, Heine muses, we had a Moses in our own day: "O Moses, our teacher, Moshe Rabenu, you the greatest opponent of slavery, pass me hammer and nails, so that I could nail our happy slaves in their black-red-golden livery by their long ears to the pillars of the Brandenburg Gates." For Heine, as for Herder, there can be no substance in any talk of "humanity" as long as there is a single slave left in the world.[18]

Freedom, then, is at the heart of what Heine and Herder made of the Mosaic message, and they assuredly agreed with Moses that anyone who asks of freedom anything beyond itself shows signs of being born a slave. At the same time they recognized with Moses (or Rousseau and Kant) that freedom in society is not lawlessness. For, if it is not to clash with justice, freedom requires standards of mutuality, shared understandings of what can be done and not done. The requirement of legal standards, however, Moses taught Herder and Heine, does not imply the division of society into rulers and subjects. Good government, as freedom with justice, *can* mean impersonal government, that is, a form of government compatible with human freedom and the dignity of the human spirit.

17. Heine, *Werke*, VII, 142–3.
18. Ibid., 143. Herder, *Werke*, XVIII, 299. Kant also remarks rather acidly on the "happy slave" syndrome. For more details see my "Aufklärung" and "Mündigkeit": Thomasius, Kant, and Herder," in *Deutsche Vierteljahrsschrift*, 57 (1983), 278–97, esp. 289–90.

With such a government in mind, Herder and Heine visualize a republic in which all share a common material and cultural life, and in which there is no permanent gulf between rulers and ruled or masters and serfs. Both variously hint, however, that such a political order is not a matter of merely rational calculation or the work of some contractual deal. But neither is it a question of revolutionary change. Every revolution, Heine trenchantly observes, creates a new tyranny, just as an opposition is successful only until it succeeds, "for after the revolution it is doomed."[19]

What, then, ensures that freedom *and* law will prevail? Here, once again, Heine and Herder speak with one voice, although darkly. For both concur that the required "something" is not a thing at all, but an indefinable, and possibly inexplicable, vigour (*Kraft*) that is not necessarily beyond human reach, but equally not within easy reach either. This somewhat mysterious power Heine described as "*ein gewisser Hauch*," a certain breath, which the Hebrews called *ruah*, the breath of the Almighty, "which remains inscrutable; it blows like a fresh breeze, and is the true harbinger of things to come."[20] This *ruah* Herder and Heine associated with the Hebrew spirit as exemplified in its most tangible form in the prophetic tradition of Israel, in which both of them saw the original soil where the idea of *Humanität* was rooted. Guarding and preserving this tradition seemed therefore the most promising way to move toward joining freedom with law within and between nations. Universal humanization is thus made contingent on the survival of a particular tradition. At the same time it was not lost on either Herder or Heine that postulating universal principles of human reciprocity within the context of a particular national tradition might pose problems in their practical application, if not in their very meaning.

Nor were they blind to the fact that the mingling of the dual strains of Jewish uniqueness and human generality amounted to something of a paradox. Here you have a small people, perhaps the most clannish of communities, proud of their seclusion even when most despised, that is supposed to determine the shape of civilization and humanity to an extent which, as Heine put it, would lead one to think that the Jews are "the only important people in history."[21] How is this paradox to be resolved? And how is one to account for this extraordinary mingling of

19. Heine, *Werke*, V, 218.
20. Ibid., 225. Herder, *Werke*, XX, 29, 118.
21. Houben, ed., *Gespräche mit Heine*, 510.

two opposite strains? With his characteristic wit, Heine offers an explanation that attributes to the Jews the rare capacity for knowing what really mattered: "At the burning of the second Temple they abandoned the gold and the silver vessels of sacrifice, the candelabra and the lamps, even the breastplate of the High Priest with its great jewels, and saved only the Bible. This was the true treasure of the Temple." The Jews were well aware of what they were doing, comments Heine, because they know the value of things.[22]

II

The veneration that Herder and Heine felt for the Hebrew spirit involved, a sort of fusion between religious sentiments and national-traditional sentiments of a secular nature. This fusion not only anticipated Zionism but also yielded pointers in the direction of tolerance and emancipation: clearly, these had to be seen as constitutional measures that combined civic inclusiveness with the recognition of particularistic distinctiveness. Thus, both Herder and Heine categorically dismissed the conversion of the Jews to Christianity – a proposed remedy to their lot – as futile and presumptuous. "Since Israel regards itself in its prayers as a people distinct from other people," Herder observed, "why should it be judged differently by the rest of the world?"[23] Heine put it even more pointedly: "Has the old Lord of Sinai and supreme Ruler of Judah also become 'enlightened' and divested Himself of His old nationality and forsaken His claims and supporters – has He given up His people for a few vague cosmopolitan ideas?"[24] Neither conversion nor the watering down of Judaism would do. Writing to a fellow member of the *Verein für Kultur und Wissenschaft der Juden* in 1823, Heine strongly voiced his dislike of the religious reform movement, fearing it would deprive Judaism of its vitality: "We no longer have the strength to wear a beard, to fast, to hate, and out of hate to suffer; that is the ground of our craving for reformation." Emancipation, Heine adds with biting irony, "does not mean a miniature form of Protestant Christianity under Jewish management – *ein evangelisches Christentümchen unter jüdischer Firma.*"[25]

22. Heine, *Werke*, V, 173; also VII, 138–9.
23. Herder, *Werke*, XXIV, 63–4.
24. Heine, *Werke*, VIII, 96.
25. Hirth, *Heine: Briefe*, I, 62.

Concerned, like Herder, that assimilation could mean the abandonment of national traditions in favour of the melting-pot, Heine pleaded for the preservation of cultural pluralism, of equality amidst diversity. Hence, once again following Herder, Heine demanded both: emancipation *and* national distinctiveness. What is more, Heine urged that the Jews should fight not merely for their own emancipation but for the emancipation of mankind as a whole. Significantly, in the same breath that he proclaimed his *credo* in humanity and global emancipation, Heine also used images that revealingly disclose the Hebraic categories of his global thinking. The emancipation is to come chiefly from France, since the French are the "chosen people" of the new religion. Paris is the new Jerusalem and the Rhine is the Jordan that divides the "Holy Land" of freedom from the land of the "Philistines."[26]

For Heine as for Herder, emancipation is not cosmopolitanism; a belief in *Humanität* does not displace the belief in *Nationalität*. And, like Herder, though in possibly starker terms, Heine warned that the gospel of *Humanität* should not be relied upon to cure antisemitism or any other lingering kind of phobia or jingoism. At times it is indeed doubtful if Heine believed in *any* remedy. "If even Christian *dogs* displayed a feeling of *Rischess* (loathing) against Jewish dogs," he bitterly jokes in a letter, "what can one expect from the Christian middle classes, let alone from the even more antisemitic upper classes?"[27] Yet, whether or not he considered antisemitism ultimately curable, he saw in Jewish emancipation, rather than in conversion, not the demise of a distinctive Jewish identity, but a safeguard of its continued existence. "Promote, accelerate the emancipation, that it may not come too late, that it may come while there are still Jews in the world who prefer the faith of their fathers to the welfare of their children."[28] And, although he had his changing moods, Heine never wavered in his solidarity with the persecuted. When on holiday at the North Sea, he was asked why he showed so little interest in hunting. His answer was succinct, in its typically acerbic way: "My forebears did not belong to the hunters, they belonged to the hunted."[29]

In surprisingly similar terms, Heine agreed with Herder in his diagnosis of persecutions of every kind, attributing their cause to institutional

26. Heine, *Werke*, III, 488.
27. Hirth, *Heine: Briefe*, I, 89–90.
28. Heine, *Werke*, VII, 293–4.
29. Ibid., III, 102.

deficiencies, particularly in the legal system, which, in turn, were symp-
toms of a lack of political maturity rather than of strictly human defects.
Appropriating Herder's organismic images, he declared (in 1844) that
"the state, like an organic body, would never acquire complete health as
long as one part of it, and be it only the little toe, suffered from an ailment."[30] Clearly, Heine, like Herder, saw a direct correlation between
the treatment of the Jews and the civic development of a state. "All those
laws that treat the Jew worse than a beast," Herder remarked, "indicate
the barbaric constitution of a state."[31] At the same time Herder did not
conceal the fact that legislation was not enough. What ultimately was
required was a metamorphosis of attitudes, a "common culture of the
soul" following a true change of hearts.[32]

Viewed in this manner, the persecution of any group or nationality
might well be traceable to defects in a country's legal system, although,
more fundamentally, persecution, as oppression of every kind, is a social
problem and a problem of individual attitudes. When he considered it
as a social problem, Heine was inclined to believe for a time that a solution might be found in a new social philosophy such as a communist
"world revolution" – a concept he is reputed to have coined –, thinking
that it might do away with nationalist rivalry and religious persecution.[33]
At other times, however, this belief was alloyed with doubt about such a
revolution succeeding in changing people's hearts. Would it not merely
serve as a disguise for further oppressions, for persecution of those who
do not fit in, such as writers and outsiders like himself? Would it not
simply replace one set of inhumanities with another?[34] Few of Heine's
words express this uneasiness more vividly than the lament of the Rabbi
of Bacherach at the gate of the Jewish ghetto: "See my beautiful Sarah,
how badly protected is Israel! False friends guard its gates from the outside, and inside its guardians are frenzy and fear."[35] What friend, and
what remedy, then, can be trusted?

Above all, Heine became increasingly suspicious of glib universalism,
the sort of thing Herder dismissed as empty cosmopolitanism. Unless
each nationality is respected, he agreed with Herder, no genuine humanity is to be had. One simply could not put one's entire faith in ideol-

30. Ibid., VII, 283; Herder, *Werke*, XXIV, 71–4.
31. Herder, *Werke*, XXIV, 71.
32. Ibid., XIV, 284.
33. Heine, *Werke*, X, 64–5.
34. Ibid., VI, 172–3.
35. Ibid., IV, 34.

ogies that claimed universalist solutions. Not long after Heine's death, those who had absolute confidence in such panaceas had to admit that they were sadly mistaken. For it became only too evident that anti-semitism and persecutions of every sort were not peculiar to this or that ideology or political regime. The Dreyfus affair in France certainly demonstrated that Jew-baiting was entirely possible even under liberalism. Similarly, communists, offering cures for humanity's diverse ills, also showed little hesitation in attaching collective guilt to Jews and other nationalities whenever it suited them. Regrettably, and not all that rarely, people in the minority had to face up to the truth that they had almost as much to fear from Heine's "false friends" as from their self-declared enemies. To be sure, universalist principles are a necessary basis for emancipation of the oppressed; at the same time, they cannot be trusted as a warrant for national survival.

III

What emerges clearly enough in both Herder and Heine, then, is that there can be no humanity for the Jews, or the rest of mankind, without full emancipation, and no genuine emancipation, without the acceptance of diversity and the plural existence of distinct groups, nationalities, and religions. However, what precisely *is* humanity, understood not simply as an aggregate of people, but as a particular quality, a quality that uniquely characterizes humans in the singular and the plural, in all their works and aspirations? Neither Heine nor Herder was a systematic thinker, and neither offers a coherent or unambiguous account of an admittedly elusive concept, yet both succeeded in enriching its moving or evocative effect to a remarkable degree.

Despite his erstwhile proclaimed religious indifference, Heine's espousal of "humanity," like Herder's, sprang from deeply religious sentiments. To be sure, care must be taken to differentiate here between membership in an institutional denomination and a credal commitment to ends whose meaning or value is incomprehensible outside a framework of transrational belief. Contrary to a widely held view that Heine returned to the faith of his fathers only late in life, my own impression is that Heine's religious thinking, albeit in a highly personal and unorthodox form, underwent no drastic revisions in essential substance. What he says as a young man concerning his sense of credal commitment finds recurrent expression to his dying day. There seems therefore little ground for doubting the sincerity of Heine's confession that the lines "Jerusalem, should I ever forget thee, let my right hand forget her cunning" forever haunted his mind.[36]

Oddly enough, although Herder was professionally associated with institutional Christianity, he entertained religious sentiments that at heart scarcely differed from Heine's ostensibly irreligious stance. For example, Herder's lament that Christianity failed to remain what it originally was as a Jewish sect – what he calls a "free philosophy" or a purely ethical creed – could easily have come from Heine's own pen. For, implicit in the lament is their shared conviction that a truly universal *Humanität* cannot be imprisoned in any *one* institutionally organized religion. Whether or not, therefore, Heine was intimately familiar with Herder's religiously founded thinking on humanity, he most likely agreed with him that, had Christianity remained a free and unorganized world-view, it would have formed a rallying cause that all peoples could have cherished.[37]

Above all – and of the highest relevance to our purpose – both Heine and Herder refused, as previously indicated, to view "humanity" as a denial or termination of "diversity," in sharp contrast to cosmopolitan conceptions of humanity in France, Germany, and elsewhere. Nor was there for either any dialectical *Aufhebung* (synthesis) of the Hegelian or Marxian variety, in that Heine and Herder insisted on both particularity *and* universality, in their utmost distinctiveness and permanence. If I may borrow a phrase from Jacob Talmon, for each of them the uniquely particular "refuses to be swamped and swallowed by the universal."[38] The unique and particular is the existential given, the ground upon which we stand, the anchorage of our identity as distinct individuals and members of distinct collectivities. An individual does not choose to be born a Jew, a Chinese, or an English person. Choice has its place in the human scheme of things, as have goals and purposes; but to whatever end we aspire, we do come from somewhere. We reach out from where we are and from who we are. This reaching out – to which I want to apply the notion of *methexis* – is, accordingly, not taken out of thin

36. Israel Tabak, *Heine and His Heritage* (New York: Twayne, 1956), 140. Heine's inner Jewishness apparently had no need for the observance of religious rituals. I cannot quite accept, therefore, William Rose's suggestion that Heine's resolve to have no masses sung and no kaddish said on his mourning days contained a "stirring of regret." See William Rose, *Heinrich Heine: Two Studies of His Thought and Feeling* (Oxford: Clarendon Press, 1956), 156.

37. Herder, *Werke*, XIV, 320; see also XX, 159, 264–5.

38. Jacob L. Talmon, *The Unique and the Universal* (New York: G. Braziller, 1966), 123.

air, but is embedded in an existential *matrix* that is the bedrock of our distinct identity.[39]

It appears, then, that neither Heine nor Herder thought of "humanity" or *Humanität* as an *absolute* universal that surpasses in every conceivable sense the particularity of the here and now in a state of total disconnectedness. On the contrary, they stressed its connectedness as a performative principle, which enters into and enriches human aspirations within their particular milieu and sphere of endeavour. And, being such a peformative principle, *Humanität* is not beyond the possibility of undergoing change in its form and range of applicability or of being contested in concrete situations in which it is invoked and applied. While, for both, the ethical thrust of *Humanität* embodied universal and abiding values, the concrete or particular interpretation, emphasis, and functionality of these values could assume divergent complexions and differ from society to society, or even *within* a society, as it could also vary from age to age. The disclosure of what precisely *Humanität* means at any time or place depends, therefore, in their view (as I understand it), not on rigid formulations or clearly definable theoretical concepts but rather on a practical understanding of, or sensitivity to, what it is to be human in diverse situations or human encounters. Perhaps what such sensitivity foremost involves – negatively expressed – is an enlarged imaginative grasp of the pervasively painful and humiliating.

Heine's, as much as Herder's, optimism about the universal attainment of "humanity" understood in this way, was recognizably guarded, equally conscious as they were of the difference between capacity and actualization. *Humanität*, in its universal implementation in the particularity of time and place, was clearly *not* simply a given; it was an act of

39. The earliest connotation of *methexis* in terms of inspirational values is to be found (to my knowledge) in the work of the Greek poet Sappho. Plato used the concept to explain the relationship between his notion of "idea" as a universal and the particular phenomena of the sensory world. This understanding of *methexis* was further elaborated by neo-Platonic thinkers such as Proclus (*c* 420–85). By the time it came to be employed by Vicenzo Gioberti – who was greatly influenced by Vico – during the eighteenth century, *methexis* generally had the meaning I associate with it; namely, the capacity of humans to participate in both the physical and the metaphysical world. It is within this meaning that Herder speaks of humans as the probable connecting link between two worlds (XIII, 194–9). The ethical striving for humanity, on this understanding, involves the attempt to bring into line the existential or empirical with the transcendental or metaphysical or, in more general terms, the "is" with the "ought." In the present context, *methexis* is thought of as the impelling conceptual link between the existing given and the aspired-to-be.

ethical willing, involving freedom, choice, and the burden of individual or shared responsibility. Indeed, the burden of responsibility was for both possibly the most significant, in that it involved a basic component of "humanity" itself. For, to choose a course of action for which one is reluctant to assume responsibility is to misjudge, if not to ignore, the intrinsic limits of one's concrete humanity – a point on which more will be said in the following essay. That is why Heine and Herder so emphatically celebrated Moses' love of freedom *in conjunction with* his veneration for law and right action. It was this simultaneous cherishing of liberty and morality that implied for both Heine and Herder a consciousness of the burden of choice which, in turn, presupposed the acceptance of generally valid principles of personal conduct. If anything, therefore, could define humanity in operation, it was the combination of free choice and full acceptance of the responsibility for one's choice.

IV

It is not my purpose in this chapter to trace in detail Herder's more coherent and Heine's more diffuse approach to "humanity."[40] But I believe it is of interest to elaborate somewhat the points of contact or divergence in their approaches, and to indicate the extent to which their interpretations of the dual strain of particularity and universality within the Hebrew tradition helped to confer upon the concept of *Humanität* a significance that was at once novel and profoundly problematic.

Heine, no less than Herder, realized that "humanity" was a complex idea that embraced in its meaning empirical as well as normative ingredients and thereby uneasily combined what humans are and what they aspire to be, their "nature" as well as their "culture," mere being as well as conscious becoming. At the same time they agreed on what it did *not* mean. "Humanity" had nothing whatsoever to do with "facile cosmopolitanism" (as they called it) because it offended their intuitive flair for diversity and colour. Although they upheld the belief in the essential oneness and ethical equality of mankind, regardless of race, religion, or nationality, they shrank from making "humanity" conditional upon the denial of ethnic, linguistic, or religious differences. It was clearly one thing to denounce exclusive and excessive nationalism (as they both did), or fanaticism, or dogmatism, but it was an altogether different

40. In particular, Herder's *Humanitätsbriefe* (*Letters Toward the Advancement of Humanity*), *Werke*, XVII and XVIII.

thing to decry distinctiveness and diversity. This much emerges from the account traced so far. But the matter goes deeper than that.

In their philosophical anthropology both Heine and Herder display an acute awareness of the duality of human nature. Herder actually speaks of an inherent contradiction in the human condition. A human being is simultaneously the inhabitant of two worlds. As an animal he can satisfy his wants, and there are people, Herder concedes, who wish for no more; for them, as for the rest of living creatures, contentment is within reach. Yet those who seek a nobler goal find everything around them imperfect and incomplete, since that which is most noble has never been accomplished on this earth. An animal's innermost purpose is always realizable; it *is* what it is meant to be. Man alone is in conflict with himself and the world around him.[41] Herder posits four anthropological characteristics as defining properties of man's inherent duality: (1) the consciousness of his own inadequacy; (2) the capacity for speech and, through it, the ability to articulate this inadequacy; (3) the existence of choice in place of sheer necessity; and (4) the possibility of choosing ends to counter this inadequacy, ends that transcend, or even oppose, strictly physical needs and desires. And it is the fourth quality, Herder's juxtaposition of physical sensuality and transcendent spirituality, that is closely parallelled in Heine's antithesis between "Hellenism" and "Nazarenism."[42]

Hellenism, for Heine, refers to the affirmation of physical nature and material enjoyment, whereas Nazarenism refers to the elevation, if not glorification, of the spirit. At first Heine sought to divide people in terms of one or the other, but eventually came to realize (chiefly within himself) that Nazarenism and Hellenism could easily dwell in one and the same soul, either one assuming predominance at any given time. Although in his earlier writings Heine tended to favour Hellenism over Nazarenism, he subsequently admitted that he was wrong, that he had mistaken the brighter colours for greater wisdom, whereas it was Nazarenism that possessed a deeper and more mature understanding of the human predicament.[43]

41. Herder, *Werke*, XIII, 194–9. (Transl. in F.M. Barnard, ed., *Herder on Social and Political Culture*, Cambridge: Cambridge University Press, 1969, 280–1.) Concerning Herder's discourse on the human capacity for speech and the formation of concepts, see his *Essay on the Origin of Language* (*Werke*, V, 28–47.) See also XIII, 181–8.

42. Herder, *Werke*, V, 28–30; see also XIII, 109–14, 142–50.

43. Regarding Heine's changing interpretation of the sensualist-spiritualist dichotomy, see Hanna Spencer, *Heinrich Heine* (Boston: Twayne, 1982), esp. 59, 119–22.

We noted earlier that the paramount respect for law as the embodiment and arbiter of right conduct seemed to Heine and Herder the most distinctive hallmark of the Hebrews as a "holy people." And what impressed them most about this law was the fact that it was not the work of rulers issuing edicts, or even the collective expression of political will, but the creation of an invisible power. Unlike the material objects produced by personified deities, it was an abstract power that gave birth to an abstract, impersonal, and transcendent *idea*, the idea of "right acting" – as Matthew Arnold has called it, in opposition to the idea of "right seeing" that he identified with the Hellenic ethos.[44] Like Heine, Arnold used the dualistic distinction as a method of emphasizing divergent priorities in a people's set of values, referring to them as the "points of influence" between which "moves our world," and the understanding of what it is to be ideally human.[45] And for both men it was the moving force of the abstract idea of *right* acting that was of greatest fascination, together with the idea of *free* acting – as embodied in the Mosaic Law – which, in their fusion, constituted for them the normative essence of the concept of humanity as a performative principle.

What we make of "humanity," therefore, depends chiefly on whether, in Arnold's words, "it is by doing or by knowing that we set most store."[46] And while Herder and Heine did not exactly apply this pespective, they unmistakably opted for interpreting the concept as a guide for *action*, deriving it, by their own admission, from the Hebraic tradition of free and right acting. Not surprisingly, both were – similarly to the Hebrews, and unlike the Greeks, who, according to Arnold, so glibly talked of perfection – forever troubled with the difficulties that appear to block perfection: "the obstacles ... fill the whole scene, and perfection appears remote and rising away from earth, in the background."[47]

The Nazarene or Hebraic understanding of "humanity" as a universal idea is, accordingly, linked to perfection not so much as an attainable

44. Matthew Arnold, "Culture and Anarchy," in A. Dwight Culler, ed., *Poetry and Criticism of Matthew Arnold* (Boston: H. Mifflin 1961), 466.

45. Ibid., 465.

46. Ibid., 467.

47. Ibid., 469. Samuel David Luzzatto (1800–1865), Italian-Jewish scholar, a contemporary of Heine and Matthew Arnold, also contrasted Hebraism and Hellenism, but rejected the idea of viewing Hellenism as diametrically opposed to Judaism. Luzzatto maintained a continuous correspondence with Leopold Zuns (1794–1886), founder of the *Verein für Kultur und Wissenschaft der Juden*, which numbered Heine among its most active members during his student days in Berlin.

fixed goal, but as an ongoing quest of reaching out, of moving toward ends in one's daily existence, in a struggling pursuit of goals that may forever remain unattainable. It is precisely this notion of *striving* that forms the recurrent theme in Herder's and Heine's vision of humanization. In essence, it is a process of becoming in which the particular is an active and integral part of the aspired universal. Separating this process of practical striving from envisaged ends seemed to both of them self-defeating. For it implied that there was no intrinsic value in the process itself – in *how* things are done – so that the goal of right-acting would become divorced from its mode of attainment; and, in the event of this happening, there would be no guarantee at all about the morality of "humanity" *in action*.

One could possibly argue that there is not one conception of humanity in Heine and Herder, but at least two: one chiefly concerned with what humans are capable of achieving in the course of historic development; the other focused on the normative goals themselves. Yet, while it may be analytically useful to disentangle in this way two distinct components of "humanity," it may also misleadingly suggest that Herder and Heine actually did keep them apart, or that they *wished* to keep them apart, when in fact it was the constant intermingling of the empirical and the normative dimension, as well as the tension characterizing it, that intrigued them above all. Their mutual interaction, not their separation, typified for them "humanity" as a *process*, as an ongoing movement of self-enactment or becoming.

The evident reluctance to separate "fact" and "value" in their treatment of humanization is already foreshadowed in their idea of "freedom" (mentioned earlier), an idea closely associated with their conception of *Humanität*. For the possession of freedom is seen simultaneously as both a necessary fact defining action *per se* and as the essential property qualifying it as moral. In the former sense freedom consists in the ability to choose and in the consciousness of this ability; in the latter sense freedom forms the basis for the attribution of responsibility in regard to the ends chosen. One explains freedom causally, the other teleologically. Being able to choose, humans may, it is true, legislate themselves into beasts, as Herder frankly recognized, or they may renounce their freedom altogether, as Heine bitterly lamented.[48] Nonetheless, the abuse or renunciation of freedom is not, if freely chosen, devoid of moral responsibility; if one chooses to misuse freedom or

48. Herder, *Werke*, XIII, 148; Heine, *Werke*, VII, 143.

abandon it, one still acts as an autonomous being, though one may be said to have disclosed a lack of humanity in having done so. Heine agreed with Moses that a person who prefers slavery to freedom, in loving the chains that fetter him, forfeits an essential part of being fully human.

Autonomy, thus understood, therefore forms a basic postulate in Herder and Heine's conception of *Humanität*, a conception which for both embraces the possibility of "man being his own god upon earth," as Herder put it.[49] To be sure, man's belief in himself as an autonomous agent capable of attaining his full humanity in and through his capacity for choosing moral ends requires ultimately an act of faith that, as Kant conceded, goes beyond reason and empirical proof; it requires a conceptual leap, in other words, that defies the methods of logic and natural science, since these eschew questions of ultimate meaning.

But whether or not the leap of freedom into "autonomy" is causally explicable, it arguably presupposes the capacity of choice as such. And, if it does, it is not entirely detachable from what Heine distinguished as humanity's Hellenist nature, that is, its "empirical" components. Thus, while ends or purposes are not *derived* from human bodily needs or desires, in some sort of cause and effect relationship – since ends or purposes have a certain self-sustaining existence of their own – they cannot wholly be disconnected from what people actually aspire to. At any rate, both Heine and Herder preferred to think that there *were* links, in view of which desires and purposes could as easily join in harness as clash. In other words, they thought of desires and purposes – as they thought of physical needs and spiritual ends, or nature and culture – as processes of symbiotic interaction, however beset these processes were by latent fragility, due to their inner tensions.

v

Unlike Herder, who saw in the symbiotic fragility and tension of autonomous humanization a serious, if not tragic, predicament of the human condition itself, Heine was inclined to view it as closer to comedy than

49. Herder, *Werke*, VI, 64; see also XIV, 322–4; XVII, 120–1. Herder conceived of human autonomy in a theistic context as well as in a context of individual self-embeddedment, in contrast to a conception of unencumbered selfness. On this problematic fusion in Herder's idea of *Humanität*, see Ulrike Zeuch, "Herders Begriff der Humanität," in *Vom Selbstdenken* (Heidelberg: Synchron, 2001), 187–98. I discuss the difficulty of applying a *pure* form of autonomy to politics in *Democratic Legitimacy: Plural Values and Political Power* (Montreal: McGill-Queen's University Press, 2001).

to tragedy, and spoke of it as the eternally ridiculous (*ewig-lächerliche*) in the human condition, by virtue of its "cosmic incongruity."[50] This divergence lends to Heine the appearance of a coolly detached thinker, whereas Herder, more given to philosophic brooding, projects the image of a thinker seething with righteous indignation. A story that Heine tells with undisguised relish (in his third Börne book) poignantly illustrates this apparent contrast of attitudes.

At an important meeting of German revolutionary republicans Börne had his watch stolen. But, instead of lamenting the loss, Heine reports, Börne rejoiced over it. Börne's hopes for the revolution are said to have risen appreciably in the knowledge that the German revolutionaries possessed their own pickpockets, since he had long been tormented by the thought that his party was composed only of honest people who, because of their honesty, would never achieve anything.[51] Although Herder was keenly conscious of the gap between *Humanität* as a credal idea and *Humanität* as an implemented idea, he would have expressed utmost shock if he had been told that honesty could obstruct the attainment of worthwhile ends. For he left little doubt that, for him, only ethical means would render the achievement of ends truly moral. Hence, to separate ends from means seemed to him self-defeatingly absurd.

At the same time, the contrast between Heine and Herder may well be more apparent than real, a matter of style rather than substance. It might, therefore, be a moot point whether Heine's sense of the incongruously ridiculous truly amounted to his seeing human failings and human foibles with more aloof eyes or to his being, in his seeming flippancy, less genuinely convinced of, or less seriously concerned with, the moral unity of ends and means.

What is manifestly beyond argument, I feel, is that Heine, quite as much as Herder, recognized the intricacy of the human condition to an extent that prevented either from conceptualizing "humanity" as a clearly definable *state* rather than an uncertain and evolving *process*. And, in view of this, it may perhaps not be wrong to conclude that they sought to transform the concept from a fixed goal into a moving purpose, or from a contemplative idea – in its Platonic sense – into a constitutive principle of ongoing becoming.

Needless to say, this radical shift in its traditional meaning did little to reduce its inherent complexity. For, not unlike the prophetic messianism of the Hebrews, *Humanität* is now taken to move humans into acts

50. Heine, *Werke*, V, 197.
51. Ibid., VI, 166–7.

of striving, in which the ends, while capable of being envisaged, remain forever uncertain of attainment. I suggested, therefore, that, so conceived, *Humanität* could be said to strongly approximate the notion of *methexis*, in that it assumes the form of an activating principle which, rather mysteriously, joins the temporally given with the infinitely aspired, the uniquely individual with the shared universal, and the collectively national with the collectively supranational within a relation of symbiotic fusion. I apply the word "mysterious" to this fusion because it joins what commonly are held to be irreconcilable opposites, involving the physical *and* the metaphysical, the tangibly palpable *and* the elusively transcendent.

And I believe it was precisely the merging of these opposites that held for Heine, as for Herder, an extraordinarily persistent fascination. Possibly this was so because the opposites seemed simultaneously rooted to them in the secular here-and-now as much as in the sacred yet-to-be.[52]

52. More simply, perhaps, this might have been so because both were highly imaginative thinkers, with a nose for the seemingly paradoxical.

4

Humanism and Titanism: Masaryk and Herder

IT IS, I believe, no exaggeration to say that the similarity between the ideas of Thomas Masaryk and those of Herder is at times breathtaking.[1] Perhaps the most characteristic affinity lies in their common tendency to bring together concepts that usually are held to be in dichotomous tension, "dialectically" opposed, if not altogether contradictory. In this chapter I want to pursue further the idea of "reaching out," which I have associated with the concept of *methexis*, by focusing on conflicting pulls within human self-understandings, tensions that have a direct bearing on the enactment of the ideal of *Humanität*. It is the central thesis of Masaryk's philosophical anthropology, as that of Herder, that the polarity between humans' seeing themselves as autonomous, self-directing agents and, simultaneously, finding themselves to be instruments or victims, dependent on others, is particularly prevalent in modernity. And both men view this polarity as the crucial source of obfuscation regarding one's sense of identity and one's sense of inter-relatedness, causing a constant vacillation between mastery and powerlessness, between boastful titanism and fragile humanism.

I

Comparative discussions present snares that are not easily eluded. Let me make clear, therefore, that in what follows I have no wish to suggest

1. Alexander Gillies, in "Herder and Masaryk: Points of Contact," *Modern Language Review*, XL (1945), 120–6, writes: "No more instructive or illuminating approach to Herder can be found than in the writings of Thomas G. Masaryk, the philosopher-President" (120). The theme of the two men, Gillies observes, was fundamentally the same: the diagnosis and cure of modern ills. And the cure, for Masaryk and for Herder, says Gillies, was the same too: the doctrine of *Humanität*.

that Masaryk was a mere carbon copy of Herder. Although Masaryk handsomely acknowledged his intellectual debt to Herder – especially with respect to the theme of *Humanität* – there were a number of other influences at work. What Masaryk, like other Slav nationalists, deeply appreciated was undoubtedly Herder's celebration of the Slavs' role in history.[2] Indeed, he regarded Herder's ardent support for the Slav cause as evidence for the spiritual retransmission of the Czech Reformation and the legacy of Jan Hus and Jan Amos Komensky (Comenius) – a view doubtlessly open to question.[3] What, however, is beyond challenge is that it was Herder's pro-Slavic sentiments in the *Ideas* that originally attracted Masaryk to Herder, as they had attracted his Czech and Slovak predecessors. Beyond challenge, too, is the fact that among the major thinkers in Germany Masaryk rated Herder above Goethe and Kant, and did so, according to his own account, because he found Goethe wanting in ethical conviction and Kant too aprioristically rationalistic.[4] In one important respect, however, the resemblance between Masaryk and Herder breaks down: Masaryk actually accomplished what Herder could only dream of. Instead of leading a life actively serving the public good which would put a Solon or a Lycurgus to shame, Herder found himself confined to the inkpot – as he himself complained.[5] And although he did carry out some educational reforms as school superintendent in Weimar, his record as a doer is a pale reflection of Masaryk's record.

In *Modern Man and Religion* Massaryk speaks at some length of Herder and points out four themes that had attracted him to his thought: (1) Herder's doctrine of *Humanität*, in that it suffuses the concept with the manifold diversity of human aspirations instead of identifying it with a single and unchanging ideal, and, no less significantly, in Masaryk's estimation, in that Herder relates the concept to religion instead of opposing it to religion; (2) Herder's theory of causation and

2. Thomas Garrigue Masaryk, *The Making of a State* (New York: Stokes, 1927), 421.

3. Yet, in spite of maintaining the transmission theory of the Czech Reformation, Masaryk was not uncritical of the Messianic historical role of the Slavs as a whole. In this respect he clearly parted ways with a number of earlier Herderians such as Josef Dobrovský, Josef Jungmann, Jan Kollár, Pavel Josef Šafařík, or Karel Havlíček.

4. Masaryk, *Modern Man and Religion* (Freeport, N.Y.: Books for Libraries Press, 1938, reprint 1970), 274–5. In point of fact, Masaryk borrowed the term "titanism" from Goethe's *Faust*, in order to characterize the image of a totally unencumbered self for whom there are no limits. See also ibid., 90 and 200–2 (henceforth cited as *Religion*).

5. J.G. Herder, *Sämtliche Werke*, ed. Bernhard Suphan 33 vols. (Berlin: Weidmann, 1877–1913), IV, 346. For an English translation, see F.M. Barnard, *Herder on Social and Political Culture* (Cambridge: Cambridge University Press, 1969), 64 (hereafter cited in parentheses).

continuity in history and its attempt to combine the idea of humanity's self-determination with the idea of an overarching providential order; (3) Herder's vision of the Slavs as the bearers of a cultural and ethical mission; and (4) Herder's belief in the ultimate compatibility of particularism and universalism in the interpretation of nationality.[6]

Although I shall focus on the first theme, I shall, in varying degrees, touch also on the other themes listed, since these, by and large, are but extrapolations, if not actual entailments, of the principal theme of humanity.

II

For both Masaryk and Herder "humanity" has at once ethical and ontological connotations, in that what human beings might be is seen through the prism of what they are, by virtue of being *human*, and the limitations this implies. Furthermore, as I indicated, Masaryk's conception of humanism, in contrast to common understandings of it, shares with Herder's the necessity of a religious context, albeit in an unorthodox, non-denominational sense. Thus interpreted, religion, for both of them, is an essential source of human self-understandings that seek to escape the traps of both resigned fatalism and deceptive titanism. Admittedly, in elaborating upon "religion," Masaryk is much clearer when describing the *function* of religion, or in pointing out what religion is not, than when telling what it is. Religion is to provide the norms or standards that enable individuals to come to terms with the limits of what existentially they *can* do and what ethically they *ought* to strive for. In a word, it is to guard against what Masaryk calls *titanism*, to which he ascribes three chief (and interrelated) pitfalls: the assumption of tasks for which one is unable or unwilling to take personal responsibility; the indulgence in acts grounded in wishful thinking or delusions of grandeur; and an utter loss of measure – a total failure to keep "scale" in mind. Titanism, therefore, is to be viewed as the very opposite of authentic humanism. Masaryk sees its threat most acutely in the relation between the sexes; he finds titanism to feed on the male's imagined superiority over the female, in his treating women not as a subject of intrinsic worth like himself but purely as an object of his desires.[7] Man's

6. Masaryk, *Religion*, 121–4.

7. The theme of titanism forms the third part of *Religion*, 215–315 and is further developed in the third volume of Masaryk's *Spirit of Russia* (New York: Barnes and Noble, 1967), esp. ch 15. "The titanic superman can only tolerate woman as subman [sic], because of whom he feels himself most vividly a superman" (260–1).

treatment of woman is therefore an important indicator of *humanita* for Masaryk and, as in the case of Herder, the touchstone of true civilization. Not surprisingly, humanism is for both closely interwoven with civic institutions in general, of which religion forms a vital component; indeed one almost gains the impression that religion figured even more importantly for Masaryk than for Herder, the professional churchman. This *is* rather startling, since Masaryk is best known as a statesman and politician who played a leading role in the founding of Czechoslovakia after World War I, and, before that, as a member of the Austrian parliament.

Was, then, Masaryk's emphasis on religion a purely political stance, an opportune move, lacking any deep convictions? I very much doubt the truth of this interpretation, although Masaryk himself almost lent credence to it by retrospectively claiming (during his presidency) that all he ever thought and wrote was politically motivated.[8] Admittedly, too, in his later years, *humanita* increasingly became associated in his works with the virtues of political democracy. Yet this in no way alters the fact that Masaryk did not so much as mention democracy throughout the greater part of his philosophical and sociological writings or his university lectures.[9] It may, therefore, be closer to the truth to regard his vision of democracy as the culmination of his theory of *Humanität* rather than as its source. Still, whether or not his humanist thinking was inherently political, his dominant interests were unmistakably human-centred. What human beings are, what they ought to be, and what they might attain to be, as individuals and in acting with others: these certainly were themes that occupied him most intensely throughout. Above all, the question of *choice* centrally engaged his mind as the paramount condition of both human autonomy and human responsibility.

At the same time, for him, human autonomy was not unbounded. And this was so, Masaryk explained, because (a) humans are not isolated monads, and (b) moral ends are not a matter of purely subjective choosing. In making this argument, he remarkably echoed Herder's thesis that no one had made himself by himself alone, or decided entirely subjectively what ends are worth pursuing.[10] Moral goals, Masaryk reiterates, are not wholly, or even for the most part, the *product* of

8. Karel Čapek, *Hovory s T.G. Masarykem* (Prague: Borový and Čin, 1936), 282 (subsequently cited as *Hovory*).

9. Milan Machovec, *Tomáš G. Masaryk* (Prague: Melantrich, 1968), 12.

10. Herder, *Werke*, XIII, 343–8.

human choice, since they *confront* individuals as objective values and self-sustaining ends.[11] Masaryk's human-centredness was therefore qualified; and what qualified it was religion. Commentators who have seen in his religion a mere prop seem to me mistaken. Religion, I believe, was vital for his conception of humanism, and conferred on it a meaning that was at once premodern and nonsecular, as it was – especially when later linked to democracy – typically modern and secular. Indeed, it is precisely this mingling of two distinct traditions that characterizes Masaryk's ethics, his philosophical anthropology, and his philosophy of history; and it does so as strikingly and problematically as it does Herder's.

Religion virtually *structures* the content of Masaryk's humanism in that it critically enters cognition and perception for him, and thereby actively shapes the mode in which humans grasp the "outside" of their existence, as it in turn provides the anchorage for their "inside," their feeling and consciousness of selfhood *vis à vis* others. As a result, humans acquire in and through religion a sense of being as such, together with a sense of the distance between themselves and others, as well as of the obstacles that lie between what they are and what they could or should be, in themselves, and in relation to others. Directly and indirectly, too, in this encounter with "God, humans, the world, and our own selves," religion generates an awareness of *limits*, a realization of the boundedness of human existence and human agency. And it is in *recognizing* these limits that Masaryk, again like Herder, sees the true meaning of human freedom and human autonomy. Hence, to ignore the limits that religion brings home to us is not to promote humanism, it is to invite titanism.[12]

Masaryk, as one commentator has put it, always fought "on two fronts."[13] On the one hand, he struggled against irrationalism and

11. Masaryk, *Moderní člověk a náboženství* (Prague: Laichter, 1934), 245. See also *Religion*, 207–8: "You are carrying on a fight – but master of it all you are not, and without a master you can see for yourself that it cannot go on; you are fighting, but precisely through this fight of yours you recognize that master; you are a general defending, or perhaps only a private, nothing more. You are not God. Who, then, is that master?"

12. This is the central idea in Masaryk's doctrine of titanism, developed especially in *Religion*, ch 3. See also his *Die philosphischen und sociologischen Grundlagen des Marxismus* (Vienna: Manzscher Verlag, 1899; reprinted Osnabrück: Otto Zeller, 1964), 456–63, (hereafter cited as *Grundlagen*). See further *Hovory*, 243, and Masaryk, *Der Selbstmord als sociale Massenerscheinung der modernen Civilisation* (Vienna: Konegen, 1881), 143–5, (hereafter cited as *Selbstmord*).

13. René Wellek, "Masaryk's Philosophy," *Essays on Czech Literature* (The Hague: Mouton, 1963), 66.

mythic religion and, on the other, against dogmatic rationalism and positivism. Although Masaryk conceded, perhaps even stressed, that rational methods are indispensable in the striving for *truth*, he nonetheless held them to be insufficient for the discovery of *meaning*. And since people cannot accept a world in which they see no meaning, they turn to unreason and utter fancy; disillusionment with rationality and the sciences further drives them to disenchantment and despair and, from there, to magic. They fall victims to pseudo-science, to what has become the "religion of modernity."[14]

At the same time, Masaryk refused to accept Kant's dualism of science and morality. Kant was aware of the threat that science posed to human self-understandings as autonomous and moral beings, as was Masaryk, but he saw no way out of the dualism. Masaryk, on the other hand, somehow wished to believe that there was no inherent conflict between true religion and true science – that, although each may uncover different aspects of truth, they both contribute to the emergence of one and the same truth.[15] Together, he seemed to hold, they *can* disclose the source of true causes and true meanings. It is only the belief that science can achieve by itself what religion must supply to it that leads to pseudo-religion, which blurs rather than illuminates meaning and creates the illusion of limitless possibilities and infinite progress.[16]

Unfortunately, it is not clear in what sense science and religion reveal the same truth or, for that matter, what Masaryk meant by "truth," although he generally identified it with factual or empirically verifiable statements.[17] What *is* clear is that he is most anxious to warn against jumping too glibly to conclusions, against assuming a causality that is prone to reductionism, particularly in the analysis of human action. We cannot hope to understand or explain human agency by wholly concentrating our attention on antecedent psycho-physical conditions, uncontrollable instincts, social and economic pressures, or unconditional commitments.

14. Masaryk, *Religion*, 55; seel also *Selbstmord*, 115–17, 170–2, and *Grundlagen*, 460–81, 498.

15. Masaryk, *Religion*, 55–61.

16. Ibid., 62–75, 204–9.

17. For a most perceptive interpretation of Masaryk's conception of truth, see Erazim Kohák, "To Live in Truth: Reflections on the Moral Sense of Masaryk's Humanism," in Milič Čapek and Karel Hrubý (eds.), *T.G. Masaryk in Perspective: Comments and Criticism* (New York: SVU Press, 1981), 37–61. In part it also contrasts with my interpretation.

While this kind of causality may enable individuals to take cover behind such reifications as class or mass society, or behind duties imposed by superior authority or membership of parties, it cannot serve as a basis for autonomous action.[18] We cannot rely on "instinct," on "causes" and "duties," if we want to view ourselves as resonsible agents. To make any such "reasons" the sovereign of human agency is to solicit moral chaos.[19] Sources of moral action are not like mechanical causes; to think on these lines is to mistake ethics for engineering. "Why," asks Masaryk, "are Marx and Engels against capitalist exploitation? Merely because the capitalist system is economically unsound? Or, rather, because it offends our feelings of humanity, in that we find it *altogether wrong?*"[20] If whatever people do inexorably results from causes over which they have no control, then individual self-direction and, with it, individual responsibility are meaningless notions. In order to act in the proper sense of acting, people have to know what they are doing, for what reasons and upon what principles. To find things right or wrong, not technically but morally, we must have some idea of right and wrong, a moral consciousness, that enables us to judge and evaluate choice. Masaryk does not belittle the role of feelings in action or moral choosing, since, like Hume and Herder, he cannot view reason as the sole moral causality. Nevertheless, he does not equate feeling with blind impulse to an extent that would deprive what we do of a basis upon which it could be judged.[21]

Clearly, the central point of Masaryk's argument here is the issue of accountability. We cannot account for our actions if we literally do not know what we are doing or why; some knowledge is therefore necessary at the time, and in retrospect, of why we did what we did, if we are to be able to accept responsibility and, in consequence, refrain from overreaching ourselves – from biting off more than we can chew – and avoid ignoring the limits within which we *can* act responsibly. This, in essence, according to Masaryk's religious understanding of humanism, defines one's performative humanity and distinguishes it from irresponsible titanism. But, it may be asked, what *are* the limits of our capacity to act?

18. Masaryk, *Ideály humanitní* (Prague: 1901, 9th ed. Prague: Melantrich, 1968), 17; Čapek, *Hovory*, 227–9; see also *Grundlagen*, 498–500.

19. Masaryk, *Grundlagen*, 499.

20. Ibid., 486; see also 149–50, 176–8, 227–30, and Masaryk, Česká otázka (Prague, 1895; 6th ed. Prague: Čin, 1948), 342–3.

21. Masaryk, *Religion*, 209–11.

How are we to know the boundaries of accountable autonomy? What, indeed, does it mean to act upon accountable principles of one's own? If humanity itself is not the measure of things, who or what is?

In attempting to come to grips with these questions, Masaryk reveals his *qualified* belief in human-centred humanism. And it is precisely in formulating this qualified humanism, a humanism tempered by religion, that Masaryk most impressively discloses his remarkable affinity to Herder's philosophy of *Humanität*.

III

Like Masaryk, Herder affirmed the principle of indivual self-direction and personal accountability, and, again like Masaryk, expressed serious misgivings about its exclusively secular and rationalist underpinnings. This is not because he was the inveterate antagonist of the Enlightenment that he is at times taken for, but because he questioned the excessively "universalist" and "progressivist" understandings of the inherited concept of *Humanität* in the Age of Reason. We are not rational automats, nor are we capable of global brotherhood, of lovingly embracing millions of our fellows – as Schiller sings in the "Ode to Joy" – for no human love is as extensive as that.[22]

Likewise, Herder objected to the belief, widespread in his age, that enlightenment was a smooth and cumulative process. Every advance has its price, since whatever new path is chosen is purchased at the cost of excluded alternatives. While we may indeed fancy ourselves more advanced by having at our disposal inventions unknown to our forbears, not everyone who uses them has the knowledge or the skill of the inventor.[23] Every advance, too, knits a new pattern of thinking and acting; new techniques create new needs, and these in turn generate new problems – new hazards as well as new opportunities. Few inventors know or indeed *can* know, let alone determine, to what use their inventions might eventually be put. Intentions frequently have unexpected consequences, and humankind can be no greater ass than when it tries to play God.[24] These are typically Herderian insights into historical and cultural processes – to which subsequent chapters will return – as they are part and parcel of his philosophy of *Humanität*. It is to the intellec-

22. Herder, *Werke*, V, 513–54 (189–211).
23. Ibid., XIII, 371 (315).
24. Ibid., 372–3 (316–17); see also V, 557 (214).

tual credit of Masaryk that he was among the first to pay tribute to Herder's pioneering contribution to cultural anthropology and intellectual history, and it was undoubtedly *via* this route that he came to adopt (and adapt) Herder's conception of "humanity" in conjunction with its religious component.

Humanität, then, is not simply indiscriminate love, the cumulative advancement of global happiness, or continuous progress. Augmenting knowledge or skills may be well and good, but, in itself it adds neither value nor meaning to human action. There is, Herder urges, another "causality" at work. By virtue of being an inhabitant of nature *and* culture, a person is simultaneously subject and object, agent as well as instrument, and thus a creature of choice *and* necessity. In other words, humans, having "a will of their own," are not only subject to law but are also "a law unto themselves."[25] In possessing freedom of choice, they are therefore not only determined but also determining. All this is fully acknowledged by Masaryk. However, as with Herder, qualifications, too, have their place. For, whatever freedom human beings have is neither unconditional nor absolute. Like love, freedom is not unbounded. To be effective and meaningful, it correspondingly requires *scale*, a space of its own.

What troubled Herder most, accordingly, as it did Masaryk, was not sanguinely unqualified optimism regarding progress *per se*, but a lack of a sense of measure, a tragically defective grasp of limits in considering what it is to be human. It was therefore, as Herder put it, the first germ of attaining a true consciousness of our humanity, as also of our effective freedom, to recognize the limits within which we *can* choose, within which we *are* agents.[26] Language and religion go together for Herder, and both, in his view, promote the attainment of the consciousness of limits. Of the two, language constitutes for him the basic causality, in that religion seems to him inconceivable without the existence of language. Language enables us to form concepts, to reason and to think, to have and share feelings, attitudes, hopes, and fears. Without language, consciousness itself would not be what it is. And *with* consciousness, or its first emergence, religion is born. Herder stipulates that while language is, as it were, the soil in which religion grows, religion, in turn, is the source on which a consciousness of limits feeds.

25. Herder, *Werke*, XV, 133; XVII, 143; XVIII, 339.

26. Ibid., V, 134–47 (170–7). This is a major thesis in Herder's influential essay *On the Origin of Language* (1770).

"Humanity" and "freedom" only assume meaning, on this argument, once we attain consciousness of the limits within which we can impose our own will and choose our own ends. "The strongest and most free among humans perceive this most deeply and yet they strive on."[27] Although Herder does not go so far as to *equate* freedom with the recognition of objective necessity, he does insist that the idea of limitless freedom is incompatible with the idea of being human. We may, as humans, be a law unto ourselves, but we are no monads; and although we may choose for ourselves, our choice is not unbounded. To make self-direction or autonomy contingent, therefore, on the complete absence of limits, influences, interferences, and restraints, is to lose sight of what it is to *be* human.[28]

All the same, and however limited the domain of human choice, exercising choice does demand a measure of freedom, just as *accountable* choice demands a measure of acting rationally, in the sense of engaging practical reason. But, as Herder stresses, and Masaryk after him, such practical reason must not be confused with "reason" as a separate "faculty" conceived as an independent entity or organ of the mind. Reason, Herder makes clear, is neither a super-faculty that majestically reigns sovereign, nor an innate, self-sustaining "automaton" (Herder's term).[29] Echoing Locke, Herder persistently affirms that reason is acquired, that it is formed by experience, and thus does not exist *a priori*. Being itself the fruit of experience, reason cannot instruct us before we have the experience; being itself formed, it cannot causally form us. Yet no one, no member of humankind as a whole, can live long enough to acquire enough experience to gain absolute or perfect rationality.

The matter goes deeper, however. Even if absolute rationality or perfect knowledge were attainable or, as Kant proposed, were identifiable with the possession of universalizable principles, this would not of necessity enhance our capacity to make choices or, for that matter, *moral* choices.[30] For example, in having to choose between telling the truth to the secret police and saving innocent lives, knowing universalizable maxims would, by itself, be of little avail. Precisely when we most need to know what we ought to do, general principles may fail to guide us. Kant, it is true, was not saying that universal maxims were point-blank pre-

27. Herder, *Werke*, VIII, 201–2.
28. Ibid., V, 134–7 (170–2).
29. Ibid., V, 29–47 (130–41); XIII, 143 (264).
30. Ibid., V, 554–86 (211–23); XIII, 145, 345.

cepts for actual conduct in his attempt to define what *sort* of reasons could qualify as admissible moral criteria; all the same, he seems to have implied that if humans were perfectly rational they would, by definition, *know* what to do. In that case, however, Herder felt, choice would not burden them, since moral action would be like solving a mathematical problem to which there was but one correct solution.

This line of reasoning evidently presupposes that knowing and acting necessarily go together, that knowing in fact *entails* acting, so that any-one with perfect knowledge would implicitly know how to act rightly and, knowing it, would of necessity act in accordance with that knowl-edge. In that event, acting rightly would no longer involve the process of weighing diverse and frequently competing alternatives which, as Herder points out, we normally associate with having *im*perfect knowl-edge. On the other hand, if knowing is one thing and acting quite another, as both Masaryk and Herder maintain,[31] then even *perfect* knowledge does not render choosing and the enlistment of will dis-pensable. If, therefore, *we* have to determine what we ought to do in the face of competing alternatives, *choice* continues to remain the basic causality, and not knowledge (*Wissen*) as such, cognition (*Erkennen*) as such, or the degree of rationality in judgment. And, once this is granted, it follows that the complexity of moral agency lies indeed first and foremost in choosing, in deciding what to do, and all the more so when we are confronted with multiple solutions to any one problem. For we then realize most starkly that to act morally *means* choosing, and that to choose may cause pain precisely because we may face options that clash, not simply because some are good and some evil, but because *several* may be good.[32]

It is principally this insight that forms the bedrock of Herder's as well as Masaryk's pluralist approach to coming to terms with the problem-atic nature of moral agency. That Masaryk could have been following J.S. Mill here rather than Herder is of lesser import, as Mill had made no secret of his indebtedness to Herder.[33]

If, then, we accept Masaryk's and Herder's account of moral agency, we cannot but grant that the relation between rationality and morality is

31. Masaryk, *Religion*, 208–9.

32. For a similar contemporary exposition, see Isaiah Berlin, "From Hope and Fear Set Free," in Henry Hardy (ed.), *Concepts and Categories* (London: Hogarth Press, 1978), 173–98, esp. 195–7.

33. For an expression of J.S. Mill's feeling of indebtedness to Herder, see his *On Bentham and Coleridge*, ed. F.R. Leavis (London: Chatto and Windus, 1950).

less direct, or a good deal more tenuous, than a number of philosophers in their time (and ours) appear to have assumed, or even than Kant, in his pre-critical period, seems to have believed. Herder was among the first of modern thinkers to insist that maximizing rationality (however defined) does not mean maximizing morality. This insistence, together with the recognition of the multiplicity and possible incompatibility of values, ends, or principles, marks a decisive break with the mainstream of thought in his time. Reason, Masaryk agreed, may tell us *what* we are about, and (possibly) also *why*, but it does not instruct us that we ought to do, what we rightfully should do, nor does it *make* us do it.[34] By saying, therefore, that someone acts rationally, we could be merely describing how, in what manner, a person says, believes, or explains things; we do not necessarily, however, imply that it was the right thing to say, believe, or bring about. Hence, insofar as *Humanität* or *humanita* is a moral idea, it cannot rest on reason only. And, since Masaryk as much as Herder failed to see how reason itself could generate principles of moral causality, their common critique of Kant's thinking on this score is not altogether surprising. Certainly, Herder's comments on Kant's postulates of practical reason add force to Masaryk's contention that *humanita* in action – as the exercise of moral choice – cannot dispense with assumptions that, in essence, are religious rather than rational.

In the *Metakritik* Herder argues that Kant's postulates of practical reason are flawed by a fundamental and fatal contradiction: "If it is unconditionally necessary," Herder states, "that you always obey the moral law because *reason* commands it, and because it it is your maxim to obey a moral precept thus commanded, then surely it [reason] should suffice."[35] Why, then, he asks, does Kant bring in God? To confuse the issue? "Clearly, you abrogate the law of reason as soon as you enlist the aid of an extraneous and unknown Being (*Wesen*) that you had to concoct (*erdichten*) in order to confer upon that law practical validity. But, in so doing, you admit that it is *in*sufficient, that it is null and void."[36] The fact that Kant had to enlist religion to press reason into service as a moral causality proves to Herder two interrelated points: that practical reason by itself is not sufficient to ground moral action and, second, that only religion structurally serves to make a moral precept tangibly intelligible and practically effective. To appeal to rationality, therefore,

34. Masaryk, *Religion*, 69–75, 205–10.
35. Herder, *Werke*, XXII, 288.
36. Ibid.

as though it were some kind of moral filter, simply will not do. Acting upon reason, while it helps to define human agency as accountable agency, nevertheless does little to define substantive morality, just as acting upon reasons of one's own defines self-directing autonomy without shedding light on the difference between acting rightly and acting wrongly.

I V

It is one thing, therefore, to regard self-directed action and reasoned choice as formal requirements of accountable conduct, but not necessarily the same thing to identify observance of these formal requirements with substantive morality. According to Masaryk and Herder, at any rate, rationality alone need not be morally binding, unless it definitionally implies morality. Such implication, however, has so far not been established by *argument*; usually the convergence of rationality with morality is presupposed and, in this sense, hypothetical, and not categorical. That much both make clear, by denying that autonomy or rationality by themselves are able to produce ethical humanism in the absence of recognizably moral sanctions. In turn, such moral sanctions are for both Herder and Masaryk virtually inconceivable outside some framework of religious beliefs.

Given they are right in taking this position, the supportive moral framework must of necessity be viewed as an extraneous framework if it is to work in the service of ethical humanism. In this event, however, Kant's claims on behalf of rationality and autonomy seem fatally undermined. Of this Kant himself was by no means unaware, it appears, in asserting that whatever function religion may serve in generating moral conduct does not make religion a *constitutive* basis of moral action. No doubt Kant was worried about admitting religion as a constitutive basis, for fear of confusing action guided by custom and tradition with autonomously moral action. Such confusion would amount to equating passive and largely unreflective conduct with conduct based on actively chosen maxims. From this (Kantian) perspective, one simply cannot have it both ways: one cannot uphold individual autonomy and personal accountability as touchstones of humanism and at the same time claim authority for religiously entrenched standards as the basic guides of being moral. Does not veneration of religious beliefs, let alone blind obedience to these – or, for that matter, uncritical acceptance of any hallowed norms or customs – *stifle* individual choice and thereby invalidate its moral content? Is not freedom from the constraints of such external sanctions, therefore, as Kant maintained, the only condition under which moral autonomy and moral responsibility can find valid expression?

These questions are not easily put to rest. There can be no doubt about the risk of tension between the simultaneous affirmation of a secular belief in human self-determination and a religious belief in a divinely ordained world. Clearly, if religious precepts, hallowed traditions, or customary norms, are to assume primacy, if they are to *ground* the conception of ethical humanism, then an authority other than the self-legislating individual *does* come into play. Such an authority undeniably *is* an external authority, and its acceptance does create a problem for individual autonomy, as Kant correctly recognized. Religious standards of conduct are things to be discovered, not created; they are not born within an individual but are something into which the individual is born, and are therefore in a real sense external. Similarly, to mean anything at all, traditions have to be authoritative; otherwise they are nothing. A tradition that ceases to command respect and compliance ceases to be a tradition. Is, then, the acceptance of religious standards tantamount to a denial of autonomy?

To Masaryk, and Herder before him, this argument seems to have involved a false dichotomy. And, whether or not it actually did, it assuredly seems somewhat elliptic. For neither advocated blind acceptance of religious norms, nor did either insist that conduct governed by religious precepts is self-evidently moral, or that choosing ends within a framework of accepted traditions ensures the pursuit of moral ends. What both do appear to think is that religious standards *could* guard against wholly subjective forms of choosing, and *could* serve as reminders of the existence of others, thereby reducing the danger of solipsism or titanism. Religious standards, in short, are seen to provide perimeters of choice; and while such perimeters undoubtedly amount to constraints, the recognition of such constraints need not imply the denial of moral autonomy. Rather, the acknowledgment of constraints betokens for both Masaryk and Herder that "humanity" as a principle of action must take cognizance of the fact that human existence, including human freedom, is not unbounded.

To a real extent, therefore, *Humanität*, as humanization, involves a process of human striving in which autonomous self-direction is of a piece with autonomous self-restraint. If this makes "autonomy" somewhat muted, it seems a price Masaryk and Herder are not unwilling to pay in upholding their thesis that the concept itself entails an ineradicable tension, a tension that is better faced than obscured. And, however "religion" is interpreted precisely, it appears in their view to offer the only way by means of which the scope *and* the limits of human self-determination can find expression, and in which the principles of individual freedom and individual responsibility can be reconciled. Take away the context of transcendent standards, and you will find most humans adrift; forced upon themselves alone, they cannot cope with their autonomy. In their despair, Masaryk asserts, they create, or turn to, Titans, secular supermen, who displace the gods of their forbears. In thus vicariously bolstering their faltering faith in themselves, they simultaneously shake loose from the moorings of their lives as ordinary humans. Fervently seeking to be more than themselves, they in fact become less than themselves, until, finally, instead of rising above themselves, they are faced with nothingness, with the spectre of abject nihilism. Idols overtake the gods they think had failed, only to use and destroy their own creators.[37]

More or less obliquely, Masaryk and Herder disclose that modernity is beset with difficulties no less potentially tragic than the redemptive hopes of earlier epochs. And whether or not they correctly assess the values of a premodern and presecular age, they effectively sound a warning about the danger of ignoring time-honoured signposts that remind humans of their finitude. In so doing, they seek to prove that outside an ongoing tradition of one kind or another, there is no known way of combining our consciousness of self-direction with our consciousness of dependence and boundedness.

In effect, therefore, both men are pointing to a serious hiatus in modern self-understandings, to a possibly unbridgeable gap between subjectivity and objectivity, autonomy and heteronomy, or self-direction and other-direction. In Herder's words, while each of us "is a microcosm in himself, he cannot exist by himself alone." Similarly, although we are, as humans, the authors of our own history, we have not made it "out of whole cloth." To transcend, if not bridge, the gaps in our "oneness" and the gaps in the purposive consistency of our changing states, we cannot dispense with inherited categories of thinking and feeling,

37. Masaryk, *Religion*, 206–12, 253–5; see also *Grundlagen*, 152–8, 458–63; *Selbstmord*, 198–9, 220–2; and *Spirit of Russia*, III, 215–25.

and have to make use, therefore, of "borrowed language" from those who had preceded us.[38]

Masaryk saw in the belief in God a certain safeguard against the loss of purposive meaning in the here and now and the loss of continuity with a past in which, through faith, humans were not troubled with a fractured sense of identity to the extent they are in modernity. Hence, premodern humans were less exposed to the danger of a false or nonauthentic humanism, to what he describes as titanism. Having lost the sense of continuity with this past, however, humans strive to over-reach themselves; filled with overweening pride in their own unaided capacities, they seek to reinvent themselves. This attempt, Masaryk fears, is bound to flounder; humans will lose their bearings, mistake the imperfect for the perfect, the false for the true, and the profane for the holy. Trying to super-moralize themselves (as Herder put it), they will in reality ex-moralize themselves.[39]

Although neither Masaryk nor Herder categorically denied that "humanity" was attainable without any religious beliefs, they both firmly presumed that, in its absence, hopes for human redemption would run the risk of utopian expectations whose non-fulfilment would herald an age of dehumanization and decadence.[40]

Ideally, Masaryk, like Herder before him, strove to bring secular values to religious concerns and religious values to secular concerns. "What a wonderful thought it is to apply religion for the benefit of man and society," wrote Herder.[41] The better it succeeded in this, the better it could further an authentic humanism. "The purer a religion was," he therefore declared, "the more genuinely it could enhance a process of humanization; indeed, the degree of its doing so could be the very touchstone of its intrinsic worth."[42]

At the same time, to bring about the joint causality of self-direction and providence, of human autonomy and a divine order, to which Masaryk referred as *synergism*, was one thing; but to identify "religion" with a particular church or creed was quite another. Masaryk, is quite

38. On the passage as a whole, see Herder, *Werke*, IV, 37; VIII, 210, 226, 314; XIV, 227. Cf. Karl Marx, *The Eighteenth Brumaire of Louis Bonaparte, Selected Works* (London: Lawrence and Wishart, 1968), 96.

39. Masaryk, *Religion*, 295–7; Herder, *Werke*, XXII, 276.

40. Masaryk, *Selbstmord*, 198–9, 220–2; Čapek, *Hovory*, 272–3. Herder, *Werke*, XIV, 320; see also XX, 159, 264–5.

41. Herder, *Werke*, VI, 63.

42. Ibid., XVII, 121–2.

explicit on this point: church and religion are not one; religion unites, but theological dogmas divide, breeding fanaticism and intolerance. Herder made almost identical remarks: religion was not a matter of external organization; rather it was the innermost concern of each individual and, thus, inalienable; every person, therefore, is to be his or her own priest.[43]

These convictions were for both the supreme message of the Reformation, the heritage of Jan Hus and Martin Luther; religion was extended selfhood in action, the coming into play of individual conscience and the consciousness of one's duties to others. For Masaryk, Christ's morality was always *social* morality, one that projected God onto one's neighbour. It was His principal lesson, best learned from Him directly rather than from the Church that speaks in His name.[44] Both make clear, however, that projecting God onto others is not a "natural" inclination. It is, rather, an effort of the mind and the will which, if regularly practised, grows into a disposition, a particular outlook, to which Herder applied the term *Gesinnung*. And for him as for Masaryk, Christ was above all a teacher of such a *Gesinnung*, regardless of whether or not the label "Christian" was applied to his teaching.[45]

In essence, this *Gesinnung*-religion was a social ethic, the central issue of which Herder identified with *Mitgefühl* – a feeling of solidarity with others that was meant to be at once universal and particular:[46] universal, in that it was to contain the most general and encompassing sentiment that human beings were capable of experiencing; and particular, in that it demanded a concrete setting of application. The projection of God onto one's neighbour implies accordingly the operation of a *concrete* universal, the constant interpenetration of the universal and the particular. By virtue of this interpenetration, the manifold experience of particulars receives its configuration, or *Gestalt*, as a distinctly human mode of

43. For a critical analysis of Masaryk's idea of synergism, see Hanus J. Hajek, *T.G. Masaryk Revisited: A Critical Assessment* (New York: Columbia University Press, 1983), 29–37. Herder, *Werke*, XV, 130–1.

44. For a critical discussion of Masaryk's religious thinking from the perspective of contemporary Christian theology, see Otakar A. Funda, *Thomas Garrigue Masaryk: Sein philosophisches, religiöses, und politisches Denken* (Bern: Lang, 1978), 121–44.

45. Masaryk, *V boji o náboženství* (Prague: Jan Laichter, 1904, 2nd ed. 1927), 27. Herder, *Werke*, XIV, 320; XX, 159, 191, 264–5. For an interesting account of Masaryk's own religious beliefs, see Friedrich Thieberger, "Masaryk's Credo and the Jewish Religion," in Ernst Rychnowsky (ed.), *T.G. Masaryk and the Jews*, trans. Benjamin Epstein (New York: Pollak, 1944), 48–73. See also Čapek, *Hovory*, 264–5, 272, 278.

46. Herder, *Werke*, VIII, 296.

perceiving and reacting. Although Masaryk and Herder both acknowledge that universals cannot be assimilated to particulars or, for that
matter, particulars to universals, they do postulate their recurrent and
reciprocal *Wirkungszusammenhang*, their unique intercausality.

V

The idea of an ongoing reciprocal interplay between the universal and
the particular within the concerns of humans as individuals and collectivities characterizes, then, in a strikingly similar manner, both Masaryk's
and Herder's humanism and nationalism. But neither had any illusions
about translating this interplay into the hard currency of political reality
within or among states. And since both allowed ideas of humanity and
nationhood to be susceptible to diverse and changing interpretations,
they readily conceded that their practical application could involve
conflictual opinions and clashing sentiments. They therefore equally
pleaded for tolerance; indeed it would not be wrong to say that "tolerance" was a built-in requirement of the envisaged "translation," and an
integral part of their pluralism.[47]

To be sure, translating the concept of humanity from an abstract idea
into an operative idea has, like any other conversion of a philosophical
paradigm into a performative principle of action, its obvious dangers.
For, rarely, can an idea or ideal wholly escape the risk of distortion, if
not corruption. As "levers of action," lofty claims or goals could therefore easily turn into mere slogans or weapons of party politics in the
struggle for power.[48]

At the same time, these dangers, though real enough, should not detract from Masaryk's and Herder's groping for an authentically dynamic
form of applied humanism. This groping launched upon the world a

47. Masaryk, *Česká otázka* (Prague: Čas, 1895, 4th ed., 1935), 337–52, 373–8. Masaryk
stresses patience as the quintessential requirement in politics, and sees in it the means for
gradual, peaceful development in place of "utopian revolutionism." See also Čapek, *Hovory*,
307.

48. Masaryk, *Id. humanitní*, 13–14, 55–60, 104–5. See also Čapek, *Hovory*, 112, 228–9,
244–6, and Masaryk, *The Making of a State*, 336–40. Antonie van den Beld gives a fascinating
account of this problem in "Masaryk's Morality of Humanity and the Problem of Political
Violence," in *T.G. Masaryk in Perspective*, 191–201; see also his *The Political and Social Philosophy of Thomas G. Masaryk* (The Hague: Mouton, 1975). Roman Szporluk, *The Political
Thought of Thomas G. Masaryk* (New York: Columbia University Press, 1981) is an excellent
companion volume to van den Beld's study which is embedded in a frame of reference that
is a good deal more urbane and comprehensive than comparable monographs of this kind.

number of exceedingly intriguing, though structurally highly complex, notions: the recognition of a difference between ethics and religion and at the same time the problematic insistence on their interpenetration; second, the affirmation of autonomous self-direction as the condition of individual accountability, despite the admission of an ineradicable degree of existential boundedness; third, the embeddedness of *Humanität* as a performative principle within the particularity of distinctive traditions of thinking and acting, even in its thrust toward transcending them; and, finally, the thesis that means are never "just means," insofar as any route chosen for the attainment of an end must be as ethically justifiable as the end itself, in that the manner in which it is pursued is part and parcel of whatever is to be achieved.

In connection with the *mode* of change in any transformation from what is into what is to be, it may be worth noting that Masaryk, while in total agreement with Herder in viewing the concept of *Humanität* as a dynamic notion, went out of his way to stress that change, as a deliberate move to alter things, must be seen as occurring within a context of meanings and values that have, as it were, a life of their own. If *everything* is subject to change, Masaryk observes, if ethical values are wholly relative to given times and places, as if they were purely their "results" or "products," bereft of any intrinsic content of their own, then we have no benchmarks to guide us, no way of appraising where we are going or where we hail from. "First come things, therefore, then development."[49] The observation is of particular importance because it gives emphasis to the distinction between applying a perspective of historical contextualism and applying a wholly relativistic ethic. This distinction has at times been overlooked in assessments of Herder's pluralist approach to cultures and societies, by imputing to Herder the view that one value was as good or as worth pursuing as any other. This, I feel, is an illicit extension of his cultural relativism, and Masaryk did well to correct, albeit indirectly, a serious misrepresentation of Herder's value pluralism.

Instead, what Herder sought to make clear (and Masaryk perfectly understood) is that every generation has to recognize anew what needs to be done to promote humanity.[50] For this kind of knowledge is not the cumulative knowledge of science and technology. Knowing what is to be

---

49. Masaryk, *Grundlagen*, 76; see also 547, 555; further, *The Making of a State*, 444–9, 454–9, 465–75.

50. Herder, *Werke*, XIII, 196 and XVII, 138. Masaryk, *Ideály humanitní*, 13–14, 55–62; seel also Čapek, *Hovory*, 295–9.

done in order to be genuinely human within the particularity of the here and now is a form of discovery which, in its coming about, almost invariably raises new questions of its own, if it does not also intimate the sombre realization that some questions may never be resolved, or wholly resolved. It was principally this sombre historical insight that prompted the *guarded* optimism of both men. But, guarded or not, the optimism of neither was so subdued as to make him give up hope that his gospel of active humanism would induce people to search hard and persistently for viable answers, and to apply them, whenever they were uncovered, with utmost vigour and honest dedication, in the service of humanity.

Even in moments of minimally sanguine optimism, however, Masaryk, I feel certain, would have been willing to settle for Herder's injunction in one of his *Humanitätsbriefe* that "not to get worse, we continuously have to strive for the better."[51] Only Masaryk might possibly have redescribed this injunction, using his own terminology, by warning that if we want to avoid being titanized, we had better make sure to get humanized.

---

51. Herder, *Werke*, XVIII, 370. For a most thoughtful discussion of Herder's fusion of *Humanität* with religion, see Ernest A. Menze, "Religion as the 'Yardstick of Reason' and the 'Primary Disposition of Humankind' in Herder's *Ideen*," in *Vom Selbstdenken*, eds. R. Otto and J.H. Zammito (Heidelberg: Synchron, 2001), 37–47. For a comparative discussion of Herder and Kant on this point, see Susan Shell, *The Embodiment of Reason* (Chicago: University of Chicago Press, 1996), 183–9.

5

Humanity and History:
Causation and Continuity

HERDER'S SPECULATIONS ON HISTORICAL CAUSATION are insepara-
bly bound up with his doctrine of humanity, a doctrine that, at least in
part, was intended to respond to what he, and Masaryk after him, diag-
nosed as the most serious ailment of modernity: the bipolar tension between a sense of mastery and a sense of dependence. On the one hand,
modern humans are emboldened to think of themselves as some sort of
Titans, while, on the other, they are constantly made aware of the limits
of their mastery, and of the extent to which they are in need of others.
Even staunch advocates of autonomy such as Rousseau and Kant were
struck by the simultaneous existence of these contrary understandings
of the self. Rousseau ascribed this malaise to the discrepancy between
escalating wants and the capacity to meet them, and Kant attributed it
to advances in science, which inspired human confidence in the possibility of controlling the cosmos, while at the same time undermining
human faith in self-direction – they goad people to fly, as they simultaneously clip their wings, causing them, the "masters" (as Masaryk put
it), to think of themselves as mere products of supra-human processes.[1]

This paradox in the human condition induced Herder to combine
two seemingly opposite, if not equally paradoxical, conceptions of *Humanität*: on the one hand he sought to "activate" it by converting the inherited idea into a practical principle of action and, on the other, he
tried to qualify it, in order to reconcile the notion of free agency with
the notion of boundedness, in the hope of lessening the risk of both

1. This is one of Rousseau's central themes in *Emile*; for a more detailed discussion of it,
see my "Will and Political Rationality in Rousseau," *Political Studies* (1984), XXXII, 369–84,
or Jack Lively and Andrew Reeve, eds., *Modern Political Theory from Hobbes to Marx* (London
and New York: Routledge, 1989), 129–48. Regarding Kant, see my "Self-Direction: Thomasius, Kant, and Herder," *Political Theory* (1983), 11, 343–68.

unlimited titanism and abject nihilism. Herder's intense preoccupation with the problem of causation in history, apart from its intrinsic merits, was meant, therefore, to demonstrate that tempering the notion of human autonomy with the recognition of human boundedness need not rule out the role of creative agency in the shaping of history or the belief in accountable conduct and moral responsibility. Transformed from a fixed and abstract ideal into a dynamic principle of action, *Humanität* was to be located in time as historical evidence that, however problematic it may seem to combine human autonomy with existential bounds, humans, in striving after goals of their own, *could* view themselves as authors of their history.

As a kind of protean manifestation of human striving throughout the ages, *Humanität*, viewed as a dynamic principle, includes, accordingly, in addition to a forward-looking dimension designed to move people into forging their own ends in history, a backward-looking dimension. And it is the latter that Herder regarded as the special interest of the philosopher of history, in that he took it to reflect the particular manner in which at any given time and place humans aspired to achieve cherished goals. It was chiefly by conferring such a historical conception on *Humanität* that Herder endowed the word with a meaning that was new in the eighteenth-century world of ideas.

This novel meaning presupposed, however, two inherently distinct considerations: that human striving is of necessity purposive, and hence assumes a particular direction over time; and that this striving has a moral orientation. The former, purporting human action to be motivated by self-chosen ends, may arguably claim recognition as an empirical hypothesis; but the same cannot be said about its moral orientation. And it is far from obvious that Herder was successful in keeping these two considerations apart.

In attempting to trace the source of this recurrent ambiguity in Herder's treatment of historical causation, I shall make use of three distinctions:

(i)　The distinction between causality and continuity in nature and causality and continuity in history and human affairs generally – a distinction which, if blurred, is liable to confuse process with action, function with purpose, and fact with value;

(ii)　The distinction between purposive continuity *in* history and purposive continuity *of* history, and the potential problem of mediation between these two perspectives;

(iii) The distinction between continuity and change in the sequence of human events, and the problem posed by the notion of *development* as being composed of both continuity *and* change.

I

Failing to rigorously distinguish what ought to be from what in fact came to be or, seen from some transcendent vantage point, had to be,[2] did not stop Herder from being (with Vico) among the first of modern thinkers to see our understanding of historical causation and our understanding of natural causality as *fundamentally* different. Moreover, Herder linked (unlike Vico) understanding the causality of history with a didactic purpose. In contrast to history, which merely chronicles the deeds of kings and generals, the study of its causality could illuminate our grasp of human endeavour throughout the ages and teach us something about human attainment and human failing in their nature and causality.[3] To serve such didactic purposes is one thing; it is quite another, though, to infer that history should be used to *justify* past sufferings and struggles as being the necessary preparation for a better life in the future. Herder was appalled by any such suggestion, both as a deeply religious thinker and as a proponent of ethical humanism. Hence, he rejected out of hand Kant's suggestion (in the Third Proposition of his *Idea of a Universal History*) that people ought to toil for the sake of those coming after them. In his polemical essay *Yet Another Philosophy of History of Humanity* (1774) he dismissed such an approach (widely adopted by several contemporaries) as an apocalyptic aberration, and fiercely attacked those who viewed the past purely as a prelude to the present and judged its achievements and failings wholly in terms of current standards or in the light of supra-historical absolutes.[4]

2. J.G. Herder, *Sämtliche Werke*, ed. B. Suphan, 33 vols. (Berlin: Weidmann, 1877–1913), V, 513, (hereafter cited as Herder, *Werke*).

3. Herder, *Werke*, XIII, 256; XVI, 587; XVIII, 283, 321.

4. Herder, *Werke*, V, 524–5. Herder seems to have reached a position similar to that of Vico quite independently, for he does not mention Vico until 1797, and even then his reference to him, though eloquent in praise, gives no indication that he was aware of their similarity (XVIII, 246). Vico was little known in Germany at the time, with the possible exception of Christian Thomasius who greatly admired him for his views on Natural Law. Paul Hazard, in *European Thought in the Eighteenth Century*, suggests that some of Vico's ideas had percolated through the writings of Montesquieu, but I can find no supporting evidence for it. (See Hazard, *European Thought*, transl. J. Lewis May [London: Hollis and Carter, 1954], 246.)

Each event, Herder insisted, must be evaluated in its own right, since it carries its validity within itself, and no event, therefore, should merely be seen as a path to ends beyond itself.[5] The historian, to recognize this fact, has to relive the past, reconstruct and rethink it, in order to recapture the spirit, the thoughts, and feelings of the age in question.[6] And, to be able to succeed in entering into this *Zeitgeist* – a term Herder invented – the historian needs to develop an insight into human motivation, into what makes people tick. Herder therefore closely linked avances in historical methods with advances in psychology. The extent to which psychology became capable of attending to each minute detail under investigation would, he believed, materially augment the scope of historical understanding and, with it, the ability of the historian "to feel himself into everything."[7]

Emphatic though he was on paying minute attention to detail before reaching any generalizations, Herder nevertheless recognized that historical understanding required more than the painstaking accumulation of facts. The notion of history as an objective compilation of data was just as untenable as the belief that facts can be, or should be, made to fit into an *a priori* framework of the historian's choosing. Instead, what Herder advocated was a circumspect merging of the "objective" material with its "subjective" ordering, with a view to arriving at a coherent narrative. Ultimately, therefore, historical interpretation could not dispense with subjective judgment. "The historian could see only what *he* could see." Of himself Herder said: "I only write history as it appears to me, as I come to know it."[8] At the same time he did not question the possibility of attaining objectively valid results. If anything, the historian's awareness of how personal judgment enters into the explanation and evaluation of historical happenings might actually enhance the possibility of objectivity, insofar as it could help to minimize arbitrariness and bias, even if it could not eliminate the subjective element.[9]

Herder fully concedes, however, that the recognition of ineradicable subjectivity does mean that the only objectivity attainable in historical interpretation is *relative* objectivity. Successful thought they may be in divesting themselves of personal bias, historians must in the end rely on

5. Herder, *Werke*, V, 527.
6. Ibid., I, 137; III, 470; IV, 202–3.
7. Ibid., V, 503; see also II, 257; IV, 364; and XXXII, 58.
8. Ibid., VIII, 466.
9. Ibid., V, 435.

their own perceptiveness, their skill in marshalling evidence, and their interpretative imagination. Accordingly, Herder regarded as essential components of historical enquiry the combination of such dispositions as open-mindedness, readiness to scrutinize a multiplicity of data and, above all – human history being primarily concerned with sequences of *actions* – highly imaginative insight. The true effectiveness of such a combination of dispositional traits does presuppose, however, that the past *can* be understood in terms of causal relationships. Regardless, therefore, of whether or not the explanations that historical enquiry yields provide *lessons* (as Herder also wished to maintain), the question to be posed in the first place is to what extent, if at all, explanations in such terms are to be had.

Any answer to this question necessarily rests on a number of assumptions about causality within the universal order of things in general and causality within human history in particular. These assumptions, be they factual, in the loose sense of being empirically verifiable, or conceptual, in being derivative of some comprehensive "metaphysical" scheme of thought, vitally bear on the historical perspective that is applied, as they guide the approach to the question of intelligibility, to making sense of where, crudely put, history is going.

In this exploration Herder is frequently tempted to invoke at one and the same time the metaphysical framework that underlies his providential theory of history and the empirical tenet he posits about the purposive nature of human actions. In the light of the former, history is held to be analogous to nature; the god of nature is also the god of history.[10] Hence if unity and continuity are observable in the realm of nature, why should they fail to be discoverable in the realm of human events? Even if we have to suspend judgment about the purpose *of* history and the ultimate design of the providential order, why should we refrain from seeking meaning and purpose *in* history, since purposiveness is so manifestly observable within the human world?[11]

Herder makes no suggestion, however, that, in studying history to learn all we can about human purposes under the most diverse conditions of

10. Ibid., II, 127; IV, 200; XIII, 7–9; and XXIV, 334. Herder's declared aim was to vindicate the place of humans in the natural realm. What seems less clear is the meaning of "nature" in this context. Although Herder was not blind to the proliferation of understandings that this word had undergone (see especially IV, 181), his own use of it is hardly less ambivalent than that of his contemporaries. Nature was what one could observe, but more often it was what one wished to oberve.

11. Ibid., XIII, 7–8.

time and place, we would be able to espy *divine* purposes. The only thing
we can do with any hope of success, therefore, is to try to come to grips
with goals that people pursue for reasons of their own or in response to
opportunities and challenges as they see them.[12] In contrast to Vico,
accordingly, Herder postulates no ultimate explanations in terms of an
allegedly recognizable coincidence between divine purposes *of* history
and actual human purposes *in* history. In this respect, therefore, Herder
seems far more of a secularist than Vico, regardless of what Michelet and
others have said about Vico's secularism.[13] For Vico never doubted that
purposes *in* history were but integral constituents of divine purposes *of*
history. To be sure, people may think they are pursuing ends of their
own, but unwittingly they in truth act in accordance with what Providence ordains, since divine purposes are not external to human purposes. Divine Providence does not govern externally "like a tyrant laying
down laws ... God is not a potter who works at things outside Himself."[14]
While people act freely in pursuit of purposes that are very much their
own, they nonetheless promote what objectively "had to be, must now be,
and will have to be."[15]

Although Herder at times expresses a belief in something akin to
Vico's fusion of subjective spontaneity and objective necessity (in survey-
ing purposes *of* history), he goes out of his way in the *Ideas* to distance
himself and his search for teleological explanations from a "theological
approach" in his determination not to follow in Bossuet's footsteps.[16]
Evidently, Herder was not slow to realize that a doctrine of historical
fatalism awkwardly converged with his ethical theory of *Humanität*. At
the same time, in stressing the importance of *evaluation* as distinct from
explanation, he did presuppose the existence of an overall pattern of
teleological history, in the light of which the *course* of history – if not its
individual events – was to be assessed. His search in terms of historical
enquiry must accordingly be viewed as a composite search or, at least, a
two-dimensional undertaking. Each dimension of this undertaking, the

12. Ibid., V, 589.
13. On Michelet's interpretation of Vico's humanism, see Patrick H. Hutton, "Vico's
Theory of History and the French Revolutionary Tradition," *Journal of the History of Ideas*
(1976), 37, 241–56.
14. Giambattista Vico, *The New Science*, transl. T.G. Bergin and M.H. Fisch (Ithaca, NY:
Cornell University Press, 1948), 525. See also *The Autobiography of Giambattista Vico*, transl.
T.G. Bergin and M.H. Fisch (Ithaca, NY: Cornell University Press, 1944), 121.
15. Vico, *The New Science*, 341, 348, 629.
16. Herder, *Werke*, XIV, 569.

explanatory as much as the evaluative, is broadly concerned with tracing connections that are distinguishable by the historian's perspective that comes into play. But, whereas the explanatory search, taken wholly by itself, could be said to involve predominantly empirical criteria for evidence, the evaluative search may well have to invoke criteria that are supra-historical, be they in essence religious, in presupposing a providential design, as in Vico's case, or secularly moral as they were for the most part in Herder's case. In both cases it is hard to see how the evaluative criteria can be historically grounded or validated outside a framework of independent standards.

Arguably, however, if indeed Herder's approach to history is principally evaluative and events are assessed first and foremost by their moral content, then his plea for viewing each individual event as an end in itself is rendered less implausible, especially on the further supposition that motives for action are the central concern of any engagement in historical enquiry. For, presumably, it then makes sense to speak of an event's intrinsic worth and significance as being *determined* by the moral criteria applied to it.

What remains obscure, though, is how the notion of the *intrinsic* value of an individual historical event is to be brought into line with the notion of its *overall* significance within the stream of occurrences making up historical *continuity*. Clearly, posing this question ineluctably leads back to the question of historical causation *per se*.

II

The general idea of causation in history is that there are events which, although separate from subsequent events, bring these about by anteceding them within a relationship that is uniquely determinate. When, we say, for example that A causes B, we not only mean to that B follows A, but also that B results from A, in that A is the necessary condition for the occurrence of B. But what precisely is the nature of the link between two single events in this necessary and determinate relationship? Surely to have causal effect it must possess causal *power*. Now this causal power constitutes, as it were, if it is something external to A and B, an additional event, the separate existence of which is causally inexplicable unless we resort to an infinite regression. If, however, it is *not* something separate, then A and B cannot be separate either, for we have no way of distinguishing their separate existence. The alternative is to stipulate the existence of causal properties *within* the events themselves.

Thus, once A and B cease to represent separate events, the law of causation in the customary sense is rendered inapplicable, and the postulate of *internal* causal powers is inescapable. Hume, who rejected such a postulate, logically concluded that the law of causation was either unnecessary or unfounded. By introducing it we are not talking about something that is inherent in, or derivable from, reality. All we do and can do is to link in our imagination events that past observation has shown to occur regularly together as if they were necessarily related. Accordingly, all we *should* mean when we say that A is the cause of B is that A is regularly followed by B.[17]

At first sight Herder's own view on causation appears to coincide with that of Hume. We merely assume the existence of a causal relation, he says, with the aid of mental constructs that are based on analogy and observation.[18] Yet, on closer reading it becomes evident that what Herder questions is not the reality of causation as such but the acceptance of causation as something simple and readily intelligible. When he agrees, therefore, with Hume that finite minds may only be able to form causal hypotheses on the basis of observation of "outside" relationships between sequences that appear to reveal regularity, he does so for different reasons. For Herder *does* accept the existence of multiple interrelations (*Zusammenhänge*) that hold together, not by external links, but by virtue of their own shapes, properties, and internal powers. In effect, he therefore does assume the workings of internal causal forces. The mode of causation he thus puts forward in place of "simple causation" is that of plural causation of an exceedingly complex and varied dynamic.

It is above all this complexity that makes Herder doubt the possibility of gaining a true or complete knowledge of causal relations. For, to gain this degree of causal knowledge, we would have to be able to enter into the inner being of things – something that is clearly beyond our abilities. "Our senses do not suffice to attain this kind of penetration; we stand outside, and all we can do is to observe as closely as we can."[19] It is not difficult to see why, if internal causality is something unknowable, Hume found himself unable to accept such a postulate. But the same cannot be said of Herder. Two related reasons account for this: one is that Herder invoked his metaphysical notion of *Kraft* (a quasi-transcendent energy)

17. David Hume, *A Treatise of Human Nature*, Bk. I, Part III, sec. VI and XIV.
18. Herder, *Werke*, XVI, 522.
19. Ibid., XVI, 551.

to support the hypothesis of internality; the other is his assumption of an inherent teleology within historical processes.

Despite his declared distrust of metaphysics and his avowed aim to think as an empiricist,[20] Herder could not dispense with his metaphysical support of *Kraft*; it was not only the unifying principle of his philosophy of organicism, it was also the basic underpinning of his theological cosmology. In *Kraft* he saw both the First Cause and the subsequent energizing power of "becoming," the core of all existence.[21] And since he thought of this power not as an external force acting *upon* the universe but as an internal one acting *through* the universe, the universe itself was for him the manifestation of *Kraft*, the divine source of *Dasein*, of active being.[22]

Closely allied with the metaphysical element in Herder's theory of causation is the teleological element, the operation of change in and through purposive motion. "Cause" here is explicable not primarily in terms of origins but rather in terms of destinations, of the end toward which things are moving, so that it is the purposive direction that really matters. Discovery of the end or purpose provides clues that disclose the range of relevant or "significant" antecedents. Explaining an event as an *action* accordingly demands not so much a looking back to what preceded it as a looking ahead to what it is seeking to bring about; purposive ends decide the relevance of originating antecedents, not the other way around. That Herder wished to emphasize the causal efficacy of ends is not surprising in view of his paradigm of development, in which, as in an organism, the terminus of growth is implicit within the starting point, so that its purposive direction consists in the unfolding actualization of that which is already latent.[23]

When applied to the sphere of human actions in history, then, Herder's idea of teleological causation posits the end or ends aimed at as the driving or motivating force. Ends are seen as the sustaining source of purposive "development," which in turn implies that events in human history are principally deliberate deeds rather than purely accidental ones, so that intended ends will be the causal *reason* for their occurrence. No doubt (Herder concedes), circumstantial grounds giving rise to causal reasons may be of particular relevance here and there to

20. Herder, *Werke*, II, 326; VI, 83, 183; VIII, 267; and IX, 413.
21. Ibid., XVI, 566; IX, 371.
22. Ibid., XVI, 547–51; XXXII, 228.
23. Ibid., II, 62.

an event's total explanation; but the degree of relevance of these antecedent grounds will be determined by the purposive force of the reason itself. Even in the case of a purposive reason being the work of antecedent circumstances, it cannot be viewed as *wholly* deriving from them, for then it would be an act devoid of purpose. Reason as purpose therefore cannot simply be a function of antecedent causes. The converse, however, does not necessarily hold good. When a course of action has been decided upon, the means chosen will be those that are deemed most suitable to the purpose at hand. The series of events preceding the occurrence of an action will accordingly be determined by their relevance to the end, in the absence of which they would never have come into being at all. We would hardly go to the trouble of obtaining a passport, visa, plane tickets and so on, if we had not the slightest intention of going abroad. It is the end, in short, that occasions the occurrence of the means.

What has earlier been distinguished as the explanatory search is therefore in a sense preceded by the evaluative search in terms of the ends envisaged, since these determine the causal force as well as the intelligibility of the explanation offered. Thus seen, Herder's distinction between "cause" as a temporal antecedent and "cause" as a purposive direction is both of methodological interest in itself, and instrumentally vital to Herder's attempt to maintain a degree of causal determinism without having to subscribe to a theory of historical inevitability. He can, that is to say, thereby argue that explanations of events in human history do not commit the historian to the view that ends that were actually chosen were the only possible courses of action that were open to the agent.

Such a line of argument seems, indeed, the principal argument in Herder's approach to history, since, in this approach, he firmly rejects, despite his providential cosmology, any suggestion that what people choose to do is inexorably predetermined by supra-human forces. Clearly, had he not done so, it would hardly have made sense to argue, as he also did, that humans can learn from the mistakes of the past and, by gaining such insight, extend their capacity for choosing among the multiple alternatives. A purpose, once embarked upon, does, it is true, have a certain compelling force; yet what matters – and what Herder wants to stress – is that humans have the ability to evaluate whatever purposes confront them, before deciding whether to pursue or shun them.[24]

24. Ibid., VIII, 198.

Herder rests this ability not merely on the inherent contingency of teleological causation in history in general but also on the specific epistemological distinction he makes between human consciousness as such (*Besinnung*) and the forming of reflective judgment through *Besonnenheit* in particular.[25] And it is by means of this distinction that he pinpoints a moment in the process of choosing that is different from that of actually deciding upon what to do. For it is during this judgment-forming process before acting (or not acting) that humans may recall the past and draw inferences or "lessons" from what happenned previously under what circumstances and for what reasons. Yet, whatever consciousness is thus gained, although capable of enriching our knowledge, is not the same as feeling committed to act. Nevertheless, it constitutes the pre-condition of the reflective process that informs our purposive judgment, our disposition to pursue one course rather than another. Unlike those who identify consciousness itself with judgment, therefore, Herder interposes *Besonnenheit* as the generating medium of practical judgment. In and through this reflective process, grounds for choosing what to do are to emerge, reasons able to prompt us to decide whether or not to make things happen. People may of course act without going through such a process of choosing. One could also possibly speak of "unconscious purposes" in referring to acts of creative genius – as Goethe has done, as well as a number of romantics –[26] but to confuse this kind of acting with what normally moves people into committing themselves to a course of action seems to me a category mistake of the first order. To allow for forms of human conduct and human creativity which are not explicable in terms of reasons, purposes, or conscious choosing is therefore one thing; but it is surely rather debatable if and how such activity can be described as *purposive*.

The paramount merit of Herder's "epistemological" grounding of his teleological theory lies, therefore, in its stress on *deliberative* choice as

25. Ibid., V, 28–9, and 93, 99. To translate Herder's concept of *"Besonnenheit"* in terms of "reflection" can, however, be misleading. For "reflection" has too close an association with the Moral Sense School (which Herder rejected) and with Locke's dualism (which Herder sought to avoid). While Locke thought of "reflection" as a particular operation of thinking, Herder defined it as "the entire economy" of man's perceptive, cognitive, and volitional nature, that is, as the essential *condition* of the working of the mind in its totality and not only in thinking (V, 28–9), whereas by *"Besinnung"* ("consciousness") Herder understood the active operation of a discerning judgment that presupposed "reflection" (V, 93, 99).

26. For a brilliant account of "unconscious genius" see M.H. Abrams, *The Mirror and the Lamp: Romantic Theory and the Critical Tradition* (New York: Oxford University Press, 1953), ch 8.

the defining characteristic of purposive action, whether or not it could be challenged with regard to acts that are said to have been done for their own sake, and not in order to produce this or that result. Herder does *not* seem to have thought that ends-in-themselves fail to qualify as purposes – a position that I myself share, although it apparently *is* challengeable.[27] For I agree with Herder that ends-in-themselves are still ends and, when deliberately chosen, are no less classifiable as purposes than ends that are instrumental in promoting further goals. To be sure, intended ends may not materialize, but, unless they are envisioned, they can hardly induce anyone to act in the first place.

Indeed, in an important sense, the potential discontinuity between intended purposes and actual attainments could be viewed as a salient feature that differentiates human actions from natural processes, since, in the latter, outcomes are, so to speak, contained in themselves. On the whole Herder recognizes and upholds the contingency of purposive human action, as he also acknowledges the possibility of discontinuities in human strivings. However, when he is applying the metaphor of organic growth to human development, he is apt to do what Aristotle had done before him, and try to do too much. Whenever this happens, he seeks to retain the causal necessity, characteristic of growth, which confers perfect continuity, and seemingly forgets that purposive action has no such necessary inner cohesion. A move of this kind, I fear, simply does not come off. We can either have virtual certainty of outcomes – as in the growth paradigm – or we can have purposive choice and uncertain outcomes; but we cannot have both.

III

Despite its intriguing epistemological underpinning, therefore, Herder's teleological theory of historical causation does not altogether escape the danger of a determinism close to inevitability. Fortunately, this danger is only sporadically apparent in his reflections on purposes *in* history, and even then it is usually evident from the context that Herder's use of organic growth is indeed *metaphorical*. Where the danger of a supra-human determinism seems both real and worrisome, however, is in Herder's

---

27. My position is at variance with that of the philosopher A.J. Ayer, who holds that "where an activity is mainly undertaken for its own sake, the description of it in terms of purposes or motives seems a little out of place." See his "Man as a Subject for Science," in Peter Laslett and W.G. Runciman, eds., *Philosophy, Politics and Society* (Oxford: Blackwell, 1967), 12.

reflections on the purposes *of* history. For in attributing purposes *of* history to the working out of a divine plan within a providential scheme of things, he suggests that ends are wholly predetermined from the very outset. Such a theory of historical causation leaves little or no room for exercising options that could make a difference to historical occurrences. Only by separating teleological causation in human action from other events and processes does it make sense to speak of purpose as something that is not merely given but is also consciously chosen, in contrast to the ripening of fruit or the onset of winter.

Herder, to be sure, is not unaware of the difference between self-chosen ends and predetermined ends or between the contingency of deciding between alternatives and the necessity of being forced to put up with what is unavoidable. He knows and states that, were there no alternatives between which to choose, reflecting upon the past in order to avoid follies and errors in the future would be utterly pointless, and nothing could militate against their inexorable repetition. But this still leaves unanswered the question of how Herder manages to reconcile the recognition of contingency with the belief in an overall order of things in which the god of nature and the god of history are one and the same, so that nothing that happens is contingent and everything is inevitable?

Herder makes no apparent effort to bring about such a reconciliation; believing in a divine power that governs the entire course of events, on the one hand, and believing in the self-sustaining force of purposive striving after human ends, on the other, seemingly poses no real problem. And while he expressly makes a distinction between a theological approach to history and a philosophical one, and roundly repudiates the suggestion that even the most meticulous study of historical data can tell us anything about divine purposes, he evidently does not view this as tantamount to denying the existence of divine purposes *per se.* I am not suggesting that adopting this stance of necessity involves a fatal contradiction, especially in Herder's case, since manifestly he sees no flaw in combining autonomous self-direction with existential limits within an order not of one's own making, an order that does not rule out divine intervention – a "coexistence," to which Masaryk referred as *synergism.* Furthermore, Herder's serious attempt to advance the thesis that each event in history be treated as having its centre of gravity within itself powerfully reinforces this stance.

I shall return to the question of the place of human will in Herder's philosophy of history below. For the present it is perhaps of interest to reiterate that, in order to strengthen his thesis that no event is to be viewed only as a means only but as something that carries its own value within itself, Herder switches (in the *Ideas*) from the "stream" metaphor to the "chain" metaphor (presumably because a chain consists of individually separable links). And, although a chain would not be a chain without interlocking links, it could be said that even if a chain breaks and ceases to perform the function of a chain, its constituent links, though detached, still form individual entities.

But, metaphors aside, the drift of the thinking that underlies Herder's switch of images, does, I think, lend tenability to the idea that even in the face of discontinuity in history, events could still be evaluated by what lies *within* them *qua* intentionality, and separated from what lies *beyond* them *qua* outcomes, by regarding their intentional content as a basis of their own assessment, in abstraction of their particular outcomes. Conversely, what makes actions highly popular or even profoundly admirable by virtue of their outcomes may have little or nothing to do with what makes them intrinsically moral – or, for that matter, intrinsically despicable – if judged from the perspective of their purposive grounds in terms of motives or intentions.[28]

In view of these evaluative discrepancies, there is no necessary conflict in Herder's overall argument between maintaining that human action is purposive and admitting that what appear as sequences in history carry with them no causal connectedness. In other words, *se*quences are not always *con*sequences. In recognizing, therefore, the possibility of purposive *dis*continuity, Herder saw no compelling ground for scuttling the idea of teleological causality as a regulative principle of human striving in pursuit of ends or purposes. Just as he allowed for the lack of any recognizable coincidence between human purposes and divine purposes, without feeling the need to abandon his belief in a providential order, so he allowed for possible gaps between purposive strivings and actual attainments in history, without feeling the need to abandon his belief in purposive behaviour as the archetype of human action. And, whether or not there is a valid symmetry between these two sets of belief, Herder, apparently, perceived in them no inherent incompatibility.

In speaking of human action, moreover, Herder's concern is not only, or perhaps even chiefly, with individual action *per se*, or even individual

---

28. I go into this point more fully in *Democratic Legitimacy: Plural Values and Political Power* (Montreal: McGill-Queen's University Press, 2001). Moreover, Herder stresses that purposes are not blueprints. (V, 531–2.)

action in conjunction with the action of others. Instead, much of his philosophy of history centres on the group, and the group singled out is the *Volk* as a social continuum throughout the passage of time (*Gang der Zeiten*).[29] While his extensive use of biological imagery suggests that he thinks of *Volk* as essentially a product of nature, it is nonetheless made perfectly evident that Herder sees the source of the continuum primarily in the development of *cultural* characteristics.[30] Complex and elusive though these are, they must, Herder keeps insisting, be uncovered, in that they constitute the core of continuity in a *Volk's* changing states, its inner identity. The task of the philosopher of history, accordingly, is to discern and atomize this inner "invisible medium" which relates the past with the present, and study the mode in which it is transmitted and creatively reapplied.[31]

This function of transmitting national traditions Herder assigns to a complex process of "education" in the broadest sense. In contrast to his usual allegorical writing style, Herder seeks to return tradition (*Tradition*) and education (*Bildung*) to their literal meanings, thereby attempting to invest them with a historically grounded dynamism, which he uses principally to demonstrate two things. One is that the human world is not simply an existential given in which individuals are passively

29. Herder's interest in the development of a national consciousness – the core of what he also refers to as "national character" and "national spirit" – assumes centrality in his most mature work, the *Ideas*. But this interest can be traced to his earliest writings, for example, I, 23, 147, 261, 276; II, 8, 13, 19, 28, 32, 79, 160; III, 30, 62, 398, 414, 425; IV, 168, 213, 253, 371; and V, 134, 506, 539.

30. For example, a nation's arts and sciences are said to grow, produce buds, bloom, and wither (I, 151). In the *Ideas* the history of humanity is pictured as a series of national organisms (XIV, 67, 84). See also IV, 212, and XX, 136. Still, what he wishes to trace, principally, are such cultural features as community customs, collective memories in and through literary traditions, and folklore and folk festivals. This is in fact already clearly spelled out in the program he set out during his sea journey from Riga to France in *Journal meiner Reise* (1769). Indeed, the *Journal* is a most instructive document of his pioneering ideas on national cultures – a concept he was among the first to coin and elaborate. (See especially IV, 478.) For additional comments on Herder's travel diary, together with its translation, see my *Herder on Social and Political Culture* (Cambridge: Cambridge University Press, 1969), 26–32, and 63–113. For a young man to map out so clearly the path he was to pursue in the years that were to follow is surely remarkable in itself. Additionally, he was not only well-read at the time, he was also exceptionally critical of what he read, often posing questions (mostly highly uncomfortable ones) that had not been raised before, or raised in quite so trenchant a manner. No doubt, resolving these questions at times severely taxed his own capacities; this hardly detracts, however, from the profound merit of having raised them in the first place.

31. Herder, *Werke*, XIII, 352.

embedded, but is itself the outcome of intricate processes of affirmation and negation, processes which involve humans who understand themselves to be *agents*, that is, individuals able to move and shape things in directions they choose for themselves. The other, and related, thing is that, *because* of these prevalent self-understandings, there are no permanent or wholly repetitive constants. Tradition, therefore, is not identified with a fixed stock of inherited beliefs designed to serve authoritatively prescriptive functions, as Burke suggests, but is portrayed rather as the handing down of a given heritage that, in the process of transmission, is creatively reinterpreted. By the same token, *Bildung* is not equated with set norms, or its dissemination with mere replication; instead, it is viewed in its original sense of actively creating, shaping, or building up.

On Herder's own showing, these twofold processes of transmission enable individuals not only to receive but also to alter, to add to or take away from the transmitted, and creatively apply, rather than simply absorb what is passed on in the way a sponge absorbs water; instead, generations actively adapt as well as passively adopt.[32] Herder's expressed aim is to present transmutations of culture as processes of interpenetration entailing preservation *and* renewal without concealing, nevertheless, that these processes could be turbulent. Humans partake in this ceaseless symbiosis of the old and the new; they are at once products and creators embedded within the universe around them, which "forms and changes them," and at the same time, "awake or asleep, at rest or in motion," they contribute themselves to this symbiosis "as they make use of fire, absorb light, or contaminate the air they breathe."[33] Herder likens this symbiosis between generations and between cosmic agency and human agency to an "ocean where wave loses itself in wave" in a mode of causality in which cause and effect are no longer strictly separable, since everything is related to everything else in ever-changing combinations, "with no single wave in the stream of time ever being like another."[34]

Given this image of ceaseless and multiple fusion, it is not hard to see why Herder invokes a transcendent power and wisdom to escape the admission of *con*fusion and the futility of humans' expecting to find meaning and order within this global interrelationship, within a texture of

32. Ibid., XIV, 234; see also XII, 343–8. Although his theory of culture transmission is most closely elaborated in the *Ideas* (1784–91), it is significantly prefigured in his essays on language (1772) and philosophy of history (1774).
33. Herder, *Werke*, XIII, 253.
34. Ibid., 254, 292.

occurrences in which purposive human striving seems virtually impossible to isolate. Within this global context of history, there is, moreover, bound to be tension between self-understandings in terms of free agency and self-understandings in terms of individual inertness – humans seeing themselves as mere flies on the wheel of time, their assumed self-direction paling into a mirage. Herder, despite his belief in an overarching providential design, nonetheless agonized over this problem and wanted to believe that his modified concept of *Humanität* would help to make it less perplexing.

But whether or not Herder suceeded in reconciling a providential view of history with a secular view and indirectly thereby managed to come to grips with the bipolar tension between human mastery and human dependence alluded to at the outset of this essay, his conception of cultural transmission departed strikingly from prevalent thinking about tradition. In its light, successive generations, even in traditional societies, do not wholly assimilate what is passed on to them without engaging in a more or less subtle process of reappraisal or revaluation.[35] Herder describes these mutations as being similar to a "continuous spiritual genesis" and invests them with "genetic" and "organic" attributes. They are genetic by virtue of the generational manner of their transmission, and organic by virtue of the nature of the assimilation attending it.[36] And, in relating "the living with the dead and with those yet to come," *Bildung*, as the educational agent of these intergenerational processes, is at once the guardian of preservation and the herald of progress.[37]

I V

Language is the chief medium in this "spiritual genesis" as it is also, we noted, the most distinctive component of a people's cultural heritage. For it is through language that a *Volk*'s sense of separate identity is both awakened and perpetuated. However, if national cutlures are not passively assimilated but are creatively applied, what is it that confers on the process of transmission that causally relational unity of directional thrust which is more than the sheer temporal succession of events?

Although Herder does not provide a systematically formulated answer to this question, he indicates, mainly in the *Ideas* and in *Letters toward the*

35. Ibid., XIV, 234.
36. Ibid., XIII, 348; see also XIII, 346 and XIV, 84.
37. Ibid., XIV, 89.

Advancement of Humanity (1793–97) that he is thinking in terms of certain basic determinants by means of which it should be possible to trace significant connections in a people's history. A remark Herder makes in a work of an earlier period in regard to the manner of interaction among these determinants proves most enlightening. In the *Fragmente* (1767) he intimates that he is thinking of interactions in history in a two-dimensional sense: "horizontally," insofar as that *at any given time* a number of agents exercise upon each other a reciprocal influence; and "vertically," insofar as that by succeeding each other they interact in a *directional* manner. In the following Chapter I shall return to the details of the dynamics involved, but for the present it may be noted that Herder associated these interacting agents with three kinds of sources: internal forces, to which he applied the term "genetic," in contrast to external or environmental influences, to which he applied the term *Klima*, both of which he held to be horizontally operative. The upward propelling power of historical "motive" forces, on the other hand, Herder linked with the vertical dimension. The distinction between horizontal and vertical interaction may appear somewhat arbitrary, if not altogether fanciful, but it helps, I believe, to cast light on Herder's desire to distinguish causal antecedents from causal purposes, or originating causes from directional causes.

Most of the social and political thinkers of the century, accepting as self-evident Locke's epistemological assumption of a *tabula rasa*, turned a blind eye to innate or hereditary factors. They tended to emphasize instead the power of environmental agents to bring about the amelioration, if not regeneration, of individuals and societies. Herder by no means disregarded the potency of environmental influences. But he looked upon them as secondary factors. The primary causal agency, he insisted, was the "genetic" source, by which he understood that fundamental or core feature which distinguished one individual and, in its extended application, one *Volk*, from another. It was an inborn energy, peculiar to each individual *ab initio*, differentiating him or her from every other, quite independently of external circumstances.[38]

Herder conceded that he could neither account for the origin of this genetic force nor describe its "inner" nature, but he felt certain about its existence.[39] In it he saw the creative power by means of which an individual could assimilate and apply what had been transmitted by educa-

38. Ibid., XIII, 273, 276–7.
39. Ibid., XIII, 274.

tion within the particular traditions in which he or she was embedded. Although it is not clear which, if any, physical characteristics are associated with this inborn force, it appears that Herder had chiefly a certain mentality in mind.⁴⁰ For what he singles out as genetic characteristics in national collectivities are distinctive habits of thinking (*Denkarten*), among which differences are said to be more marked than differences of individual mentalities among members of a given nation. Accordingly, there is both a national and an individual mode of thinking; an individual is born not only *with* but also *into* a particular mentality.

The trouble with the distinction between individual and national genetic forces is that it threatens to become circular. As a result it is difficult to tell which is the decisive causal factor, the fact that an individual is already born with a given national mentality or the circumstance that he or she acquires that mentality by having been born into it; is it heredity or environment? What is more, the idea of an inborn mentality may not sit too well with Herder's epistemological anti-apriorism; and, to complicate matters further, Herder suggests that, as a result of the interaction between inborn traits and environmental influences, the inborn traits may undergo change, so that inborn and acquired characteristics intermingle or indeed wholly merge.⁴¹ Herder, it is true, made a point of stressing that, in spite of such intermingling, a "hard core" of inborn traits would survive, by proving immune to the influence of environmental factors.⁴² Clearly, Herder saw himself faced here with a dilemma. To insist on the unchanging nature of genetic sources would have involved the denial of the (much-emphasized) dynamic of historical causation. To allow, on the other hand, for the complete changeability of genetic sources would have seriously threatened, if not invalidated, the notion of a persistent identity implied by the term "national character."

A similar conundrum bedevils the excessively comprehensive sense in which Herder employs the term "climate" as a description of environmental sources within historical causation. For he evidently does not confine its applicability to meteorological phenomena; nor does he restrict it, as Montesquieu has done, to physical influences attributable to geographical, geological, or biological factors. Rather, he identifies *Klima* (somewhat sweepingly) with the total environment into which people

40. Ibid., XIV, 39.
41. Ibid., XIII, 280–4.
42. Ibid., XIII, 273.

are born, and includes in it elements of the most diverse nature: institutions of learning, constitutions, standards of living, dress, posture, amusements, and the arts, as well as natural products and culinary preferences; he even calls for a "climatology" of thoughts and feelings.[43] More perplexingly still, at times *Klima* is held to be a mere "medium" and, as such, incapable of initiating activity on its own;[44] at other times, though, it is presented as the "global sphere of interaction" that reflects the effect of the interplay between human "genetic" forces and their contextual environment. Humans are, as it were, both the cause and the effect of moulding: "Man changes *Klima*, but *Klima* also changes man."[45] Interaction thus undeniably means confusion in its most literal sense; yet confusion, so perceived, is not necessarily the same as befuddlement. Complexity can indeed be highly perplexing, and the question as to whether or not Herder's attempt to come to grips with the bewildering facets of historical causation helps toward its intelligibility does not in itself warrant its dismissal as totally meaningless.

At any rate, Herder's concept of *Klima* is of considerable interest to students of social and political development. First, it emphasizes the plurality and interrelatedness of what may "causally" bear upon the shaping of particular outcomes within the historical process, and thus, if nothing else, calls attention to the need for the utmost care in drawing generalizing inferences from occurrences in the human realm. In the second place, by the manner in which Herder insists on *organically* relating the physical and human components of social development, he went some distance beyond Montesquieu's doctrine of environmental causation. The impetus here was to bring out the contrast between the passive nature of environment, taken by itself, and its potency when "energized" (or contaminated) by the existence of humans. And, as a corollary, Herder wished to demonstrate that there is no such thing as the purely objective or the purely subjective in the encounter between source and context within the sphere of human agency. This sort of dynamic interaction (*Wechselwirkung*) was to him the essence of *developmental* continuity – an idea in which he sought to integrate "progressive" change without losing an identifiably persistent "core."

Implicit in this view was the thesis that, in the absence of a measure of interpenetration in any process of historical change, the notion of

43. Ibid., XIII, 269.
44. Ibid., IV, 205.
45. Ibid., XIII, 272.

development makes no sense. Herder felt that if a theory of historical causation cannot account for *both* persistence and change it is unlikely to account for either, and "development" would become inexplicable altogether.

V

Among the developmental agents that give significant direction to human history, Herder ranged *ideas*. They were for him the most impelling source of purposive development, if not its dominant motor power, particularly in politics. Ideas, especially if they interact with, or reinforce, other ideas and thus form what he called "a system of ideational forces,"[46] are able to revolutionize societies, and can do so more drastically, and lastingly, than many a palace revolution.[47] Ideas were first and foremost to bring about Herder's envisioned transition from "mechanical" to "organic" institutions within the social and political realm.[48] Here, once again, Herder was enough a man of the Enlightenment to hold that ideas as *reasons* would be effective causal instruments of change.

The causal power of ideas had, however, much to do with the *Zeitgeist*, the spirit or temper of an age, Herder argued. Interestingly, the work of *Zeitgeist* in turn implied for him the operation of *time* as a propelling agent in its own right: time, itself, is to give significant "shape" to the causality of ideas in history.[49] Unfortunately, in postulating time as an immanently progressive force, Herder moves perilously close to the brink of fatalism: "what time commands to happen must of necessity happen."[50] He strikes a similar fatalistic note when he discusses the notion of *Zeitgeist* itself. For he identifies it almost mystically with the "genius of humanity," with a "mighty genius," or, more ominously still, with a "powerful demon," but he stops short of drawing outright sinister inferences. Nonetheless, his rhetorical question whether the *Zeitgeist* should rule or serve

46. Ibid., XIII, 181.
47. Ibid., XIII, 186; XX, 90.
48. Ibid., XVIII, 332.
49. Ibid., XIV, 236; see also V, 505, 513; and IX, 372. But Herder resisted the temptation to look upon the mere progress of time as a sure path toward amelioration, let alone perfection. Indeed, *Auch eine Philosophie (Yet Another Philosophy of History)* was first and foremost an indictment of that idea of progress which viewed all the centuries preceding the present age as a period of darkness.
50. Ibid., XIV, 248.

reveals his uneasiness in the matter.[51] By replying that it should indeed do both, Herder does not face up at all squarely to the issue raised in the question. His alternative interpretation of *Zeitgeist* as the "sum of the thoughts, attitudes, strivings, drives, and life-forces, expressing themselves within any causes and effects in a definite course of events,"[52] while suggesting an attempt to reduce the concept to more manageable proportions, only blurs the issue further. It appears simply unresolved whether *Zeitgeist* is merely a metaphorical way of expressing the essentially empirical idea of the "temper" of a society at a given time or whether it is indeed a wholly metaphysical or transcendent concept.

But, whatever it is precisely, *Zeitgeist* plays a pivotal role in Herder's assessment of the chances for any idea or set of ideas to make any headway and, hence, for any individual or group of individuals espousing views to exert a causal force in history. At times Herder seems to believe that individuals can never hope to achieve success if their ideas cut across the prevailing bias of a community.[53] Luther's Reformation, for example, was successful, not because of what Luther said or did, but because the time was ripe for it.[54] Joseph II (of Austria), on the other hand, failed because the *Zeitgeist* was against him.[55] At other times, however, Herder puts his trust in "the few" who guide the spirit of the age.[56] Once again, so it seems, Herder is faced with a dilemma. While he is anxious to recognize individual merit and desires to accord praise to individual achievements, he is at the same time reluctant to concede that history is made by individuals.[57] In view of these equivocations it is difficult to resist the conclusion that on the basic question in this matter, the efficacy of "time" (and history with a capital "h") to act as a creative force *sui generis*, Herder was unclear and possibly undecided.

Herder's ambiguous use of the concepts of chance and fate gives rise to difficulties similar to those that result from his vacillating attitude

---

51. Ibid., XVII, 77–9.
52. Ibid., XVII, 80.
53. Ibid., XIV, 408.
54. Ibid., V, 532.
55. Ibid., XVII, 56.
56. Ibid., XVII, 79.
57. Like Voltaire, Herder had a strong distaste for "heroes" and for "glory." More often than not, however, this distaste clashed with his reluctance to view historical individuals as mere products of their times. Hence he could not, for example, resist describing Luther as the greatest teacher of the German nation (XVII, 87), or Joseph II as a ruler who had a more profound vision of the needs of his country than any other ruler at any other time (XVII, 57).

toward "time" and *Zeitgeist*. Thus, "chance" is presented as a real motive power of historical sequences in some contexts,[58] whereas in other contexts the mere possibility of chance's playing any role is categorically denied.[59] It might of course be argued that by "chance" in the former case Herder simply means that which is not deliberately willed, without denying that it is causally determined. Such an argument, however, is hardly convincing in view of Herder's tendency to identify chance with fate, and his additional lack of clarity about the concept of fate itself. For it is debatable what exactly Herder had in mind by "fate," in that at times it is intended to be simply synonymous with good or bad luck, while at other times it refers to a course of events that is divinely ordained, the work of determined intervention by Providence and hence by no means haphazard.[60]

In spite of these difficulties – the main source of controversy regarding his theory of historical causation – chance and fate mercifully play no major role in Herder's *Ideas*. Although he recognized that unintended consequences, coupled with what Machiavelli meant by *fortuna*, have their part to play, he did wish to believe that in the main the regnant human events were the work of deliberate actions in pursuit of ends or purposes that were sparked off in and through the power of ideas.

By the same token, while in his providential conception of history Herder insisted on the essential unity between the realm of nature and the realm of history, he nonetheless went out of his way to give special emphasis to the unique position of human action in history by virtue of humans' being at once observers and objects of observation. The point of this emphasis was to bring out a fundamental difference between the study of nature and the study of history. For, whereas in the study of nature causal hypotheses could be based only on the observation of external relationships, in the study of human history there was the possibility

58. See, for example, *Werke*, II, 54–5; V, 531; and XIV, 69.
59. For example, XVI, 488.
60. In *Yet Another Philosophy*, for example, chance, fate, and Providence appear to be used interchangeably (V, 531). Clearly, in his treatment of "fate" Herder is far from being consistent. There are times when he draws an emphatic distinction between fate and Providence: "Providence has entrusted man's fate into human hands" (XIV, 213); on this view, humans determine their own fate, and what appears to them as fate is in truth the natural result of their own actions. (See especially, XVIII, 405 and 410.) At other times, however, fate is identified with a hostile power, and history viewed as mainly the story of man's struggle with fate (XXIV, 326), or as objective necessity (XIV, 85–6).

of gaining an insight into the internal relations between events, in which Herder saw the embodiment of active causal power. And it was the measure of consistency in the manner of its purposive direction that indicated, in his view, the relational unity, or *continuity*, within historical causation.

VI

Like Vico, Herder realized and emphasized that, as opposed to events in nature, historical events in the human world do not just happen; they are *made* to happen. It is in this rather obvious sense that Vico's celebrated dictum that the world of man was made by man is beyond challenge. Intended or not, events in human history are what they are because people, singly or collectively, did what they did, when they did, under whatever influences and conditions, and for whatever reasons, beliefs, hopes, or fears. There is no clear evidence that Herder was aware of Vico's now famous dictum, but he drew the same bold inference as Vico had done, namely, that what humans have made other humans can come to understand.[61] Presumably, it is feelings, ideas, and purposes that other people can understand in a way they cannot understand the work of nature. And, in Herder's theory, it is chiefly through being possessors of language that such imaginatively perceptual modes of understanding – what Vico called *fantasia* – are rendered possible. Feelings, ideas, and aspirations, in finding expression through language, are, like language itself, the products of the human mind. Consequently, argues Herder, it is chiefly through literary traditions, folklore, and folksong, being creations of language, that the historian of humanity can enter into the mind and spirit of people by means of imaginative *Hineinfühlen*. And it is precisely by such "entering into" that historians of human events are able to reconstruct the causal processes that characterize history, as distinct from the natural scientist who, faced with processes characterizing nature, must entirely rely on observation from the outside, and whose causal knowledge, such as it is, must of necessity remain largely conjectural. Accordingly, that the world of human vicissitudes, unlike the world of natural phenomena, *can* be known through

61. For a most perceptive discussion of Herder's intellectual affinity to Vico, see Isaiah Berlin, *Vico and Herder* (London: Hogarth Press, 1976), xiii–xxvii, and 76n. Berlin strongly suggests that Herder did not know more about Vico's philosophy of history than what I believe the available evidence supports.

the uncovery of inner causes, in the form of motives, attitudes, and cherished ends, is undoubtedly the single most startling idea that Herder, together with Vico, launched upon modernity and its approach to human history. And what to us now may be commonplace was certainly not so at the time.

Acting on his own principle of inner relations, in the light of which nothing could be understood outside the context of its manifold interconnections,[62] Herder became involved in occasional quandaries that he found unable to resolve. In his determination to advance a causality in which he envisioned a multiplicity of diverse elements to be mutually related, he did not always observe the lines that separate politics from biology, metaphysics from empirical fact, ethics from psychology, and purposive strivings from functional processes. Similarly, it is not always easy to decide whether Herder's approach to history was merely deterministic or was outright fatalistic. Did he, in other words, believe historical events to be causally connected within a contingent mode of continuity or did he also hold them to be inevitable and therefore beyond the control of human choice? It must be admitted that the second possibility cannot altogether be dismissed. When the area of free choice is as circumscribed in his scheme of things as it at times appears to be, it is indeed hard to see how it can function at all. If humans can only be what they must be according to circumstances of time and place,[63] then surely their freedom to act consists merely in conforming to what objective necessity dictates.

All the same, Herder's distinction between causes as purely temporal antecedents and causes as directional purposes – no less than his persistent emphasis on ideas, if not ideals, and on the human capacity to act on them out of autonomous choice – hardly supports the view that he was anxious to "suppress the free play of man's intelligent will," as a once highly influential commentator has remarked.[64] It may, I feel, be nearer to the truth to say that, like others possessed of a reforming zeal, Herder may have believed that by investing the desirable with a degree of historical necessity he might succeed in making it psychologically

---

62. Herder, *Werke*, XXI, 179. Herder portrayed all human activity in historical events to be mutually reciprocal in a more or less direct manner. Perhaps the term "cross-interaction" comes closest to what Herder may have had in mind by speaking of a multiple form of interpenetration, "*wechselweise ineinander wirken.*" (See also XIV, 83–4; XVI, 488, and 546–8.)

63. Ibid., XIV, 149.

64. J.B. Bury, *The Idea of Progress* (London: Macmillan, 1920), 241.

more compelling. If a sufficient number of people could be persuaded that worthwhile ends were not utopian dreams but were the subjective recognition of what was objectively called for, there was practically no ceiling to what they would strive after and possibly attain.[65]

VII

Although in his attempt to grasp the confluence of happenings that make what we call history Herder did not consistently succeed in observing the sort of distinctions I set out in my introductory remarks, he did manage to make a strong case for the view that, despite discontinuities and incongruities, there were inner sources at work that enabled humans to feel that they *could* enact a world of their own. And while he knew and stressed that human strivings were not unbounded, and human purposes not blueprints, he nevertheless did not hesitate to combine these limitations with the belief that, by and large, humans act *as if* they were self-directed, and that, when they treasure ends, they do so out of a consciousness of having chosen them. Had Herder not thought that in some inscrutable way history and humanity converge, he would scarcely have portrayed the thrust of history as the unfolding of that *Humanität* of which humans were capable. Thus, without mistaking lofty aspirations for actual achievements, he felt certain that despite the folly, wickedness, and destructiveness that human history displays, there is also enough moral purposiveness in evidence not to lose hope in the extension of human compassion, human judgment, and human creativity in and through forms of imaginative *Wirken*.

Above all, what permeates Herder's engagement with history is the conviction that, even if perfection is out of reach, humans can and will prevent things from getting worse, once they have learned through the study of the past to deepen their *Besonnenheit*, their reflective potential, and to enhance that sensitivity which Martin Heidegger has called *Mitsein*, the perception of being in a world shared with others.

---

65. This is presumably what Friedrich Meinecke's concept of "inner necessity" could be taken to mean in this context. (See his *Die Entstehung des Historismus* [Munich and Berlin, 1936], II, 403).

6

The Dynamics of Social Cultures
and "Globalization"

WHEN HAROLD LASSWELL DECLARED in the early 1930s that "political symbols and practices are so intimately intertwined with the larger array of symbols and practices in culture that it is necessary to extend the scope of political investigation to include the fundamental features of the culture setting,"[1] he was very much a voice in the wilderness. Today Lasswell's words have become almost common-place in the vocabulary of political studies – evidence in itself of how much the discipline has undergone reappraisal in the course of seeking to come to terms with problems of persistence and change, sources of national cohesion, and the diverse bases of political legitimacy. To be sure, this evolution has not made the study of politics less taxing, but it has had the result of adding new dimensions or perspectives to its analytical vision. Above all, "culture" has, by its entry into political discourse, contributed its share to making things more rather than less daunting in their complexity.

This chapter seeks to elaborate somewhat on points I made in the previous chapter in connection with the transmission of cultures and traditions. Although Herder had no illusions about the elusive nature of the notion of culture, he managed to confer on it a meaning that was new. For, in the way he applied it, he effectively challenged the accepted essentially Bodinian and Hobbesian doctrines of law, sovereignty, and nationhood, and in so doing, remarkably presaged not only Lasswell's injunction to heed the relevance of culture patterns to political processes, but also broader themes that have assumed prominence in contemporary social and political theory. Herder's reflections on culture,

1. Harold D. Lasswell, *World Politics and Personal Insecurity* (New York: McGraw Hill, 1935), 158.

therefore, could be said to have clearly gained rather than lost in significance in the period separating his time from our own.

Here I want to focus principally on those of Herder's ideas that bear upon what has become known as a "world culture" in that it is said to characterize the particular historical unfolding associated with the notion of "global modernization." In so doing, I hope to be able to suggest that Herder's approach to the dynamics of cultural change provides some insightful underpinnings for current discussions about the tensions inherent in the conflicting impulses to preserve national cultures and to partake in a global world culture.

I

Although the intimate linkage of science, technology, and commerce with rapid progress and incessant change typifies only a minor part of the world, it has assumed the (promotional) status of a "world culture," with "globalization" as its hallmark. Leaders of emerging nations are urged to embrace globalization as a cultural absolute in order to enable their peoples to become part of the civilized world. And even if a number of them sense that the diffusion of a scientific world culture might constitute a threat to indigenous cultures, such fears are often assuaged by identifying world culture with purely "material" elements incapable of impairing the "spiritual" content of a nation's traditional values. Underlying this alleged distinction there is unfortunately a great deal of confusion about what is to be confirmed and what negated, about how much adaptation is necessary, and what form the fusion should take. Clearly, what appears as a perfectly plausible formula regarding the distinction between technology and culture in truth fails to resolve profound problems of identity – the survival of national entities and collective traditions – which may result in chaos and bewilderment, and not in the expected synthesis of preservation and progress.[2]

Two crucial misunderstandings seem to be at the heart of this confusion and uncertainty: (i) a misconception of the notion of tradition, and (ii) an erroneous belief that "spiritual" elements of a social culture are easily separable from "material" elements. I propose to deal with the second misunderstanding first, since it provides a convenient handle for contrasting the philosophy underlying it with Herder's conception of social culture. Also the first misunderstanding is symptomatic of a more

2. See, for example, Lucian W. Pye's trenchant comments in *Aspects of Political Development* (Boston and Toronto: Little, Brown, 1966), 97.

basic problem, namely, that of the relationship between persistence and change.

The separation between material and spiritual elements, in the dichotomous manner in which it is commonly made, parallels the distinction frequently made between "civilization" and "culture." According to this distinction, civilization is identified with the development of material conditions and people's growing control over forces of nature or mechanical structures, while culture is identified with people's spiritual development, in which intellectual, moral, and artistic values are the central concern. Perhaps Alfred Weber's analysis of this distinction comes closest to the theory of cultural diffusion that has gained currency among leaders of transitional societies.

In his main work, *Kulturgeschichte als Kultursoziologie* (1935), Weber classifies the chief structural components of historical development in terms of three processes: the social process, the civilization process, and the culture process. By the first, the social process, he means the recurrence of certain social sequences which, notwithstanding individual variations, reveal sufficient uniformity to yield the basis for a comparative study of social development. As an example of a social process, Weber cites the succession from kinship organization to territorial groupings. The second process, the "civilization process" consists in the accumulation of knowledge about techniques of controlling natural and material energies and resources. Weber considers the discovery of these techniques as a continuous and cumulative course of development, susceptible to the generalizing methods of science, and hence causally explicable. The knowledge and the methods and techniques involved in this process are said to be essentially value-neutral and therefore globally transferable, regardless of national differences. The third process, the "culture process," on the other hand, is *not* transferable. Culture can be understood only by acknowledging the incomparability or uniqueness of each of its manifestations, since it derives from creative spontaneity, a property that is not susceptible to the generalizing methods of science. Causal laws, therefore, have no applicability to the realm of culture. Nor can one, in Weber's view, speak of developmental stages of culture, for culture does not follow a lineal order of historical growth but occurs sporadically, defying the causal determinism and temporal dynamism operative in the realms of science and technology.[3]

---

3. Alfred Weber, *Kulturgeschichte als Kultursoziologie* (Leiden: Sijthoff, 1935). See also my article on Alfred Weber in the *Encyclopedia of Philosophy* (New York: Crowell, Collier and Macmillan, 1967), VIII, 281–2.

In contrast to Weber, Herder rejected the dualism between material and non-material activity. It is one of his fundamental ontological principles that "nature has put no bars between what commonly is called material and immaterial ... The fundamental antithesis that is presumed to exist between them is entirely unfounded."[4] Not surprisingly, therefore, culture is seen as an inseparable whole. Western science and technology are part and parcel of the Western cultural ethos rooted in the Judaic, Christian, and Greek tradition. Artefacts are as much constituents of culture as ideas, beliefs, and values. Formed to walk erect, man has his hands free to manipulate objects, and is thus capable of making tools, weapons, and objects of art.[5] On this interpretation of culture, *all* of people's activities are included, both what they do and what they *think.* Herder is not unaware that this further widens the connotation of a word whose meaning is already elusive and indeterminate enough – as he remarks in the very first pages of the *Ideas.*[6] He therefore goes to great lengths and spares no effort in order to bring the concept's application to human and social pursuits into sharper focus. And, whether or not he thereby succeeded in attaining the "modern scientifically generalized concept of culture,"[7] his relativist, pluralist, and process-centred approach did blaze significant trails.

In the next section I shall attempt to single out the strands in Herder's thinking about culture, reserving the question of what forms the integrative element of social entities as "cultural wholes" until a later stage in the discussion.

II

At a time when it was common to distinguish cultured from uncultured nations, Herder's insistence upon culture as a universal phenomenon was a novel idea. There is no such thing, he flatly declared, as a people devoid of culture. Wherever people have lived together as a group over a period of time there is a culture. To be sure, there are differences, but these are differences of degree, not of kind. "The picture of nations," he writes in the *Ideas,* "has infinite shades, changing with place and time.

4. J.G. Herder, Sämtliche *Werke,* ed. B. Suphan, 33 vols. (Berlin: Weidmann, 1877–1913) VIII, 193 and 178, (hereafter cited as Herder, *Werke*).

5. Ibid., XIII, 137.

6. Ibid., XIII, 4.

7. See A.L. Kroeber and Clyde Kluckhohn, *Culture* (New York: Vintage Books, 1963), 286.

But, as in all pictures, everything depends on the point of view or per-spective from which we examine what we see."[8] Yet, despite his recogni-tion of culture as a universal phenomenon, Herder denied that the standards and goals of human development could be subsumed under any one immutable universal. He therefore treated his contemporaries' attempts to use the concept of *European* culture as a criterion or stan-dard with utmost disdain. "To apply such a criterion or standard," he writes, "is not just misleading, it is meaningless. For 'European culture' is a mere abstraction, an empty category. Where does, or did, it actually exist in its entirety? In which nation? In which period? ... Only a misan-thrope could regard European culture as the universal condition of our species. The culture of *man* is not the culture of the *European*; it mani-fests itself according to place and time in *every* people."[9]

As early as 1769 Herder laid down what may be regarded as the basic premise of his cultural relativism. "Human nature under diverse cli-mates is never wholly the same."[10] If, he asked, we can scarcely express the individuality of one person, determine what specifically distin-guishes him and how he feels and experiences things, why should we presume to be able to survey "an ocean of entire nations, times, and regions" at one glance, with two or three categories of classification, without making even the slightest effort to enter into the spirit of their thoughts and deeds? Who can compare the different forms of satisfac-tion perceived by people in different epochs and different worlds? Each person, each period, each nation, has its centre of happiness within itself, just as every sphere has its centre of gravity.[11]

This principle of relativity has far-reaching implications. Taken to its logical extreme, it denies not only any basis of comparison, but the very possibility of valid explanation in history or any other field of enquiry. If each culture and each generation carries within itself its own immanent validity, if we have to think of the world as composed of uniquely differ-ent sociocultural entities, each with its own peculiar pattern of develop-ment, its own inner dynamic of change, it is hard to see how any general theory or even taxonomy could validly be applied as a tool of explana-tion. And, if it cannot, how can we ever comprehend or analyse a given culture? For, surely, we need at least some general concepts or categories

8. Herder, *Werke*, XIII, 348.
9. Ibid., XVIII, 247–9.
10. Ibid., IV, 38.
11. Ibid., V, 502 and 509.

in order to see and convey meaning or discover the significance of historical sequences or any complex of relationships.

Herder's way of meeting this criticism can best be discerned from his epistemological treatise, the *Metakritik* (1799), a work that was intended as a response to Kant's *Critique of Pure Reason*. The major principle Herder wished to establish in it was that there is no single thing that can be known or understood outside the context of its interrelationships.[12] Accordingly, before we can even start to analyse a thing, we have to *identify* it within a particular temporal and spatial setting. And, to identify is to explore the characteristics that govern its contextual relationships, which, in the case of social actions, essentially comprise the norms, values, and customs that are operative in any given society at a given time. Facts, by themselves, are meaningless; a chronicle or array of unrelated facts is neither history, nor sociology, nor philosophy. To understand the meaning of a particular action, therefore, we have to understand the position of an actor in a specific situation. And in order to be able to do this, we must try to relive the action, to feel ourselves into the situation surrounding it, taking into account the particular times and the juncture of circumstances. This requires, we noted earlier, both empathy and analytical imagination. Only by a careful blending of contextual enquiry and imaginative interpretation can we avoid the pitfalls of glib analogies based on *a priori* frameworks or an uncritical, naïvely factual sort of empiricism.[13]

It may nonetheless be maintained that Herder's reply to the objections raised does not adequately address the problems posed by his cultural relativism. For although contextual analysis enables us to discover what the characteristics of a particular situation are or were, the determination of their significance, and hence of their explanatory force, hinges on the possibility of drawing comparisons, however implicitly, with apparently similar situations that are more familiar to us. Still, the heuristic intent of Herder's emphasis on relativism and *contextual* understanding is of major interest in itself. For it is meant to alert us against the danger of assuming that similarities between situations in themselves establish identities, because there may well be other characteristics – and possibly more significant ones – that are not alike. This danger is particularly real in metaphorical or analogical reasoning. In practice, the degree of similarity implied by a metaphor has a wide

12. Ibid., XXI, 179.
13. Ibid., XIII, 290, V, 504.

range of variation, and this could easily cause attention to be withdrawn from unique attributes that in fact may prove to be the decisive ones. Since analogies, once chosen, have a tendency to acquire credibility through repeated use, the risk of faulty understanding or empty explanation is easily compounded.[14]

The merits of Herder's contextual relativism are in no way diminished, however, if we take into account that it sprang in part from an unmistakably polemical eagerness to combat the prevailing fascination with "universalization." For it prompted him to use a terminological belligerence suggesting logical extremes that were not intended. Certainly, in his own historical thinking Herder did not carry cultural relativism to quite such excessive lengths. Thus, although he emphatically distinguished between the mode of causation operative in nature and that operative in human cultures, he was not, for example, prepared to go as far as Alfred Weber in ruling out law-like propositions for culture-related explanations. In short, by upholding cultural relativism, he primarily wished to stress that comparative generalizations about diverse habits of thinking and acting must avoid resting universal principles on standards that are in truth purely ethnocentric prejudices. For, thus grounded, they risk being totally insensitive to the range of diversity in terms of both similarities and differences. No effort should therefore be spared, Herder urged, to study each culture historically, within its own particular interrelations, its own shapes and structures.

Before turning to Herder's attempt to use his teleological theory of (internal) development in order to reinforce his plea for cultural relativism, I would like to make at least passing mention of a widespread reaction to cultural relativism: that it entails, condones, if not stridently displays, ethical nihilism. It seems to me that such a reaction not infrequently confuses universals with absolutes. Although Herder indeed questioned the judging of cultures by a single standard of value, he would have categorically dismissed any suggestion that one value was as good as another as a vulgarized distortion of cultural relativity. Just as he did not wish to imply that social cultures are in all respects utterly disparate, so he likewise had no desire to impugn the authenticity of universals as such, properly understood and concretely perceived "within the actuality of the particular" – to borrow Ernst Cassirer's apt

14. All the same, there is a potential threat to moral standards, and Charles Larmore skillfully addresses this issue in *The Morals of Modernity* (Cambridge: Cambridge University Press, 1994).

phrase.[15] Indeed, Herder's philosophy of *Humanität* is an eloquent affirmation of the hope that ethical norms could assume the status of meaningful universals in terms of which people might recognize standards of mutuality to which they ought to aspire as human beings everywhere. At the same time he did feel that the realization of this hope was contingent upon, rather than contrary to, the acceptance of temporal and spatial relativity. Ethical universals have to be cherished and applied if they are to be effectively operative, and this, he felt, was inconceivable *in vacuo*, in abstraction from the particularity of peoples, periods, and places.[16]

In essence, therefore, Herder's emphasis on relativity and plurality in personal idiosyncrasies, social values, and national allegiances should be viewed principally as a challenge to that myopic form of universalism which inclines to judge every variant as a deviant; and, accordingly, should serve as a corrective to the fondness of burying one's head in the sand and underrating the problematic tension that can beset the relation of diverse goals and beliefs.[17]

III

An approach that so markedly highlights diversity and the immanent distinctiveness, if not uniqueness, of cultural entities cannot fail to have a significant bearing upon problems of historical development in general and political development in particular. From what we know about Herder's archetype of historical evolvement, the paradigm of causation that he favours is clearly that of *internal* development, "energized" by the pursuit of envisaged goals, ends, or purposes. Although he does not deny that external sources may bear upon configurations of social-cultural entities by promoting or inhibiting their growth, the essential driving power he sees as coming from within.[18] In Herder's teleological conception of development, however, his frequent use of the metaphor

15. Ernst Cassirer, *The Logic of the Humanities* (New Haven: Yale University Press, 1961), 25. See also my *Herder's Social and Political Thought* (Oxford: Clarendon Press, 1965, 1967), ch 5, esp. 98.

16. For a full bibliography of recent secondary literature on Herder's relativism, see Marcia Bunge, ed., *Against Pure Reason* (Minneapolis: Fortress Press, 1993).

17. A special issue, "Pluralism or Relativism?" in *Critical Review* (1997), XI, no 4 is of considerable interest on this point.

18. Herder, *Werke*, XIII, 172–88, 274–7.

of organic growth also illustrated that (as we noted) he thought of the end of the process as something akin to the actualization of what was latent or germinal in it from the outset. I have elsewhere pointed in some detail to the dangers inherent in such an approach, and have also indicated in the previous essay that applying the paradigm of natural growth to purposive development involves a category mistake of formidable proportions.[19] All the same, there is no denying that Herder's "organic" approach does reinforce his argument in support of cultural relativism. It invites us to view social and political development as the emergence of distinctive cultural wholes, as configurations, that is, which can lay claim to a separate, if not unique, form of existence in terms of criteria of its own making.

Guided by the paradigm of internal evolvement, although not ruling out processes of culture diffusion, Herder nevertheless voices doubts that emergent nations could take kindly to the idea of embracing lock, stock, and barrel, social and political modes of life that are urged on them, if not imposed, from the outside. Coupled with this insight – strikingly borne out by subsequent experience – Herder makes clear that, as a *historical* process, development takes time and assumes a high degree of complexity, being neither monodimensional nor free from internal tensions.

Anthropologists have of course realized much of this all along; yet leading policy makers have been rather slow to acknowledge that what has been advocated as "polycentrism" by nationalist communists wanting their countries to travel their own road to socialism was a desire not confined to revisionist Marxists. Nationalism may be one of the most persistent features of "world culture" but it also embodies "primordial sentiments" not unknown in pre-Western or non-Western cultures, in favour of particularistic distinctiveness.[20] In other words, the conflicting pulls of particularist and universalist tendencies are not new in the history of political development. Perhaps parochial or particularistic tendencies within diverse political cultures receive insufficient

19. F.M. Barnard, "Natural Growth and Purposive Development: Vico and Herder," *History and Theory* (1979), XVIII, 16–36.

20. See, for example, Edward Shils, "Primordial, Personal, Sacred and Civil Ties," *British Journal of Sociology* (1957), VIII, 130–45; Clifford Geertz, "The Integrative Revolution: Primordial Sentiments and Civic Politics in the New States," in Claude E. Welch, Jr (ed.), *Political Modernization* (Belmont, Calif.: Wadsworth, 1967), 167–88; and Edward Shils, *Political Development in the New States* (New York: Humanities Press, 1964), 7–8.

attention in the craving for rapid *economic* development. Be that as it may, Herder did well to alert the world to problems of culture diffusion, in particular to the tension entailed in meshing external and indigenous social cultures – the burden of his central argument. Implicit in this argument is a related insight; namely, that what is frequently overlooked or only reluctantly acknowledged is the realization that *political* development, however connected it may be with economic or other forms of change, demands recognition as a profound problem of its own.

What is it, however, that characterizes a particular social culture as a relational *whole*? The way Herder tries to come to grips with this question merits, I believe, closer examination in that it sheds needed light on the causes of disenchantment with globalization.

When Herder thought of culture as an integral whole, he conceived this "whole" not as a homogeneous or unstructured mass but as a composite which, by virtue of its inherent relational characteristics, is something more than a mere sum-total or aggregate. In an aggregate the parts are separate and unrelated, like people in a crowd, and their number can be increased or reduced without affecting the *nature* of the total, but only changing its *size*. A whole, on the other hand, is something more than the sum of its parts, and the "more" is not contained in the parts considered in isolation but arises from their interrelation and the varying degree of their integration. Herder contrasted the holism typifying culture with the atomism typifying aggregates by comparing the former with the unity of an organism. In so doing he wanted to focus on two crucial qualities: functional interrelatedness *and* self-generated activity. The coherence of a culture, like that of an organism, is consequently held to be contingent upon relations that arise from, but at the same time govern, the degree of reciprocal interaction between the constituent parts, where the parts – unlike those of a mechanical assembly – are activated by their *own* source of energy.

In other words, the distinguishing characteristic of culture, viewed as a complex whole, is the *intrinsic* creativity of its interrelated parts. And, in order to underline its *composite* nature, Herder speaks in terms not of a single organism but of a plurally structured complex of organisms. Thus, like St Thomas's "accidental whole" (as distinct from the substantial whole of a physical body) or Aristotle's concept of the state as a composite, Herder's holism is composed of multiplicity as well as unity. And although each of the component parts is considered an active whole in itself, comparable to the Leibnizian monad, it also differs from it in that the Herderian monad *has* windows; it is not wholly self-contained but interconnected.[21]

Herder's organismic conception of culture as a complex whole posits a further characteristic, which, however, is already implicit in his cultural relativism: the idea of diversity. The notion that the world consists, in society no less than in nature, of interrelated and interacting processes, each of which pertains to the whole in its most distinct individuality, is the principal theme of Herder's cosmology and one of the central theses of his philosophy of history.[22] Multiplicity is but a corollary of the postulate that infinite diversity coexists with unity in a holistic nexus *sui generis*; in plurality there is, accordingly, a tendency "striving for unity which lies in all things and urges all things forward."[23]

In asserting this, Herder is as much a child of the Enlightenment as he is its critic, since the tendency toward unity amidst diversity is not tantamount to continuous, linear progress.[24] Thus, while he maintains that diversity is capable of creating unity by creating the conditions – potentially, at any rate – for reciprocal activity, he also recognizes, and indeed emphasizes, that – just as potentially – the plurality of values does not rule out mutual *in*compatibility. It follows that tensions and irregularities must be accepted as the price of diversity; incongruities and contradictions are not mere exceptions or accidents but are the very essence of the human condition. Just as change does not *mean* progress, so a measure of unity does not *mean* total harmony. "A nation," he writes in *Yet Another Philosophy of History* (1774), even if at peace, "may display the most sublime virtues in some respects and severe blemishes in others, show aberrations, and reveal the most astonishing contradictions and incongruities. These will be all the more startling to anyone carrying within himself an idealized shadow-image of virtue according to the manual of this century, one so filled with philosophy that he expects to find the whole universe in a grain of sand. But for him who wants to understand the human heart within actual

21. The most systematic exposition of Herder's philosophy of organicism is to be found in his *Metakritik*, esp. XXI, 152–82.

22. See particularly Herder, *Werke*, XIV, 83–4.

23. Ibid., XIII, 346; see also XIV, 227; XVI, 119, 551; XVII, 116; XVIII, 302, 408; XXIV, 375; and XXIX, 133, 139.

24. Undoubtedly, the most vigorous expression of Herder's repudiation of linear progress is to be found in *Yet Another Philosophy*, esp. V, 527, 559, 564.

living circumstances, such irregularities and contradictions are perfectly human."[25]

To speak of a cultural whole, therefore, in terms of the unity of social cultures is not of necessity a way of referring to a state of blissful concord, for it may just as conceivably refer to a field of tension. More is to be said later about Herder's process-oriented conception of culture, according to which culture is seen as both the product of the past and the creator of the future, and therefore is also potentially beset with the prospect of conflict.

For the present, however, the point to be noted is that a cultural whole, for Herder, is not a "thing" at all, but a relational *event*; and, although it is a continuum, it is not unilinear, but is subject to a dialectic entailing preservation *and* innovation. A culture-continuum, therefore, is not a state, but a dynamic movement, and this movement Herder describes as a potential unity seeking actualization, and not as a necessarily existing or instant actuality. The mode of causality characterizing this contingent dynamic relationship between potentiality and actuality is depicted rather vividly in a formulation dating back to one of Herder's earliest works, the *Fragments* (1767), which I mentioned in the previous essay: "A series of causes act together, reciprocally and in succession; one wheel interlocks with the other, and one spring acts upon the other."[26] The formulation specifies an analytic distinction between two *types* of processes which, in their dynamics, are closely interwoven. In one type of process the emphasis is on spatial interactions occurring *at any given time* between culture constituents, which I earlier described as the "horizontal" dimension, whereas in the second type of process the emphasis is on historical interactions occurring in sequences *over time*, which I described as the "vertical" dimension.

I am aware that this distinction does not substantially diminish the problems attending the selection of relevant givens or directional determinants. Nonetheless, I believe that distinguishing "cause" as a situational component from "cause" as an orientational component helps to avoid confusing the notion of causal determinism with the notion of causal inevitability, as I suggested in the previous essay. In the remaining part of this section I shall briefly illustrate Herder's application of the horizontal interaction sketched in the *Fragments* to his conception of

25. Herder, *Werke*, V, 506.
26. Ibid., II, 65.

culture as a complex whole. I return to the vertical dimension of inter-action in the subsequent section, and attempt a closer analysis of the idea of interaction itself in conjunction with my comments on Herder's thoughts on *political* culture.

For the most part, Herder preferred to speak of specific cultures (in the plural) rather than of culture in general. This would, he believed, re-duce the inherent ambiguity of the concept and at the same time direct attention to the distinctive culture patterns arising from social, religious, economic, political, or geographic differences, as well as from diverse historical traditions. Although he was mainly concerned with eliciting sources of national cohesion, he recognized that there are diverse cul-tures existing side by side even within any one nation, owing to differ-ences in occupation, education, religion, social birth, private wealth, and so on. He distinguished, for example, between the culture of intellectu-als and the culture of craftsmen and traders.[27] The reason he thought of these coexisting cultures as subcultures – or more precisely, as *segmental* cultures – is that he considered the differences between, say, occupations within one nation to be less fundamental or significant than those exist-ing between the same occupation among different nations. Herder's careful formulation of this point merits, I think, quoting in full, for its methodological import has scarcely been outdated.

It is customary to divide the nations of the world into hunters, fishermen, shepherds, and farmers, not only to determine their level of cultural develop-ment, but also to imply that culture as such is a necessary corollary of a given occupation or mode of life. This would be most admirable, provided the diverse modes of life were defined in the first place. Since these, however, vary with almost every region and for the most part overlap, it is exceedingly difficult to apply such a classification with accuracy. The Greenlander who harpoons the whale, hunts the reindeer, and kills the seal is engaged in both hunting and fishing, yet in quite a different manner from that of the Negro fisher or the Arancoan hunter. The Beduin and the Mongol, the Lapp and the Peruvian are shepherds; but how greatly do they differ from each other, with one pasturing camels, the other horses, the third reindeer, and the last alpacas and llamas. The farmers of Whidoh are as unlike those of Japan as the merchants of England are to those of China.[28]

27. Ibid., XIV, 34–5.
28. Ibid., XIII, 310.

Of particular interest to our purpose is Herder's realization that segmental cultures can develop at different rates and, as a result, produce an acute imbalance capable of threatening the cohesion or "wholeness" of a society. For this realization highlights the point made earlier regarding the fallacy of unilinear development. Once again, this point has not lost relevance. Not many social theorists today, it is true, share their nineteenth-century precursors' faith in unilinear progress. Yet, this does not seemingly prevent contemporary sociologists and economists from theorizing about political development as though progress in one direction – for example, in the possession of telephones or automobiles – must necessarily correlate with the arrival of stable democracy.[29]

To put the matter differently, what Herder emphasizes here is the possible clash between coexisting cultures and forms of development. The horizontal dimension of interaction, that is to say, may involve areas of tension no less than spheres of cooperation. One crucial element in horizontal interaction, therefore, is the degree of balance between segmental cultures. Significantly, Herder remarked to this effect that it is neither the number of cultural divergences nor the progress achieved in this or that direction that is decisive for the existence of national cohesion, but the *relationship* of its constituent cultures.[30] When certain forms of culture are widely out of step with other forms – in particular if "techniques" and "values" markedly diverge – there is the danger of a crisis of identity that can give rise to alienation, if not fragmentation.[31]

Any such imbalance within "horizontal" relations cannot be wholly divorced, however, from elements in the "vertical" dimension, in which, we found, Herder accords a crucial role to beliefs and ideas and vigorously challenges the view that they are merely epiphenomenal, or not quite real, in comparison with environmental circumstances or established institutions. To be sure, he agrees that beliefs and ideas may serve instrumental functions in maintaining forms of ruling, but emphatically denies that this is tantamount to saying that they would disappear with the disappearance of such authority structures, or the other way round – that, if beliefs could be discredited as mere prejudices, the authority structures associated with them would vanish. Either mode of thinking, Herder feels, is altogether mistaken. By the same token, while

29. See, for example, S.M. Lipset, *Political Man* (New York: Doubleday, 1959, Anchor ed., 1963), 31–7.
30. Herder, *Werke*, XIV, 149.
31. Ibid., XIII, 371.

he concedes that shamans, priests, or ideologues may use myths, ideas, or religious beliefs to deceive people and manipulate them for self-serving purposes, this does not mean that myths, ideas, or religious beliefs are their own creations. Rather, it means that, being entrenched habits of thinking, they effectively lend themselves to manipulation, without ruling out that the manupulators themselves are sharing them. "They may well have been cheats in many or most places." Herder comments, "but this should not induce us to forget that they themselves were people too, and the dupes of myths older than themselves."[32]

Any attempt, therefore, to account for imbalances in social cultures in terms of ideas, values, institutions, or symbols must, Herder insists, have recourse to "vertical" forms of exploration involving historical or process analysis, in addition to "horizontal" enquiries. The horizontal dimension of interaction, which still dominates functional-situational research, taken by itself, is accordingly inadequate as an explanatory tool, if what we seek to establish is the significance and meaning of sociocultural wholes as "national" identities, or the source of friction in "globalizing" endeavours.

Similarly, Herder's heuristic principle of treating every manifestation of culture as essentially self-sustaining also enjoins us to view the mode of causality applicable to the formation and dynamic of social cultures in multiple ways. Admittedly, both the idea of two-dimensional interaction and the idea of multiple causation are inherently no more than *perspectives*, angles of viewing, in devising conceptual categories. As such they provide no guarantee of obtaining correct answers, or indeed, of even asking the indisputably right questions. At the same time, without any such perspectives or conceptual aids it is hard to see how any questions could be raised at all.

IV

What Herder's relativist and pluralist conception of culture seeks to underline, than, is the importance of a historical, process-centred approach. In and through a combination of these perspectives he proposed a way of discovering integrative sources that would enable us to speak of social cultures as national and political cultures. And it was principally toward this end that he introduced the concepts of *Bildung* and *Tradition* in their original dynamic sense of "building up" and "passing on."

32. Ibid., XIII, 307.

Accordingly, *Bildung* is identified not with a particular *state* of a person's educational accomplishments, "breeding," or refinement – its usual meaning in German –[33] but rather with an interactive process in which humans draw from and add to their particular social heritage. Furthermore, in returning to the word's dynamic origins, Herder also attempted to confer upon it a distinctly dialectic denotation. Humans, by virtue of possessing language, perceive nature not directly but through the mediation of words and ideas. By means of language they are in a position to receive and convert into their own understanding what has been "taken in." What, and how much, they thus "internalize" and apply to their own use is in part, Herder concedes, contingent on environmental circumstances; largely, however, he attributes the nature of the process of taking in to the learner's own receptive and creative powers. He speaks of the process as a continuous genesis that combines the receiving and converting ingredients, in terms of which that which is learned is assimilated and reapplied.[34]

Bildung, thus, *is* a "process" because it involves a continuum of collecting impressions and simultaneously evaluating them, so that cumulatively received stimuli incessantly undergo *creative* assimilation, a sort of conversion or redirection, differing in varying degrees from individual to individual. "One activity is increased by another; builds upon or evolves from the foregoing ... We are always in motion."[35] This motion, Herder explains, is uniquely ascribable to human beings, and it entails restlessness and dissatisfaction at every step. Forever faced with challenges, human life almost amounts to a series of new and variously different beginnings. As a result, "the essence of human life is never fruition, but a continuous becoming."[36] Manifestly, therefore, *Bildung*, the way Herder presents it, is not simply a replicative process, and it certainly is not socialization chiefly aiming at "system maintenance." On the contrary, Herder wants to see *Bildung* as the preferable alternative to abrupt cultural discontinuities that attend the replacement of societal values through their prior destruction rather than their creative transformation.

Tradition, likewise, is identified not with a stock of accumulated beliefs, customs, and ways of doing things but with an ongoing process of

---

33. Of Herder's German contemporaries, Goethe perhaps comes closest to his conception of *Bildung*, although Goethe views the process in wholly apolitical and individual terms, as "self-improvement."

34. Herder, *Werke*, XIII, 343–8. See also XIV, 84.

35. Ibid., V, 98.

36. Ibid., XIII, 182.

intergenerational transmission. And, as we noted, it entails, like *Bildung*, passive and active ingredients in the merging of the old and the new. This being so, its operation potentially involves affirmative *and* negative properties; "change" in this context means therefore the coming into being of new and specifically different constellations, and not merely the replacement of one set of conditions by a new set of the same specific type. The process of *Tradition* is by no means therefore tantamount to a smooth advance or progress, and Herder accordingly, we found, does not rule out friction. Every discovery in the arts and sciences, in technology and industry, he remarks in the *Ideas*, knits a new pattern of society. New situations create new problems, and every increase in wants – even if satisfied – is not of necessity conducive to an extension of human happiness.[37]

At the same time Herder refused to view stages of development in an outright dichotomous manner. One reason for his refusal to apply such dichotomies as traditional and modern, primitive and civilized, static and dynamic, sacred and secular was his cultural relativism. The other, and possibly still more compelling, reason was that he found them inherently unhistorical as well as in conflict with his conception of development as an interacting dynamic. Hence in place of the idea of polarity he advanced the idea of *inter-play*. Tradition and progress no longer embody two opposed entities, but a single continuum. Progress, or more precisely, change, becomes a built-in characteristic of tradition. And since the intergenerational process of transmission is held to involve the merging of negation and affirmation in a manner analogous to that associated with *Bildung*, *Tradition*, too, entails its own immanent dialectic. Change as development is, therefore, at once part of a given culture *and* the instrument for its transformation.[38]

It may be asked why *Bildung* and *Tradition*, in revealing so close a similarity, are at all set apart, since Herder also considered them inextricably related; why, in short, did he bother to distinguish between them? Herder offers no explicit answer to this question. It seems, however, reasonable to assume that he found the distinction useful in order to differentiate personally-social processes of transmission from publicly-social processes. *Bildung*, although it may lead to shared patterns of public conduct, is nonetheless viewed as a more informal process of internalization, whereas *Tradition* is closer to a more "institutionalized" or

37. Ibid., XVIII, 313–20, 331–2; XIII, 372–3.
38. Ibid., XIV, 89.

publicly sanctioned expression of internalization and, in this sense, the more inclusive term.

All the same, the interaction of *Bildung* and *Tradition* (however differentiated precisely) does not ensure that "development" within Herder's teleological model of causation would correspond to the matching of intended consequences or aspired goals with actual consequences or achievements. Undeniably, "cause" as a directional determinant in the "vertical" direction could have an important bearing on "cause" as a temporal antecedent. But this in itself, we found, does not guarantee purposive continuity between intentions and outcomes. Especially in "developing societies," in which the directional determinant will be predisposed toward drastic change and innovation, development would inject into sequences a highly incalculable element. On the other hand, this uncertainty underlines the contrast drawn earlier between causal determinism and historical inevitability, or that between *explaining* and *predicting* the dynamics of change.

What *Bildung* and *Tradition* may jointly help to militate against, however, is the danger of change's becoming wholly discontinuous. For then its meaning would be altogether incompatible with that of *development*; a social culture that has undergone complete mutation would clearly no longer be recognizably the same culture in any intelligible sense. Herder's principal point here, therefore, is to show that the problem of change and the problem of persistence are but one and the same problem. Whatever change takes place as development must accordingly take place within the continuum of a tradition. And for development to assume the form of *national* development was for Herder essentially a matter of highly distinctive modes of interpenetration between *Bildung* and *Tradition* within particular collectivities over time. The nature of this mysterious "spiritual genesis" of national collectivities, together with the two-dimensional processes of interaction in which it takes shape, absorbed Herder's interest from his earliest writings onward – a remarkable continuum in itself.

V

Startling though it is, Herder seemed to see little point in offering a definition of culture itself.[39] But the absence of a formal definition of a word he found hopelessly elusive is more than compensated for by the

39. Ibid., XIII, 4.

wealth of intimations that impressively disclose what in essence he meant by it. The dominant characteristics that emerge as basic could be summarized as relativism, pluralism, historism, a non-deterministic form of causalism (as distinct from causal inevitability), and a type of holism that embraces diversity as well as unity. Within the conceptual framework formed by these categories, culture is presented as a *relational* attribute of a collectivity, if not as the hallmark of its existence as a cohesive entity. A *national* culture, therefore, in Herder's portrayal, is the product of a relational process that is embedded in the consciousness of a shared heritage, itself further deepened by means of certain determinants that act as internal bonds of a nation's political development as an integral whole.

Herder seems particularly interested in those integrating determinants by virtue of which members of a social collectivity come to recognize not only what unites them with each other but also what distinguishes them from others. Hence, once again, his central concern is the twin problem of sameness and otherness, of identity and interrelatedness. Within this orbit of thinking he takes pains to differentiate modes or expressions of cultural integration within a nation by contrasting political culture in the broader sense with political culture in the narrower sense.[40] Structurally, political culture in the broader sense forms, so to speak, the matrix in which political culture in the narrower sense is embedded, and through which it acquires its distinctive identity, its "national character" – a term Herder coined.

As for political culture in the narrower sense, Herder thinks of it on two levels: a level of formal structures, such as legislatures, the courts, and administrative bodies; and a level of informal processes such as involve political activity itself, the degree of civic participation, and the nature of reciprocal relations in the public sphere. The physical environment is accorded merely secondary importance; it can *influence* the course of political development, but cannot *compel* it.[41] The *human* environment, however, seems a different matter. Hostile neighbours, for example, constitute an external environment most likely to rouse a people to an invigorated sense of collective identity and solidarity. "The more a group is threatened," Herder remarks, "the more it will turn upon itself

40. Herder's dissertation on the reciprocal influence of government and the sciences, crowned by the Royal Academy of Science and Art in Berlin (1779); Part I is a (much neglected) source on this distinction. See esp. *Werke*, IX, 313–15.

41. Herder, *Werke*, XIII, 273.

and the closer will be the ties of its members."[42] Still, the degree to which external hostility can strengthen the national cohesion of collectivities is, in Herder's scheme, principally contingent upon the prior existence of actual or latent bonds working *within* cultural entities.

In view of this prior requirement, Herder, not surprisingly, put greatest emphasis on internal determinants. A group threatened by hostile forces may or may not succeed in repelling an aggressor, but it will not even act as a group in the first place unless there are some foci around which individual members can rally, and in terms of which they can experience a sense of common belonging. It may be of interest to recall in this connection the importance Herder attached – against the background of the Age of Reason – to non-rational moulding agents such as myths, legends, or even sheer prejudices, and, very much in opposition to the cosmopolitan thinking of the Enlightenment, to particularism or even to "parochialism," if this can assist in the formation of national political self-identity. "If, in this development of particular national tendencies toward distinctive forms of collective happiness and self-awareness the distance between nations widens," he declares in *Yet Another Philosophy of History*, "and prejudices arise, together with mob judgement and narrow nationalism, and the dispositions and spheres of interest of nations collide," all this may be good in its time and place, for "self-esteem and happiness may spring from it. It urges peoples to converge upon their centre and attaches them more firmly to their roots.[43]

Indeed, Herder expresses regret that so little has been done to explore the intermixture of rational notions with non-rational elements that shape social and political cultures. Folklore, myths, folksongs, dances, rituals and customs, for example, are vital clues to a nation's collective "personality," its political sense of affinity.[44] Language in particular, we noted, plays a pivotal role in Herder's anatomy of political culture in its broader sense. For it is both the medium through which humans become conscious of their inner selves *and* they key to their "affinitive" understanding of the world in which they are placed. It also

42. Ibid., V, 141.
43. Ibid., V, 510.
44. Herder's early interest in this direction is evident from his travel diary of his voyage from Riga to France in 1769, which was not published during his lifetime. He resolved there to collect data from the mythology of all ages and cultures and "to examine everything from the point of view of politics," (IV, 363–4), which in fact he subsequently did in his collection of folksongs from diverse and almost forgotten nationalities.

links them collectively with the past and enables people to enter into communion with the way of thinking and feeling of their progenitors and, thereby, to take part, as it were, in the workings of the ancestral mind. Language, in short, is a living link in the chain of tradition. In his highly original essay *On the Origins of Language* (1772) Herder explains in some detail why this is so. In essence, language performs this mediating role because words describe or classify not merely *objects* but also *feelings*, and they do this not only explicitly but also implicitly *via* emotional overtones which communication acquires in the process of transmission. Particularly words we learn during infancy and adolescence carry secondary associations that are rekindled whenever we use them. And frequently these associations sway the mind more powerfully than the concepts with which they were originally linked. These "companions of the dawn of life" permeate social cultures far more than we are wont to admit, and may well prove, Herder caustically adds, more decisively important than "all political contracts and systems devised by the philosopher."[45]

Herder bemoans that political thinkers have not taken greater pains over the significance of language in the formation of collective attitudes. Notably they have failed to realize sufficiently that what really matters is not solely "what a word means according to the dictionary," but what it means in the consciousness of living people "in all its capriciousness."[46] Already in the *Fragments* (1767) Herder urges the philosopher "not to heap scorn upon the language of feeling," and in his *Travel Diary* (1769) he links it specifically with a people's political culture.[47] Indeed, in the *Ideas* he declares that a nation will survive even if it ceases to be a state if it can preserve its language of feeling as the living manifestation of its continuity.[48]

In this view, it is through language that individuals become at once aware of their selfhood and of their membership of a collective culture. So close an identification between the private self and the public self recalls the intended operation of Rousseau's General Will; at the same time, however, it also signals its transcendence. For, by stipulating a cultural and historically derived basis for political association in place of a

45. Herder, *Werke*, V, 117–36.
46. Ibid., IV, 423.
47. Ibid., I, 388; For a recent translation of this volume of the *Fragments* see Ernest A. Menze and Karl Menges, eds., *Herder, Selected Early Works, 1762–67* (University Park: Pennsylvania State University Press, 1991), here 198. See also Herder, *Werke*, IV, 429.
48. Ibid., XIV, 87.

legal construct – if not a metaphysically grounded absolute – Herder hoped to render formal authority structures less important. Much the same reasoning underlies his two-stage concept of "political culture" – a term that Herder actually uses in the *Ideas*;[49] he postulates political culture in the broader sense as both an *antecedent* and an *internal* requirement of nationhood, which manifests itself in and through a sense of cultural and civic belonging rather than the trappings of *external* sovereignty. This line of thinking is unmistakably the corollary of Herder's paradigm of development, according to which what is capable of actualization is only that which already exists in latency.

At the same time Herder was realistic enough to acknowledge that political culture was not simply a matter of preserving a common language, just as he (albeit sometimes reluctantly) agreed that the existence of a political culture could not be viewed as though it were, like a plant, purely the work of natural growth. Hence, despite all his emphasis on *evolvement*, he had to admit the need for deliberate nurturing. Even so, however, Herder was determined to oppose political *culture* as something *sui generis* to both Hobbes's leviathanic "power" and Rousseau's transcendent "will," that is, as something that was neither mechanical nor metaphysical in its origin and expression.

V I

The most vivid, and the most succinct, formulation of the origin and developmental structuring of political culture can be found in Herder's treatise *On the Reciprocal Influence of Government and the Sciences* (1779). In particular, it sheds added light on the manner in which "interaction" is meant to work *politically*; Herder, demonstrates in this treatise *how* a particular regime is embedded in a broader context, and how this context in turn impinges on the regime, "making its political culture thrive better in one setting than another." By the same token, the interaction significantly helps to form a regime's distinctly *national* character and thus "determines more closely the *seed* of the political constitution *in its widest sense* – its principles, norms, and ideals – by the finer tilling of the soil and the nurture of the seed, so to speak, without which nothing can prosper, nothing that has been sown can grow."[50]

---

49. Herder uses the term when discussing the political culture of the Hebrews (XIV, 67); this may indeed have been the earliest use of it.

50. Herder, *Werke*, IX, 311–12. This formulation recalls what Herder says about "development" itself as a continuum of tradition and change (XIV, 89). The italics are Herder's own.

Significantly, the constitution, in its widest sense, is held to articulate a particular *ethos* that acts as the leaven of a nation's political culture in its maturing stages toward a specific governmental regime. But, whereas interaction (*Wechselwirkung*) within the broader context of political culture refers to interrelations between human and non-human sources, such as geographic and meteorological influences, interaction within the narrower context refers to expressly human creations such as laws, civic representation, and the demarcation of governmental authority. Implicit in the distinction between interaction in the broader political culture and interaction in the narrower political culture is Herder's determination to call attention to an obvious, yet not infrequently overlooked, recognition that only some form of *human* activity (including thought and its product, ideas) is capable of reciprocal interaction, either horizontally, insofar as at any given time people influence each other directly or indirectly, or vertically, insofar as this influence involves a sequential-historical dimension. I regret, however, that stating Herder's account of historical interaction in this bland manner fails to convey the vibrancy that throbs through his portrayal of it in the *Fragments* in terms of interlocking wheels and intermeshing springs, and which succeeds in virtually making one *feel* the force of the incessant activity pervading it.

As to the hub of this activity, which commonly is associated with "government" itself, Herder has little positive to say. Although he grants that government as the central authority of a collectivity may formally be seen to serve the symbolic function through its chief magistrate or head of state as, so to speak, "the abstracted collective emblem of the nation as a whole,"[51] he has nothing but scorn for hereditary rulers or any form of absolutist political authority.[52] Kant's dictum that man is like an animal needing a master to rule and control him[53] provokes Herder's angry retort that man is man only if he no longer needs a master in any real sense. The idea that humans *need* a strict master, Herder adds, presupposes that they are feeble or under age and therefore incapable of managing their own affairs; or that they are wild detestable creatures demanding a tamer or minister of vengeance.[54] No less vehemently, Herder rejects the concept of government as the legitimate wielder of physical power. The institution of *any* central political power is for him

51. Herder, *Werke*, XIII, 453.
52. Ibid., XIII, 377, 383.
53. Immanuel Kant, *Idee zu einer allgemeinen Geschichte in weltbürgerlicher Absicht* (1784), *Gesammelle Schriften* (Berlin: Preussische Akademie der Wissenschaften ed., 1902–), VIII, 23.
54. Herder, *Werke*, XIII, 383–4.

not the beginning but the collapse of politics, an obvious symptom of social decay and political bankruptcy.[55]

It would seem that Herder could see no difference between the *use* of power and its *possession*; at any rate he argued as if the mere existence of power in itself constituted the erosion of politics as a pursuit worthy of humans who are both adult and free. This complete rejection of even the *ultima ratio* conception of coercion may (perhaps rightly) be judged as utterly unrealistic. At the same time it should be borne in mind that Herder did not rule out the power of ideas and values but only that of physical force. Likewise, he recognized the power of sentiments of solidarity derived from participation, since in that case he envisioned power as widely shared and, in view of his political pluralism, as widely diffused – not all that different, perhaps, from Robert Dahl's notion of *polyarchal* power.

Herder's attitude to bureaucracy was no more favourable. He had little faith in it as an instrument in the creation or preservation of a participatory culture of politics or a sense of patriotism and civic belonging. Its hierarchical structure, based on seniority rather than talent or vision, its endemic hostility to change, its arrogance and conceit stemming from the belief that public officials know best what is good for the populace did not enamour bureaucracy to Herder as a branch of government.[56] Odd or not, this viewpoint is not as unrealistic as it may seem, neither within the context of eighteenth-century Germany, nor with reference to the more recent scene in some ex-colonial countries.[57] Even in the United States of America "an enormous amount of national development took place" before bureaucracy had to any appreciable extent been established.[58]

Politics, in short, did not principally mean "government" for Herder. He saw it not as an "instrument" but as an *activity*, an associative pursuit of ends that was not exclusively bound up with the state. As soon as there are family relations, he declared, there is some form of politics.[59] And since he viewed a polity as but an extension of the family – the same sort of plant, only with more branches – "family" and "polity" are differ-

55. Ibid., XIII, 319–22.

56. Ibid., XIII, 384–5; XVI, 48.

57. See, for example, Ralph Braibanti, "The Civil Service of Pakistan," *South Atlantic Quarterly*, 58 (1959), 258–304, and Joseph La Palombara (ed.), *Bureaucracy and Political Development* (Princeton: Princeton University Press, 1963), 360–440.

58. La Polambara, ibid., 55.

59. Herder, *Werke*, IX, 313.

entiated not in kind but merely in degree.[60] While this denial of a fundamental difference between family relations and civic relations involved Herder in a number of perplexities, it also signalled an important departure from the still common identification of the political with one specific type of organization such as the state.

What, then, was for Herder the essence of *political* culture in the narrower sense? A good many aspects that are now connected with government, such as social welfare, education, and employment, Herder associated with his notion of "humanization," with the creation of conditions that befitted life as human life, and hence considered these facets as components of *social* cultures.[61] Political culture proper, on the other hand, he essentially linked with civic participation, an engagement in public life as a *citizen* that as for Rousseau and others before him, was at the heart of political freedom. This emphasis on participation evidences once again the measure of Herder's almost prophetic vision. At least this is what the modern reader must feel when he or she is told that, if there is one aspect of the "new world political culture" that is plainly discernible, it is "a political culture of participation."[62] Herder's participatory vision of political culture in the narrower sense consisted of a historical process within two stages that he distinguished in terms of what may be identified with a "transfer" and a "goal" culture respectively.

The transfer culture corresponds broadly to Herder's idea of "aristo-democracy" that I have previously sketched, and which refers to the period of transition from what has been called "subject political culture" to "participant political culture."[63] Herder envisaged it as a transformation from elitist tutelage to democracy in the form of public education oriented toward ways of thinking that could provide the basis for societal reciprocity and the sharing of certain social values. Herder assigned the task of guiding this educational transformation to "aristo-democrats," popular leaders whom he looked upon as what we now call role models, that is to say, exemplary people, distinguished by virtue of their intellect and character rather than their wealth or property. However, unlike Plato's guardians and philosopher-kings, aristo-democrats

60. Ibid., XIII, 384. Aristotle, by contrast, is emphatic in stressing that the distinction is a difference in kind, and not simply a numerical difference. (*Politics*, I, chs 1, 3; and III, ch 4.)

61. Herder, *Werke*, IX, 407; see also IX, 401–8; XVI, 601; and XXX, 234.

62. Quoted from Gabriel Almond and Sidney Verba, *The Civic Culture* (Princeton: Princeton University Press, 1968), 4.

63. Ibid., 19.

are intended as a purely transitional expedient, for their function is not to rule, or to perpetuate their rule, but merely to establish civic conditions that will render their future leadership dispensable.[64]

The assumption underlying this conception of political leadership is, to be sure, highly debatable, because the world has so far not come across many politicians anxious to make themselves dispensable at the earliest possible stage. But, to be fair, Herder had no illusions about the difficulties that may attend the political transformation from tutelage to democracy. He granted that there may be "some disorder and a good deal of disagreement," that "men are not always honest," and that "the institutions as they emerge may be far from perfect," yet nonetheless he asked, "is it healthier or more beneficial for humanity to produce only the lifeless cogs of a huge, wooden machine ... in which men are forced to rot and decay during their lifetime, or to arouse and activate living energies?"[65]

Evidently, maximum popular participation mattered more to Herder during this transfer culture than elitist efficiency – not that he correlated absolutism with efficient government. "Those who feel they are accountable to no-one," he wrote toward the end of the century, "must shoulder the blame for our political disorders ... A state cannot be a healthy polity unless all members share a sense of civic responsibility."[66] Thus, while Herder's conception of aristo-democracy has unmistakably utopian overtones, and its underlying assumptions about the motivation of political leaders are questionable (to say the least), there is nonetheless more than a grain of realism in its anticipation of later "populist" pressures toward "grassroot" politics, more meaningful civic reciprocity, governmental accountability, and popular participation in public affairs.

The *goal* culture that was to emerge from this transformation was to witness the disappearance of the state as an administrative machine and its replacement by a pluralist diffusion of government, where "government" would be virtually tantamount to what Herder (in the *Ideas*) called *Zusammenwirken* (joint endeavour), in that it would manage to operate without coercion or central direction of any sort.[67] It is not

64. Herder, *Werke*, XIV, 217.
65. Ibid., V, 516; seel also XIII, 340–1. J.S. Mill argues similarly in *Representative Government*, ch 8.
66. Herder, *Werke*, XVIII, 309.
67. Ibid., XIV, 227.

necessary for our purpose to decide whether or not this almost eschatological vision of the ultimate end of political development is even thinkable as a *political* society. What, however, is of considerable interest, I feel, is the paradigm of participation that it projects. A brief comparison with Rousseau's vision of political participation may bring this point into sharper relief and, at the same time, disclose two distinct variants of the democratic ethic.

While Rousseau's scheme favours participation within a closely knit and highly centralized framework, Herder's scheme puts forward participation within a diffuse framework of diverse bases of activity and power. Moreover, for Herder it is largely the group rather than the individual that constitutes the nuclear unit of political association. Within this group-pluralism, the most active political participants and effective sources of multiple power are the representatives of diverse groups and institutions that sustain the political culture in the narrower sense. They are chosen by their peers as the best persons for certain projects; but their sphere of competence and range of power is strictly limited, and starts and ends with the tasks that have been allotted to them.[68]

Rousseau's scheme, no less than Herder's, manifestly rests on voluntarism and coordination rather than on compulsion and subordination; but by vesting power in the "sovereignty of the people" as a single totality, and by putting emphasis on unity and the centrality of authority, it seems prone to inhibit rather than promote the expression of diversity and dissent. And yet, though potentially illiberal, its paradigm of participation may well have greater appeal to emerging nations or democracies in that they view their undertakings as emergency operations.

To be sure, the idea that maximum popular participation may be the cornerstone of both democracy and the so-called world culture has been questioned by a number of political analysts. But whether it is dismissed as an empty slogan or salvaged as a useful myth, for many people political participation is not just a lofty ideal, beautiful to behold, but also a goal within possible reach. They may disagree about the timing of its attainment, but nevertheless cherish it as a conviction they would not easily surrender. Besides, whether they disagree over the timing alone or also over the style of the goal culture of participation, any such disagreement is bound to entail a searching reappraisal of the democratic ethic *per se*, regardless of whether or not "globalization" has any concrete

68. Ibid., XIII, 376.

meaning or recognizably tangible appeal. And it may well come to be the case that in the course of this reappraisal Herder's paradigm of participation could prove of as much interest as Rousseau's.

VII

As a result of eighteenth-century "rational" progressivism and nineteenth-century "evolutionary" progressivism, the notion of "globalization" has become culture-impregnated. Together with "development" it has assumed the status of a universal value, if not that of an incontestable absolute and, as such, virtually performs the role of a *symbol* of modernity. In this role it has undoubtedly fired the aspirations of a growing number of new nations toward becoming participants in a "world culture." What is more, the idea of culture integration in this sense has become almost indistinguishable from a transmutation of the concept of culture itself. Thus, for Antoine de Condorcet, Thomas Paine, and Thomas Jefferson, "culture" became tantamount to the "march of civilization" as an inexorable process. Barbarism was to recede before it; the diffusion of scientific knowledge and technology was to replace philosophy, in that there would no longer be anything to guess about. Much confidence was also expressed in the transferability of cultures from more to less developed countries. Indeed, Condorcet predicted that the latter, after importing the know-how, would actually overtake the former, by having learned from their mistakes.[69] With this hopeful message the idea of globalization as a "world culture" was born.

By the time "globalization" had entered the vocabulary of contemporary discussions of culture dissemination, two other concepts had, however, entered the world stage: nationalism and participation. And while Herder may be said to have had a hand in the emergence of these new entries, he nevertheless also provided a timely antidote to the seemingly boundless confidence in the "march of civilization," by drawing attention to the formidable unknowns that happen to be involved, as well as to the immense complexity of whatever *was* known.

Above all, Herder left no doubt on three vital points. First, the move toward a world culture embraced values that could prove exceedingly problematical to reconcile. Second, "development" need not simulta-

---

69. J.A.N. de Condorcet, *Esquisse d'un tableau historique des progrès de l'esprit humain* (1794). I discuss it in more detail in "Culture and Civilization in Modern Times," in *Dictionary of the History of Ideas* (New York: Charles Scribners, 1973), I, 613–21.

neously mean economic progress, administrative efficiency, military prowess, or political advancement, just as changes in any of these directions would not necessarily rate as being equally important. Fervent nationalists, for example, might have a scale of priorities very different from people striving for the attainment of civil liberties or a more equitable distribution of welfare or standard of living generally.[70] Choices would clearly have to be made, Herder warned, and the cost of excluded alternatives would have to be incurred. Third, he rather perspicaciously anticipated that the heralded march of civilization was likely to bring about what have become known as crises of rising expectations, the core of many current discontents.

The themes touched upon in this chapter undeniably bristle with conceptual perplexities – not least because "culture" itself is so elusive a term – but I do believe that Herder's suggestive insights have profoundly helped to enrich our understanding of processes of culture formation, culture diffusion, historical interaction, and societal integration.

Thus, however inadequately Herder may have attained what contemporary theorists of culture fancy to be its "scientifically accepted" meaning, I do believe that, apart from students of the history of ideas, those more specifically interested in the dynamics of social cultures may find in Herder's reflections a good deal to intrigue them and to ponder on. Put more negatively, while I would be loath to go so far as to claim that he has established for all times what "culture" is, I might conclude, with some assurance, that he has prodigiously contributed toward clarifying what it is *not*.

No doubt, Herder's fondness of the metaphor of growth – as typifying *internal* development – together with his contextual relativism, is capable of giving rise to difficulties which, like the philosophical problems connected with his theory of historical causation, may defy resolution. On the other hand, Herder's multi-faceted approach helps to bring out shades and nuances of seeing and perceiving that otherwise could well have been lost. Two resolves, I think, figured most prominently in this approach. One was Herder's determination to adhere to his basic principle of historical and cultural inquiry; namely, that no thing could be grasped outside its interconnections within and over

---

70. Intense nationalists do not ask themselves whether or not they are more competently governed, economically better off, or in the possession of greater civic liberties, in one political setting rather than another. Sudeten-German nationalists in pre-war Czechoslovakia or Palestinian nationalists in present-day Israel did not and do not entertain such "rational" calculations.

time, "horizontally" and "vertically." The other resolve was "to resist at all cost the German disease of deriving everything, whether it really follows or not, from purely formal propositions."[71] I am not sure which was the strongest resolve, but I have a hunch that it might have been the second, the determination to resist the "German disease," judging by Herder's intense hostility to Kant's "metaphysical *a priorism*."[72]

71. Herder, *Werke*, IV, 445.

72. This was Herder's main line of attack in the *Metakritik* (1799) against Kant's *Critique of Pure Reason*. Of considerable interest, from an anthropological perspective, in this connection, is a recent monograph by John H. Zammito, *Kant, Herder, and the Birth of Anthropology* (Chicago: University of Chicago Press, 2002).

7

*Historical and Political Consciousness:
Herder and Rousseau*

IN VIEW OF HIS EMPHASIS ON "INTERACTION" in his philosophy of history and culture it is scarcely surprising that Herder should have seen a close link between people's consciousness of history and their self-location in the world. What *is* surprising is that relatively little has so far been written about Rousseau's influence on Herder's reflections on history. To be sure, there are significant divergences; yet both were at one in the belief that an awareness of the past powerfully bears upon one's sense of identity, both as an individual and as a member of a context of others. What follows is in essence an attempt to explore the grounds on which both men thought that an enhanced consciousness of one's identity, in and through one's grasp of historical roots, could produce a shift in one's self-understanding from being a *subject* to becoming a *citizen*.

I

Neither Herder nor Rousseau before him could accept that humans should act in the dark, not knowing who or what they are, or whither they are going, within the flux of events called history. It might perhaps not be wrong to say that Herder as much as Rousseau (if not more so) *needed* history as an instrumentality toward creating no less than what amounts to a *revolutionary* consciousness as the source of a drastic trans-formation of people's self-understandings. History was to demonstrate that the passing of time *demanded* a metamorphosis of selfhood *in con-junction* with the world in which the self was embedded. Both Herder and Rousseau go to history, therefore, not for its own sake, principally, but rather in order to enlarge their vision of human possibilities.

The study of history, then, would have two paramount results for both of them. First, it would further people's reflective self-identification and self-location within time, space, and a context of others; and, second, it would make them realize that they were not meant to be merely passive observers, but that they could also think of themselves as active participants. For the most part, therefore, "self-understanding" has to do with such questions as Who am I? What can I do? Where do I fit in? What am I to others? or What are others to me? And, since history portrays humans essentially as doers, "self-understanding" also implies a growing awareness on the part of individual selves that they possess the capacity to gain control not only over their private existence but also over those aspects of public life that directly or indirectly impinge on themselves.

Of the two thinkers, Herder is the acknowledged pioneer of the idea that historical consciousness (*Geschichtsbewusstsein*) is the necessary presupposition of historical *understanding* in the sense that Wilhelm Dilthey has interpreted as *Verstehen*, but he is less acknowledged as a political philosopher. Rousseau, by contrast, has his unquestioned place among the great in political thought, but is not usually linked with speculations on the meaning or use of history. An incidental purpose of this essay, therefore, is to redress the balance somewhat.

In the endeavour to derive lessons from history Herder seems, surprisingly perhaps, the more optimistic, in that he is inclined (especially in his providential moods) to confer upon the overall thrust of history an ultimately positive quality. Thus, whereas Rousseau used history largely to sound warnings against the ever-present threat of corruption, Herder, though eschewing any belief in linear progress, nonetheless viewed the passing of time itself as an active force in the promotion of humanization (*Humanität*). Considering "time" to be intimately identifiable with the "pressure of ideas" (*Drang der Ideen*), he suggested that ideas have (or acquire) in the course of history a life and dynamic of their own which carry a distinctly teleological thrust, able to convert purposes *of* history into purposes *in* history.[1] Whereas Vico invoked Providence to

---

1. J.G. Herder, *Sämtliche Werke*, ed. B. Suphan, 33 vols. (Berlin: Weidmann, 1877–1913), XIII, 186. The mediating potential of ideas in bringing together purposes *of* history with purposes *in* history is strikingly echoed in Hegel's "cunning of reason," in that ideas – which, for Herder, include ends, values, and beliefs – are objectified as quasi-independent forces; they are said to press on humans by way of recurrent "impulses" (Herder uses "pressure" and "impulses" interchangeably) and thereby operate as agents of teleological causation in history. For a more detailed discussion on what appear to be sharply contrasting approaches to the idea of purpose in history between Herder and Vico, see my "Natural Growth and Purposive Development: Vico and Herder," *History and Theory*, 18 (1979), 16–36.

juxtapose these twofold purposes, and their hidden fusion, Herder intimated their mediation through "ideas," and, thereby, the possibility of humans themselves' being their "own god" in history.[2]

Rousseau, though showing less interest in history as a subject for philosophical reflection, nevertheless reveals remarkable insight when he does turn his attention to history, and expresses views that strikingly go against the current of historical thinking. Thus, *contra* Voltaire, Rousseau puts major emphasis on the "valleys" of history, asserting that it is they rather than the "peaks" which yield true glimpses of human possibilities and most add to human self-understandings. The valleys, the broad stretches of happenings, show best how people inject themselves into processes of history. Against the backdrop of the state of nature, as the arch-exemplar of the genuinely authentic, Rousseau wants people to realize how much that is so highly prized among the peaks of civilization is but sham and show. Historians, especially, seing the "stage without any longer being able to act on it, as simple spectators, disinterested and without passion," are in an excellent position to tell us something about our fellow-beings, and do so as their judges, "and not as their accomplices or their accusers."[3] They should, therefore, glancing backward, and being some distance away from occurrences, be capable of assessing action and distinguishing the genuine from the spurious.

II

Most intriguingly, Rousseau anticipates what Marx and Engels were to call "false consciousness," by focusing on self-deception as the most

---

2. Herder, *Werke*, VI, 64; XIV, 210. No doubt, the notion of ideas pressing upon humans in particular directions has a transcendental ring to it. At the same time, when people speak of themes or motives dropping in on them (what in German is appropriately called *Einfälle*), they speak of an experience common enough to artists, writers, and composers. Evidently, within creativity, the ordinary and the extraordinary coalesce.

3. J.-J. Rousseau, *Emile*, ed. A. Bloom (New York: Basic Books, 1979), 237. (*Oeuvres Complètes*, ed. Pléiade, Paris, 1959–69, IV, 525–6.) Subsequent references are to this edition, cited by volume and page after the translated source. Herder most likely first learned from Kant, when he studied under him in Königsberg, of Rousseau's use of historical retrospection in the mediation of the future. Indeed, Kant was among the few of Rousseau's contemporaries who correctly understood his use of the "state of nature" as a means of distinguishing the genuine from the spurious. While Voltaire's interest in history embraced social and economic activities, Rousseau was not wrong in stating that, as Isaiah Berlin has confirmed, it was the "peaks, not the valleys, of the achievements of mankind" on which his historical inquiry was riveted. See Berlin's *The Crooked Timber of Humanity: Chapters in the History of Ideas*, ed. H. Hardy (London: John Murray, 1990), 51–2.

corrosive force throughout human history, judging it to be even more pernicious than mendacity. At once fascinated and repelled by its corruptive potential, he sees genuine self-enactment constantly imperilled by it, since it warps values, blurs the truth, and undermines reason. Words are by far the most offending source, in that they often not only *happen* to deceive, but are indeed *meant* to deceive, for rhetoric is frequently empty, and spoken truth false truth. Unlike words, deeds *are* authentic, and transparently so, in that they speak for themselves. If, therefore, we want to know humans the way they truly are, we must see them act.[4] That is where history comes in. In history, from the vantage point of hindsight, human actions are laid bare, freed from the disguise of words. What is more, Rousseau argues, even words, historically viewed, appear now in a new light. Instead of helping to conceal what people are up to, they disclose the difference between "what they do and what they say," so that one is able to "see both what they are and what they appear to be." Indeed, Rousseau adds, "the more they disguise themselves, the better one knows them."[5]

Unlike Herder, Rousseau takes a poor view of ideas as such. Deeds alone yield a basis for judging past events, and it is through deeds that one may discover the real meaning of ideas, opinions, and beliefs. Only in this indirect way can the historian evaluate the ideals that men and women profess to cherish. Outcomes, to be sure, do not necessarily correspond to what was intended. Rousseau is alive to this possibility, but nonetheless insists that it is precisely the historian's task to determine how genuine professed intentions are, and to what extent their lack of follow-up truly reflects strivings that had miscarried. It appears that only the historian is effectively able to uncover the degree of deception and self-deception that beclouds human deeds, and thus to reveal the excess of falsehoods over truths, or the triumph of truth, sincerity, and authenticity over lies, clouded judgments, and sheer ignorance.[6]

4. Rousseau, *Emile*, 237 (IV, 525–6).
5. Ibid.
6. For Rousseau most existing states were fraudulent contraptions designed to fool the many for the benefit of the few. The historian is to detect such false claims and thereby puncture public lies. See his *Discourse on the Origin of Inequality*, ed. G.D.H. Cole, *Social Contract and Discourses* (London: Dent, 1946), 204; henceforth cited as *Inequality* (*Oeuvres*, III, 176–7). Herder, similarly, views history as a sort of world-court in which, as (subsequently) in Schiller's conception of history, historians are called upon to act as judges, to distinguish true claims from false claims, and to decide which, on balance, do prevail, or should have prevailed.

How the historian is to discern the true and authentic reasons for an occurrence solely by riveting attention on accomplished deeds seems puzzling at first. It transpires, however, that deeds are of interest to Rousseau only as historical actions when they evidently contrain dispositions or motives as their generating source. Clearly, for Rousseau as for Herder, history is inseparable from psychology; the study of the past is essentially a study of the human heart. The historian's success, consequently, lies precisely in eliciting the true springs of action; this, and this alone, betokens for Rousseau the true measure of historical understanding.

Unfortunately, defects in historians themselves or in their methods could mar the benefits that a study of history might bestow. One of these defects is the odd if not perverse selectiveness of historians; it inclines them to "paint people's bad sides more than their good ones," since these have a far more dramatic impact on them than the peaceful pursuits of daily life.[7] Revolutions and catastrophes absorb their interest rather than whatever brings forth well-being and serenity of mind. "So long as a people grows and prospers calmly, with a peaceful government, history has nothing to say of it. History begins to speak of a people only when, no longer sufficing unto itself, it gets involved with its neighbours' affairs or lets them get involved in its affairs."[8]

The upshot of this selectiveness is a fatal misreading of reality. What in truth is deterioration is taken for amelioration, and decline is taken for ascent. A people that appears illustrious is in truth on the brink of disaster. The trouble is that historians begin where they ought to finish; they ought to be silent where they are the most eloquent. Yet, precisely about those matters in which human life shows itself at its best or political government is at its soundest history is mute.[9] Rousseau denies, therefore, in opposition to Hobbes, that history, as it is commonly found, discloses what humans in general are, or that it helps to yield so-called laws of human nature. Focusing almost exclusively on the wicked and famous, on the startling rather than the quietly honourable, historians *fail* to tell us about those deeds which, for the most part, define the quality of human virtue. Humanity, Rousseau concludes, cannot be judged by the criteria of historical selection and historical recording; history, while pointing to the possible, does not

7. *Emile*, 237 (IV, 525–6).
8. Ibid., 238 (IV, 526).
9. Ibid.

instruct us about the generally necessary or even the commonplace and ordinary. Although we may learn from it, we cannot deduce principles of universal applicability.[10]

Apart from being selective, historical findings are loaded with bias. Facts are not merely selected facts; they are also value-laden, since bias, known or unknown, enters into the historian's judgment. "The facts described by history," Rousseau states, "are far from being an exact portrayal of the same facts as they happened. They change form in the historian's head; they are moulded according to his interests; they take on the complexion of his prejudices."[11] What is more, the historian's bias frequently is not a purely personal bias; for, like everybody else, the historian cannot escape the prevailing currents of the times – Herder's *Zeitgeist* – so that these surreptitiously colour a historian's assumptions and fashion the pattern of historical thinking.[12] While, in his most cynical moods, Rousseau rates historical findings at their best no higher than being among several lies the ones that most closely resemble the truth, he does recognize, in more sober moods, that, despite the fluidity of what separates facts from interpretation, historical judgment need not be altogether bereft of values that are genuine values, or of conjectures that are "reasonable conjectures."[13]

In other words, while pointing to all sorts of shortcomings in the recording of events, Rousseau urges caution but not outright nihilism. For he is aware that, although a historian's perspectives are prone to distort facts, without perspectives of one kind or another there could be no historical judgment. Somehow, therefore, a balance has to be struck between having perspectives that are too rigid and having no perspectives at all. Clearly, if perspectives are too rigid and exclusionary, the same object, viewed from different perspectives, could never be the same, or even remotely the same. If, among spectators looking at a play, each sees an entirely different play, there is no way of knowing if they indeed watched the same show. Relativism, thus pushed to its extreme, confers upon facts as many faces as there are perspectives of viewing them. Even if nothing had changed, all would appear different, and for no reason other than that the eyes of the spectator had undergone a change.[14]

10. Ibid.
11. Ibid.
12. Ibid.
13. Ibid.; see also *Inequality*, 172, 190 (III, 142–5, 161–3).
14. Rousseau, *Emile*, 238 (IV, 527).

On closer reading it appears, however, that it is not so much the risk of relativistic distortion that worries Rousseau most. Rather, it is what might be described as the danger of misplaced concreteness. History, insofar as it for the greater part records only "palpable and distinct" facts, facts that can be fixed by names, places, and dates, leaves unknown those occurrences whose causes, being slow and cumulative, cannot similarly be set down. "Often one finds in a battle won or lost," Rousseau declares, "the reason for a revolution which, even before this battle, has become inevitable."[15] Dramatically startling events mislead us to attribute to them a causality they do not truly posses. In Rousseau's own words, "war hardly does anything other than make manifest outcomes already determined by moral causes which historians rarely know how to see."[16] Too interested in fitting causes into preconceived systems, they prefer what they think to what they see. Noticing only the palpable effects, they *impose* causes rather than *discover* them. Furthermore, because they only see the surface of things, they mistake dressed-up reality for true, unadorned reality; they see people in certain selected moments, when they are on parade, dressed up in their parade clothes. As a result, they depict an actor playing his role portraying the costume rather than the person.[17]

III

Just like Montaigne before him and Herder after him, Rousseau searched for causes working within the human psyche. For, as we have seen, despite all the emphasis on accomplished deeds, the basis and source of historical judgment lie in uncovering motives and intentions. Good historians will therefore follow their subjects everywhere, for people frequently hide their real design.[18] Only by revealing the hidden, by uncovering the concealed, can the historian hope to lay bare the true nature of human deeds. But this is not all there is to it. For Rousseau is not unaware of the fact that humans acting in concert with others are not motivated in the same manner as they are when acting by themselves. One would, therefore, know the human heart very imperfectly if one did not "examine it also in the multitude."[19] So, in order to understand

15. Ibid., 239–40 (IV, 529–30).
16. Ibid., 240 (IV, 530).
17. Ibid.
18. Ibid.
19. Ibid.

human dispositions and human intentions in their diversity, we have to do both: we have to study "men or people," when they are assembled, in order to judge them individually, and we have to "study man" as an individual, "in order to judge men" acting with others. In either case, however, historians must not be overly concerned with "propriety," for if they are, they will neither see nor want to see what stares them in the face; unadorned reality will totally escape them. They will continue "to put on costumes and pass cords over pulleys," mistake decline for growth, degradation for improvement, and self-destruction for self-perfection.[20] In the end historians, like the rest of us, will no longer see with their own eyes, feel with their own hearts, or judge with their own reason.[21]

But, even if historians were to heed Rousseau's strictures, this would not remove a recurrent source of despondency on his part. In sharp contrast to Herder, who, we noted, looks upon "time" itself as a potential force for better things to come, Rousseau agonizes over the sheer passing of time, in that he sees in it a potential source of advancing deception and depravity, of an increase in unhappiness together with a mounting loss of innocence. Herder, to be sure, also has his moments of doubt and melancholy, and talk of the world's ceaseless amelioration irritates him most aggravatingly;[22] yet in few of Herder's writings do we come across the degree of almost tragic foreboding that Rousseau betrays. And although Herder agrees with Rousseau that every change carries risks, and that alternatives displaced may involve losses that exceed gains, he nonetheless wants to think that a synthesis might be forged between progress and preservation, between the demands of commerce and industry and the demands of *Humanität.*

If Herder, therefore, saw at least a chance for humanity's self-transformation over time, Rousseau could never altogether suppress his anxiety over attempting to make the world over; he could not quite overcome the fear that much that at first promised to yield improvement would in the end prove detrimental to the lot of humankind. Efforts seeking to provide effective solutions, to make things work, almost invariably backfire, for they threaten to injure or destroy what gave

20. Rousseau, *Emile,* 240–2; see also Rousseau's *Discourse on the Arts and Sciences,* ed. Cole, 129–32, 140–2; henceforth cited as *Arts and Sciences* (*Oeuvres,* IV, 529–34; III, 15–20, 27–30).

21. Rousseau, *Emile,* 244–55 (IV, 535–52).

22. For more on this point, see my *Self-Direction and Political Legitimacy: Rousseau and Herder* (Oxford: Clarendon Press, 1988), ch. 10.

them life and inner value in the first place. Change always involves tremedous risks, risks that are not calculable in the way that problems are in geometry. Methods that are eminently applicable to mathematics, or to science generally, are therefore not at all appropriate when applied to the realm of human affairs and the understanding of human history. Indeed, they may be worthless, and principles that are held in high regard in the former prove disastrous in the latter.[23] Although Rousseau certainly believed that the study of history might enhance human self-knowledge, he at the same time rejected the idea that each century cumulatively added its enlightenment to that of preceding centuries. Human self-understanding, he felt, simply does not work like this; for, inherently, its scope of development is strictly bounded.[24] Political self-understandings likewise have their limits, and it is unwise to have buoyant expectations about infinite improvements, as, for example, about the prospect of finding a form of government that would put laws above men. "I frankly confess," Rousseau writes toward the end of his life, "that I believe that it is not to be found."[25]

Unlike Herder, who, as he grew older, displayed an increasing confidence in the future, Rousseau became progressively more sceptical. Whatever, therefore, sustained his belief in reason as a means of averting chaos or total destruction, was a thoroughly chastened faith. While he did not think that the *philosophy* of reason would cease to command universal lip-service, he could not suppress his fear that the *application* of reason would sooner serve the perfection of deception than the cause of enlightenment. In effect he foresaw a highly manipulative use of reason, a rationalized form of deception, that would succeed better than ever before in distorting our vision, until we would no longer know whether we believed what we saw or saw what we wanted to believe. Rousseau's prize essay of 1750 (on the arts and sciences) is one of the most eloquent indictments of naïve progressivism, as of all that is spurious, glib, and meretricious. As were Herder and Tocqueville after him, Rousseau was particularly suspicious of projects that used fanciful rhetoric invoking progress, liberty, and equality, when in truth they

23. Rousseau, *Emile*, 268–75 (IV, 567–79). See also Rousseau's letter to Deschamps of 8 May 1761, in *Correspondance Complète*, ed. R.A. Leigh (Geneva and Oxford: The Voltaire Foundation, 1965–86) VIII, 320.

24. See Rousseau's Letter to Mirabeau of 26 July 1767, in C.E. Vaughan, *Rousseau's Political Writings* (Cambridge: Cambridge University Press, 1915), II, 159.

25. Vaughan, *Rousseau's Political Writings*, II, 160–1.

were merely trying to conceal tyranny and adorn the chains that were to bind us – and bind us far more banefully than the unadorned chains of the most despotic of tyrants.[26]

I V

And yet, notwithstanding Herder's qualified optimism and Rousseau's qualified pessimism regarding the portents of time itself, the contrast must not be overdrawn. Herder, no less than Rousseau, demanded authenticity in the recording of past events, and emphatically made a distinction between history as it actually happened and the way it is told. "Is this England's history as it occurred or is it what Mr. Hume thinks should have occurred?"[27] Similarly, anyone reading his scathing attack on the complacency of the Age of Reason in *Yet Another Philosophy of History* cannot have the slightest doubt about Herder's (acknowledged) debt to Rousseau in the manner in which he expressed his own apprehension about the sanguinely rising expectations of the benefits of philosophy, knowledge, rationality, science, trade, and technology. Quite as much as Rousseau, Herder was conscious of the price of these advances. Modern people travel in ships, but how many can *build* a boat? Every change, every advance in techniques, knits a new pattern of thinking and acting; it creates new needs and generates new problems.[28] This, we noted, is the gist of Herder's theory of displaced alternatives. And though it is perhaps less gloomy about change *per se*, or less bent upon painting an absolutely dismal picture of its outcome, in its main thrust it is not a great deal more hopeful about the augmentation of human happiness in the train of human advancements. If Herder nonetheless in his later years wanted to believe (and wanted others to believe) that gains would ultimately outstrip losses, he most likely did so because the humanist in him managed to subdue the sceptic.

In his emphasis on the historical causality of purposive motives, too, Herder remarkably echoes Rousseau's speculations on history. Like Rousseau, he wants to enter the inner person, trace the deeper source of human aspirations, in order to penetrate the minds of other people and periods and discover the purposive direction in it all. And, again like Rousseau, he seeks historical understanding, in the main, as a

26. This is the thrust of Rousseau's argument in *Arts and Sciences*, 120–1 (*Oeuvres*, III, 6–8).
27. Herder, *Werke*, III, 466–70, esp. 469.
28. Ibid., XIII, 371.

means, and not as an end in itself. The real point of historical under-standing for both, therefore, is not chiefly to find explanations, but rather to evaluate and judge events in the light of their intrinsic mean-ings, values, and principles within expressions of creative (or destruc-tive) strivings. The mentalities, intentions, or motives underlying these strivings are viewed, however, not as antecedents in the mechanical sense of "cause," but as guiding criteria for ascribing praise or blame, the presence of which is a matter not of physical fact but of conceptual properties that lend themselves to evaluative judgment.

That conceptual properties have their own cognitive and causal force is the basic claim Herder makes in his philosophy of language and hu-man history. He traces their source to the human capacity for speech and, through it, to a consciousness of others as *others*, and of time as *his-tory*. In turn, a consciousness of others and of hisotry implies for Herder an awareness of *distance* and an awareness of conscious activity within social space as well as within the temporal chain of human existence "linking the first thought of the first human mind with the last thought of the last human mind."[29] Discovering *meaning*, therefore, is not the same as discovering general laws of causality in the physical sciences. Also, it is not simply finding out "what is" but "what it is like" to discover meaning and purpose in *experiencing* history. Once again, there are unmistakable points of contact with Rousseau, although Herder is not only more emphatic on the need for historical empathy but also more obviously anxious to persuade and assume the role of reformer, urging the study of past activities as a means of avoiding their mistakes in the shaping of the future.

The main assumption underlying Herder's reforming endeavour to link historical consciousness with the improvement of social life is the belief that human nature is not an inexorable given, through and through, but is something capable of being nurtured or cultivated. Like Rousseau, Herder firmly presumes that true reform demands the nur-ture of appropriate dispositions and, in turn, a matrix of suitable institu-tions. In both cases, however, it is not clear how, if the cultivation of individual dispositions is to *follow* the creation of an institutional matrix, the latter could come about in the first place. This problem oppressed Rousseau, but Herder suggested it could be surmounted by means of his idea of "interplay" between *Bildung* and *Tradition* or, more broadly, be-tween forces pressing for change and forces pressing for preservation.

29. Ibid., VI, 64, XIV, 210.

While for Rousseau a similar interactive process of contextual self-development is at all feasible only as a *moral* process within a politically integrated and legitimately grounded community, it seems for Herder bound up with a perfectly *natural* process, in terms of anthropological-social evolvement. For, although self-understandings occur *within* individual selves, they are in truth inconceivable outside a context of others, and such a context is as natural for humans as air, sunshine, trees, and meadows. Without this context, our understanding of ourselves would most likely never awaken in the first place.[30] What we know about ourselves, accordingly, is essentially a function of the continuous interaction between the self's "inside" and its "outside," thus, becoming fully human is a sort of contextual *Wirkungszusammenhang*, a matter of multiple interactions, *at once* natural and social.[31]

It is precisely this contextual dynamic that Herder puts foward as a critique of Kant's *Critique of Pure Reason* in his *Metakritik* (1799). Viewing the growth of individual self-understandings as part of the overall process of human self-development or *Bildung*, Herder treats *Bildung* as inseparable from *Tradition*. Only thus can continuity be preserved and, at the same time, *Tradition* be prevented from becoming a jailer who, imprisoning values, thereby warps and enfeebles them, depriving them of their inner life, so that they are no longer in harmony with what people in truth authentically feel about them, even if the norms upholding them nominally still prevail. From the hermeneutics of contextualism that Herder applies to culture and history it therefore follows that, although norms may remain the same, their perceived meaning and significance would no longer be the same – a point that recalls Rousseau's central theme in the *Discourse on the Arts and Sciences* about the gap between appearances and genuine being. Possibly buildig on this theme, Herder writes that each belief, each custom, each principle, retains an inner life and outer recognition only if forms of acting and thinking carried over from the past mesh with goals pointing forward within the minds of people here and now, so that past and present interblend.[32] And it was the belief in the possibility of such interblending that markedly sustained Herder's *credo* of dynamic humanism.

Continuity and change, therefore, in their delicate balance hold out the promise of humanization for Herder, that is, of a trend with strongly reforming overtones. Rousseau, unable to advance a similarly hopeful

30. Herder, *Werke*, XXI, 152.
31. Ibid., 179–82.
32. Ibid., V, 28–30, 93, 113–14, 134–5; XXIII, 321.

dialectic, offers by contrast an essentially negative prognosis, in view of which even illiberal elements enter into the envisioned process designed to ward off the acceleration of corruption. Unlike Herder who, we noted, *could* entertain the hope that conscious striving after *Humanität* would act in the service of reform, Rousseau, for the most part, could not help viewing the future as anything other than a likely harbinger of evil, an ever-threatening seducer whose corrosive work could at best only be halted. It is, above all, this difference in projecting the "lessons" of history into the future that sets apart their reforming mood, or, at any rate, their readiness to inspire confidence in doing the world over.

v

Regardless of their contrasting ways of looking ahead, Rousseau and Herder both fully shared the view that looking back into the past was an essential route to "finding oneself." For it provided that sense of identity through an inner link with one's ancestors, through which selves could situate themselves within the particular milieu into which they have been born – defining their self-location within the larger scheme of things. Although Herder in important directions put a sharper edge on this inner cohesion with the past, Rousseau had already gone some distance in deriving nationhood from the existence of a prior consciousness of a common affinitive culture. And it was this idea that nationalists subsequently were not slow to latch on to. But if Rousseau thus launched upon the world the conviction that people, in gaining consciousness of themselves as *a* people, could raise themselves up into a self-governing entity by an act of concerted will, Herder may be said to have both detracted from and enlarged upon this belief, by putting less weight on a collective *will* and proportionately greater weight on an affinitive *culture*.

In view of this divergent emphasis, Rousseau is frequently contrasted with Herder as a *political* nationalist, whereas Herder is seen as an essentially *cultural* nationalist. I have in an earlier chapter tried to show why I believe this opposition between political and cultural nationalism to be overdrawn, and that, if there are (as there undoubtedly are) differences between Rousseau and Herder, they do not derive from one being non-culturally political and the other non-politically cultural.[33] Instead, as I

33. I touch on this point in the (above) essay on "Cultural Nationalism and Political Romanticism," and develop it in more detail in "National Culture and Political Legitimacy: Herder and Rousseau," *Journal of the History of Ideas*, 44 (1983), 231–53.

see it, the two approaches represent variants of national legitimation, with Rousseau accentuating the act of *creation*, assisted by the founding initiative of a superhuman lawgiver, and with Herder stressing gradual *emergence*, a political process that is closer to organic growth or natural unfolding.

This variation stems, I believe, from their contrasting historical presuppositions. For Herder there never was, nor could have been, any human life outside the context of kinship groups, and he therefore saw no point whatsoever in Rousseau's solitary man of nature – not even as a hypothetical construct. In short, the natural origin of human existence is of necessity a "contextual" origin, because a human being, in being human, *needs* a context of others, and that context is primarily the nuclear and extended family. Significantly for Herder – and insufficiently recognized by those who see in him the father of modern nationalism – no state, not even the nation state, can ever wholly displace (or replace) humanity's original context. The nation, therefore, does not displace families, clans, tribes, on other primeval groups, but is *continuous* with them and, in this literal sense, is their extension – as natural a growth as the family itself.

In Herder's scheme of things, accordingly, membership in a state is not direct but mediated. While for Rousseau citizenship is a matter of undivided loyalty to the state, for Herder it is perfectly compatible with *plural* loyalties, with a diversity of allegiances. The nation, for him, is no monolithic rock; it is more like a mountain chain, in being, as we observed, a composite ensemble, which, in biological terms, is more like a *complex* of organisms than a single organism. Yet, in spite of its manifold layers, a nation is held to possess inner cohesive forces, by way of shared modes of thinking, enabling a distinctive manner of collaboration (*Zusammenwirken*) among its members.[34]

The other consideration that underlies Herder's differing position is his insistence that bonds among members of a nation are not, as with Rousseau, the work of a separate and ahistorical act of will, but are rather the outcome or "product" of historical growth, that is, of something that only awaits ripening through time. To be sure, Rousseau does not ignore the element of time; indeed he stresses no less than Herder that the time

34. Herder, *Werke*, XIII, 347. *Wirken* and *Zusammenwirken* are key concepts in Herder's *Yet Another Philosophy of History* and the *Ideas*. Unfortunately, neither word is precisely translatable; to render the former as "having an effect" is rather stilted, and the latter as "collaborate" rather wooden.

must be ripe for certain measures to succeed. However, Herder goes further; he postulates latent common understandings, deeply rooted in a people's psyche, its collective soul, which merely need awakening. No lawgiver, no social contract, is therefore required to convert a nation in itself into a nation for itself.[35]

Consistent with this doctrine, Herder's envisioned transformation from hereditary tutelage to democratic self-government is comparable to a process of historical evolvement, inducing him to speak of "decay" from above and new "growth" from below. It is only during the aftermath of the French Revolution that Herder painfully discovered that historical change is not at all like natural change – that decay from above does not necessarily ensure growth from below. This disovery was not only painfull but also embarassing; for the new realization somewhat undermined his dismissive attitude toward Rousseau's bringing in the mysterious figure of a lawgiver. All the same, even when he had to concede that some form of political intervention was called for to prepare the "soil" and "sow the seed," Herder went out of his way to make sure that his political "gardeners" came from the nation itself. Although exceptional in many ways, they are nevertheless not like meteors that arrive from nowhere, without roots among the people they are meant to guide.

How, precisely, these popular leaders are to emerge, Herder fails to disclose. Their appearance, therefore, seems almost as mysterious as the appearance of Rousseau's lawgiver. But Herder wished to believe that what I earlier called the transfer culture was a matter not of collective *will*, but of history and common ways of thinking and feeling. Although a degree of voluntarism is taken for granted, the real driving force is seen in the historical process itself. The popular leaders, the "aristo-democrats," merely help to accelerate this ripening process, but they themselves are not viewed as its culmination. Indeed, the intervention is intended as a purely temporary affair, and its guiding function strictly limited in time as it is in scope. Primarily it is meant to stimulate reform from below through universal *Bildung*, a course of development, to enable people to walk by themselves, and *themselves* forge the laws and institutions they want as *citizens*.[36]

35. I make use here of Hegelian terminology in order to point out the difference between the unreflective existence of collectivities and their self-conscious existence. Only the latter seems for both Rousseau and Herder a suitable grounding of *political* self-understandings.

36. Herder, *Werke*, IV, 454; XIII, 149; XVIII, 33; XXXII, 56.

Underlying this approach is Herder's conviction that the ordinary folk are in truth the most precious part of the nation, and not the stupid, inarticulate mob, they have been thought of hitherto. This qualitative approbation, rather than a strictly majoritarian principle, seems uppermost in Herder's vision of the rightful polity. And it was above all this qualitative approbation that was to provide the ideological impetus for the agitation in support of "national self-determination" in Central and Eastern Europe – an agitation which in effect telescoped the argument for cultural self-expression with the argument for political self-government.

V I

The political self-understandings, then, which a consciousness of history was to mediate, and toward which Herder, as Rousseau before him, directed his thought, carry the conviction that it is ordinary people, and not aristocratic and dynastic rulers, who are the source of a nation's rightful existence. What Herder and Rousseau differ about is the decisive moment in history that gives birth to the transformation of existing nations into rightful nations. It appears that for Rousseau this moment is essentially a matter of ahistorical willing, of a consensual determination to found such a rightful association, whereas for Herder it is essentially a matter of historical maturation, of *unfolding* in its literal processual sense. It is perhaps not surprising that Rousseau, in keeping with the idea of instant creation, therefore favours the mechanical image of a structural "body," while Herder favours the organic metaphor of a plant, the result of growth and gradual ripening.[37] In point of fact, Herder liked to imagine the world as a garden in which nations grow like flowers, blossom, and bear fruit in their utmost variety. "Republics," he says, "are like plants which are grown from seed."[38] And, whereas for Herder the whole is not separate from or superior to its parts, it is for Rousseau inherently different and ethically superior, just as the general will differs from and qualitatively transcends the will of all.[39]

It is not really difficult to find reasons for the divergence in doctrinal emphasis. Although Rousseau is by no means unaware of the role of history in the formation of civil society, he virtually abandons historical evolvement when it comes to founding the rightful polity; moral will, not

37. Rousseau, *Social Contract*, Bk. I, ch. 7 (*Oeuvres*, III, 362–4). Herder, *Werke*, XIV, 84.
38. Herder, *Werke*, IX, 375. The "garden" is at once the symbol of human creativity and a representation of human interconnectedness with nature. See also XIII, 341 and 384.
39. Rousseau, *Social Contract*, Bk. II, ch. 3 (*Oeuvres*, III, 371–2).

history is the dominant causality. History is a useful instrumentality in disclosing human propensities, but it is not a path that itself leads to moral willing and moral acting. Herder, on the other hand, attempts to maintain a strictly historical stance throughout, by linking the emergence of self-government directly with a people's historical self-awakening. And, as we observed, Herder, unlike Rousseau, ascribes to history, conceived as the sheer passing of time, an ultimately positive function. Humans, on this view, *can* put their faith in the future, if not in the short run, nevertheless in the long run, once they realize that history, so to speak, is on their side. Rousseau, by contrast, feels he is in no position to preach such a faith; while he recommends the study of history as a means of acquiring greater self-knowledge, history itself, as the passing of time, contains for him no promise of rightful self-enactment, individually or collectively. Similarly, the growth of national cultures, though a necessary foundation for political cultures, implies no maturing process of legitimacy itself, no subjection of will and action to the paramountcy of moral principles. Cultures refer to the soil and its cultivation; they do not determine the product. These is for Rousseau a cut-off point, at which *making* takes over from *growing*, and at which the "engine" of will replaces the "thriving" of a plant.

These (by no means negligible) differences aside, political association for both, to be legitimate, has to rest on active membership, on individuals' participation in concerns that relate to them as *citizens*. And the possibility for such a *civic* consciousness to come into being is for both thinkers, albeit to varying degrees, bound up with a collective historical memory entering people's sense of individual *and* national self-location. This fusion, to be sure, is in itself only the potential basis of a truly shared *political* consciousness, but directly or indirectly it *could* act as a spur toward injecting a revitalizing spirit into "public opinion" as Rousseau envisioned it.[40]

Yet, whether or not the idea of such a fusion succeeded in giving rise to a "revolutionary consciousness," it undoubtedly had a momentous impact on public thinking. The result of this impact assumed, however, two sharply contrasting forms. On the one hand, it heralded a massive upsurge of people's individual self-assurance and, with it, the historical shift from command to contract, from concession to right, and from subject to citizen. Collectively it emboldened those who hitherto counted for little – *within* a nationality or *as* a nationality – to feel that they mattered and that

40. Rousseau, *Social Contract*, Bk. I, ch. 8; Bk. II, ch. 12; Bk. IV, ch. 7; *Political Economy* (G.D.H. Cole ed., *The Social Contract and Discourses*), 235, 240; *Preface to Narcissus* (*The Miscellaneous Works of Mr. J.J. Rousseau* (New York: Burt Franklin, 1767, repr. 1972), 138.

they indeed had every ground to think that they *should* matter. And it was this individual and collective self-discovery that forged the transition from the state-nation (as Meinecke put it) to the nation-state, from the domain of dynastic rulers to the self-authenticated commonwealth. On the other hand, however, it involved a radical switch from ideological individualism to ideological holism. Henceforth, a person could be fully human only as part of a "whole." Conversely, for a state to be a proper state its inhabitants were expected to be, and feel themselves to be, integral components of a distinctive associative culture, of a collective self of its own.

Parallel, therefore, with the marriage of historical and political consciousness, individual and collective identities underwent a transformation in a direction which, while it pointed to the resolution of the problem of two (potentially clashing) moralities that Machiavelli so acutely brought to the attention of the preceding are, at the same time posed the worrisome uncertainty of whether collective oneness may not come at too high a price.

To say this is not to imply that Rousseau, any more than Herder, was a nationalist in the sense in which the word is commonly understood today. Nor was either of them insensitive to the baffling human predicament of at once needing others and being at the mercy of others who may harm and abuse us. Therefore, while forming an association such as the state may humanize us, it may also corrupt us and make us dependent on each other in onerous ways. In view of this predicament, is it possible for a person to attain self-fulfilment through self-enactment without injury to others or, conversely, can a person associate with others without sacrificing his or her individuality? *Can* people unite and still remain free?

These are troubling questions which undeniably bothered Herder as they had bothered Rousseau before him. In attempting to come to grips with them, each in his own way suggested a reappraisal of individual self-understandings. And, although in this attempt neither can be called or thought of as a conventional individualist, likewise neither can be called a collectivist in any recognizably contemporary sense. For, while both saw in a people more than a mere aggregation of individuals, in insisting on embedding the individual within the context of a shared cultural matrix, they were careful not to confuse *relation* with *identity*. The contextual setting that was to call forth sentiments and symbols of a new social reality was an *associational* reality, intended to involve the symbiosis of two distinct entities, of selfness and otherness. And, even though it was meant to give life to a selfness that viewed its individual good as bound up with the good of its fellows, the selfness as such was to remain intact in its entirety, both as humans and as citizens, including their respective rights and freedoms.

VII

It is above all this symbiosis of selfness and otherness that lends Rousseau's and Herder's search for rightful association its distinctive character as well as its problematic causality. Distinctive, because it postulates a metamorphosis of both individuality and sociability, enlarging the former and narrowing the scope of the latter to those we can tangibly recognize as our "fellows." Problematic, because, as Rousseau disturbingly remarked, the effect would need to become the cause.[41] All the same, these novel meanings of extended individualism and circumscribed altruism critically underpinned for both the conceptual fusion by virtue of which right and law, rulers and ruled, and subjects and citizens were to be one.

The fact that neither felt unduly daunted by his redefinition of oneness and otherness or by the problematic causality of the suggested transformation could be so chiefly for three reasons: their belief that emphasizing nationhood need pose no threat to humanity; second, their profound distrust of overly high-pitched calls for cosmopolitanism despite their recognition of universal values; and, third, though relatedly, their extraordinary sensitivity to questions of scale.

To start with, both Herder and Rousseau denounced mutlinational empires in favour of national entities founded on an affinitive culture of their own. Rousseau, indeed, made no secret of his hunches about the (necessary) demise of the great monarchies of Europe, while Herder welcomed the French Revolution as the dawn of a new world of distinct nations and, simultaneously, as the prelude to better international relations.[42] Second, while supporting the idea of international cooperation, they nonetheless dismissed a craving for universal *citizenship* as a misguided chimera wholly beyond the grasp of the ordinary mind. Finally, although they were reluctant to be dogmatic about the optimum size of nation-states, they both left no doubt about their personal preferences. Herder never ceased to recall the city-state of Riga, "in which 'well merited' meant more than

41. Rousseau, *Social Contract*, Bk. II, ch. 7 (*Oeuvres*, III, 381–4).

42. Rousseau, *Emile*, 194 (*Oeuvres*, IV, 468–9). Herder writes: "These events undoubtedly open one's mouth and overwhelm one's soul," and, on another occasion, he adds: "Speaking for myself, I cannot deny that, of all the remarkable events of our Age, the French Revolution has appeared to me by far the most important." (In a letter to Jacoby of 11 November 1792) (H. Düntzer, *Aus Herders Nachlass*, 1856, II, 298–301); see also Herder, *Werke*, XVIII, 314.

'well born.'"[43] Geneva, throughout, sustained Rousseau's hope that a public self could be a legitimate self, in that the city's size was such as to provide the chance for civic solidarity and a sense of civic belonging.[44] Riga and Geneva, therefore, paradigmatically served as approximations to the attainable, if not as symbols of the potentially ideal.

To be sure, whatever expectations Rousseau and Herder entertained in the direction of the envisioned symbiosis were no more than an inkling of what *might* be achievable. For neither underrated the hiatus that separated vision from reality. Even so, each felt that the potentially realizable needed stating to make it at all thinkable.[45]

Although, unlike Rousseau, Herder is usually not thought of as a political philosopher, I would like to suggest that by his deft blending of historical consciousness with a distinctly national and civic culture he managed to complement, and possibly enrich, Rousseau's doctrine of political association, according to which nation and *patrie*, sovereign and citizen, the socially useful and the politically rightful, were to form one seamless whole. By making the past of one's national origins the basis of both one's personal self-discovery and one's discovery of relationship to others, Herder held that, through this twofold self-recognition, human mutuality would acquire tangible substance and meaning. The point to note is that, in its basic origins, this mutuality is *not* chosen; it is not an act of will, but is rather a reflexive finding of oneself within a community

43. Herder, *Werke*, XVII, 391, 413. Herder's early works were written in Riga, the Baltic port, then part of Russia, where he had his first position as a clergyman after completing his studies at Königsberg during the 1760s, the crucial period of Rousseau's influence on Kant, Herder's favourite teacher, who inspired his own interest in Rousseau.

44. Rousseau refers to Geneva as "a State, in which all the individuals being well known to one another, neither the secret machinations of vice, nor the modesty of virtue, were able to escape the notice and judgment of the public; the pleasant custom of seeing and knowing one another could make the love of country rather a love of the citizens than of the soil." *Inequality*, 144 (*Oeuvres*, III, 112). The immense importance Rousseau attached to "scale" is borne out also in his essays on Corsica and Poland and in his *Letters from the Mountain*. The "Dedication to the Republic of Geneva," with which Rousseau starts his *Discourse on Inequality*, is a most eloquent declaration in support of a state's smallness. (*Oeuvres*, III, 111–21).

45. For Herder a sense of "extended selfhood" – a combination of imaginative feeling and imaginative seeing – implying *Mitgefühl*, or sympathy through empathy (what Kant called an enlarged mentality), constitutes the essence of ethics as social morality (*Werke*, VIII, 296). The greater part of his most interesting and original essay "Vom Erkennen und Empfinden" ["Of Cognition and Perception"] (1778), is an elaboration of this line of thought regarding human mutuality. As is the case with Rousseau, extended selfhood is bounded, as is citizenship, in its sentiments and its reciprocal rights and freedoms. In this connection, see J.G.A. Pocock, "The Ideal of Citizenship since Classical Times," *Queen's Quarterly* (1992), 99, No. 1.

of language. And a communal language, for Herder, is not, as we observed, merely a means of external communication at any given time – horizontally, so to speak – but, and a great deal more powerfully, a vertically operative link with the past. More powerfully, because language for him was first and foremost an instrument of self-expression involving the internal formation of thoughts and feelings. Accordingly, the self-formation (*Bildung*) of individuals, as they grow up in a particular cultural milieu, consists in acquiring words to express what they think and feel. In this process they draw on a common heritage, passed on and treasured by previous generations, not only in the speech form of daily use, but also in that of song and poetry. And, significantly, this common heritage, in and through language, is something everyone can partake in, and do so with an ardour that is as deeply-felt as it is egalitarian. As we noted in the Introduction, Herder referred to this domain of language as "a realm of democracy which tolerates no tyrants."[46] It is a type of property that all can share equally within a nationality, and of which they must not be deprived. For, to rob people of this property is to rob them of their inner selves, their existential humanity as thinking and feeling creatures.[47] Herder identified this distinctive character of thinking and feeling with a people's *Denkart*, which, to him, was the bedrock of their sense of belonging and, by extension, the foundation of their solidarity as a nation.

46. See above, Introduction, n13. Accents and dialects in the spoken language do admittedly disclose class distinctions and differences in education – in some nations more than in others – but this does not necessarily apply to the vertical dimension of language transmission in the intergenerational manner and the sentiments it involves. Children as well as adults are here equally free and able to feel attached to songs of the past or to the poetry of their forebears.

47. Herder, *Werke*, XVII, 59: "Truly, just as God tolerates all languages of this world, so too should a ruler tolerate, nay honour, the diverse languages of his subject peoples." So writes Herder in one of the *Humanitätsbriefe*, in which he censures Joseph II of Austria for having been insensitive to the different nationalities of his subjects and their sense of pride in their own distinctive cultural traditions, and above all their native languages. For, as I indicated in the previous note, and pointed out earlier, Herder associated with languages more than the dictionary meaning of words. Words do not merely denote *things*, they also connote *feelings*, both directly and indirectly; Herder described these emotive associations of words as the "companions of the dawn of life," and these emotional meanings and overtones form a living link with the thinking and feeling of past generations, connecting those who learn the words with "the workings of the ancestral mind" of those who preceded them. (See above, ch. 6, ns 45 and 46.) Herder's recognition that sentiments of solidarity produced by shared language traditions are not, however, the same as a sense of reciprocity produced by just institutions is strikingly echoed in George Kateb, "Aestheticism and Morality: Their Cooperation and Hostility," *Political Theory*, 28 (2000), 6.

Herder's historical vision of a sense of belonging as the quintessential sustenance of human association, together with Rousseau's (more systematic) political doctrine, set in motion self-understandings in the light of which nothing in society was ever the same again. While neither was prepared to turn his back entirely on the ideals of the European Enlightenment, each in his own manner fostered a communal ethos that could not but impinge on conventional notions of both individualism and universalism. Herder, in part following, in part transcending, Rousseau, succeeded in giving birth to modes of public discourse without which present-day variants of claims to national recognition and political legitimacy would be hard to grasp and even harder to account for. In the main he did it by seeking to match a historical consciousness with a cultural consciousness and a cultural consciousness with a consciousness of social reciprocity. Admittedly, Herder did not *identify* this social reciprocity among members of a nationality with civic membership of a state; he denied, however, that a state which ignored the existence of national self-understandings, or declined to respect the distinctiveness of such self-understandings, could be thought a rightful state.

Language, although it was an important bridge between individual self-enactment and the enactment of the self-constituting nation, was nevertheless not the only bridge, or the only path, to the politically just society. That much Herder made abundantly clear, as I have observed throughout the book. As in Rousseau's thinking, there was also in Herder's no ambiguity about the fact that cultural foundations traceable to common linguistic traditions were alone simply not enough to bring into life the *political* nation, regardless of undeniable ambiguities about the precise requirements of the modern *nation* state or the nature or the degree of sovereignty it could command internationally.

Nationalists of the subsequent era no doubt thrived on such ambiguities, but one can hardly blame Herder or Rousseau for that. For neither had much use for generalizing dogmatism, let alone for sheer utopianism, just as neither thought that their teleological arguments should be taken for performative blueprints.

Index

agency: as self-direction, 9; and embeddedness, 103; and limits, 93–4, 99, 130; with others, 8, 33–4, 156–7, 174; and providence, 100–1; and rationality, 97; and traditions, 99–100, 103, 120–1. *See also* joint agency

Althusius, Johann: on the Mosaic Covenant, 22n15

analogy: and reasoning, 136–7

aristo-democracy, 33–4, 47–8, 155–7, 175–6

Arnold, Matthew: on right acting, 80

authoritarianism; and myths, 10–11, 144–5

autonomy: and boundedness, 94, 98–9

Ayer, A.J.: on intrinsic ends, 116

beliefs: instrumental and intrinsic, 144–5; and ideas, 125, 142, 144–5, 162

Berlin, Isaiah: on Voltaire, 163n3

Bildung: as continuous becoming, 145–8, 171–2; as spiritual genesis, 121, 131, 140; its transmission, 5, 119–20. *See also* culture, language, and tradition

Burke, Edmund: on the French Revolution, 54; on the British constitution, 55–6

causation: in history *vs* nature, 106–7, 110, 116, 127–8; internal, 112–13, 136–8, 179–80; multiple, 141–2; through purpose, 113–14, 122, 129, 142, 170–2, 179–80. *See also* purpose

change: as development, 5, 42, 107; and persistence, 5, 42, 124–5, 131, 133, 147–8, 171–2

choice: as basic human causality, 95, 118; and reflection, 115; and religion, 98, 130

civilization: and culture, 10, 132–4

Coleridge, S.T.: on obedience, 59

Condorcet, Antoine de: on march of civilization, 158

contextualism, 99–100; and meaning, 136–7, 171–2; and relativism, 103–4, 135–7

contingency, 116–18; and inevitability, 116–17, 129, 142

core themes summarized, 15–16

cost of excluded alternatives, 92, 159–60, 170

creation: and emergence, 39, 41–2, 44–5, 48, 175–7

culture: and civilization, 10; and language, 12, 122; and nationality, 9; and nature, 8–10, 41, 46, 50; and politics, 131; and transmission, 5, 119–20, 122, 142; uniqueness, 6; universal phenomenon, 134. *See also* political culture, segmental cultures, social cultures, transfer and goal cultures, and world culture

Dahl, Robert: on polyarchy, 154

democratic ethic: variants, 157–8

Dilthey, Wilhelm: on historical understanding, 7